NATIVE AMERICAN DRAMA

The recent rise in publications and professional productions of Native American plays moves Native theatre from specific, cultural communities into larger, more generalized audiences, who quickly discover that Native plays are uniquely different from mainstream drama. This is because Native theatre is its own field of drama, one that enacts Native intellectual traditions existing independently from Western drama yet capable of extending mainstream theatrical theories. This study contends that Native dramaturgy possesses a network of distinctive discourses pertaining to Native American philosophies and relating to theatre's performative medium. Following an introduction that traces Native American theatre history from the 1900s to today, *Native American Drama* moves into a critical examination of Native dramaturgy. The study privileges voices of Native literary theorists, including Gerald Vizenor, Robert Allen Warrior, and LeAnne Howe, to introduce four Native discourses – platiality, storying, tribalography, and survivance – that intersect performative elements of space, speech, action, and movement. To demonstrate how these discourses address Native dramaturgy without reducing the multi-dimensionality of Native theatre, Stanlake applies them to Native plays, ranging from Lynn Riggs' *The Cherokee Night* to Tomson Highway's *Ernestine Shuswap*.

A leading scholar in the field of Native American theatre, Christy Stanlake approaches her work through a fusion of theory and practice. Her theoretical works in Native theatre have been published by *Modern Drama* and the *Journal of Dramatic Theory and Criticism*. She also guest-edited the recent *Nations Speaking: Indigenous Performances Across the Americas* and serves as an editorial advisor for the Alexander Street Press' North American Indian Drama collection. Her artistic ventures include working as the dramaturg for JudyLee Oliva's *Te Ata* world première, the first professional play produced by a Native nation, and directing the United States Naval Academy's 101-year-old theatre program, the Masqueraders.

NATIVE AMERICAN DRAMA: A CRITICAL PERSPECTIVE

CHRISTY STANLAKE

CAMBRIDGE
UNIVERSITY PRESS

CAMBRIDGE UNIVERSITY PRESS
Cambridge, New York, Melbourne, Madrid, Cape Town, Singapore,
São Paulo, Delhi, Dubai, Tokyo, Mexico City

Cambridge University Press
The Edinburgh Building, Cambridge CB2 8RU, UK

Published in the United States of America by Cambridge University Press, New York

www.cambridge.org
Information on this title: www.cambridge.org/9780521182409

First published 2009
First paperback edition 2010

A catalogue record for this publication is available from the British Library

Library of Congress Cataloguing in Publication data
Stanlake, Christy, 1972–
Native American drama : a critical perspective / Christy Stanlake.
p. cm.
Includes bibliographical references and index.
ISBN 978-0-521-51980-9
1. American drama – Indian authors – History and criticism. 2. Indian theater –
United States – History – 20th century. 3. Indians in literature.
4. Indians of North America – Intellectual life. I. Title.
PS153.I52s73 2009
812'.509897–dc22

ISBN 978-0-521-51980-9 Hardback
ISBN 978-0-521-18240-9 Paperback

For two remarkable Oklahomans
Mother, who taught me our state's history
&
JudyLee, who taught me to see new trails

Contents

Illustrations

Cover photograph: DeLanna Studi as Young Te Ata in JudyLee
Oliva's *Te Ata* world première, 2006. Photograph by Rex Knowles,
courtesy of Knowles and USAO Archives.

Acknowledgments

Creating this book has been a journey and, as on any meaningful journey, there have been many people and organizations who have touched my life and guided me along the way...

From my years at the University of Oklahoma (1995–1998), I would like to thank Dr. Clara Sue Kidwell, whose Native American Philosophy course blew my mind, changed the way I view performance, and has inspired my work ever since. To Drs. Geary Hobson and Alan Velie, who introduced me to wonderful writers and theorists and who always believed in the relevance of Native American theatre studies: thank you for your encouragement. Most of all, Dr. JudyLee Oliva, my mentor and life-long friend, thank you for setting me on my path and walking this road with me from time to time.

From my years at Ohio State (1998–2002), I would like to acknowledge the support of my doctoral dissertation committee, Dr. Leslie Ferris, Dr. Joy Reilly, and Dr. Dan Reff. With them I thank my advisor, Dr. Esther Beth Sullivan, who kept me on task with her generous spirit. To Dr. Tom Postlewait, thank you for challenging me to go farther and for opening new roads for me to travel. During my doctoral work on Native dramaturgy at Ohio State University (OSU), I received an Elizabeth D. Gee Research Grant and Department of Theatre's PEGS Award, which helped support the research I did on "Mapping the Web of Native American Dramaturgy," my dissertation that formed the groundwork for this book. I would also like to thank the organizations that shared their work and contributed to my understanding of Native theatre: Native Voices at the Autry, Project HOOP, and Miami University of Ohio's Native American Women Playwrights Archive (NAWPA). I specifically want to recognize Dr. Bill Wortman, who made NAWPA his labor of love and built a community of artists and scholars around it.

From my home in Annapolis, I thank my colleagues, especially Drs. Allyson Booth, Michelle Allen-Emerson, and Jason Shaffer, who were always willing to give whatever was necessary – whether that was a critical reading or a moment of empathy. To my friend Marcela Valdes, thank you for our weekly walks and talks that have proven invaluable with your advice and laughter. For his openness and enthusiastic vision, I would also like to thank Vinni Scott, producer of the Native theatre program at the National Museum of the American Indian (NMAI). My thanks also go to the Naval Academy Research Counsel for the funding it provided while I developed this book. As a civilian, theatre person working in Native studies, I am always somewhat awed and very grateful to have found advocates, here, at the US Naval Academy.

During the completion of this book, I've had the pleasure of meeting many people who have assisted me along the way. From Cambridge University Press, I would like to thank Dr. Victoria Cooper for taking a chance on this project, Becky Jones for her clear and positive advice, Chris Jackson for his skillful reading and word-crafting, Chris Hills for his production work, and Joanna Garbutt. For those many people who helped me track down production photos, thank you for taking the time to send me your images. I would especially like to acknowledge Lori Marchand, Administrative Director from Western Canada Theatre, whose excitement about artist–scholar projects is infectious; Gary Cundiff, of the Lynn Riggs Memorial, who patiently guided me through computer security to obtain the photos from his uncle's play; and the University of Hawaii Manoa's Theatre Department, which kindly joined me in a quest to track down a non-existent photo.

Several playwrights paused their busy schedules to help me gather their production photos: Victoria Nalani Kneubuhl, Diane Glancy, Marie Clements, and Hanay Geiogamah. Thank you for sharing your memories and your best wishes for this project. I know how blessed I am to work in a contemporary field that allows me to meet the artists I write about. I'd like to thank all of the Native theatre artists who have generously shared their work with me over the years and who inspire me daily.

I thank my immediate family for their unconditional love and support: my sister, Missy; my father, Gary; and my mother, Jean. I am especially grateful to my mother's keen eye for style editing. Finally, endless gratitude goes to my husband, Judah Nyden, who was willing to share our first year of marriage with a book project. Thank you, Judah, for creating a place for me to work – and for coaxing me outside when I am in most need of balance.

Abbreviations

AIM	American Indian Movement
AITE	American Indian Theater Ensemble
BC	British Colombia
BIA	Bureau of Indian Affairs
HOOP	Honoring Our Origins and People
IAIA	Institute of American Indian Arts
NATE	Native American Theater Ensemble
NAWPA	Native American Women Playwrights Archive
NMAI	National Museum of the American Indian
OSU	Ohio State University
TCG	Theatre Communications Group
UCLA	University of California, Los Angeles

CHAPTER I

A history of Native American drama

AN ORIGIN STORY

One August evening of an Oklahoma summer, a thousand theatregoers gathered to celebrate the opening night of a new Native American play. The audience came from many different communities, including: the Chickasaw Nation, a major producer of the production; the Oklahoma state government, which declared the play the inaugural event of its centennial; and the nation-wide extended family of Te Ata, a classically trained Chickasaw actor who had previously toured her one-woman performances across the Americas and Europe for over seventy years. The World Premiere of *Te Ata*, a play written by another Chickasaw woman, playwright JudyLee Oliva, was a theatrical event that represented Native American theatre's rich history and growing future.

The 2006 Equity-level, full-scale production of *Te Ata* was the first professional Native American play to be produced largely by a Native American nation.[1] The play featured some of Native theatre's rising stars: JudyLee Oliva is one of the playwrights who currently leads Native theatre's move into mainstream American theatrical venues; and DeLanna Studi, the Cherokee actor who played the title role, has captured national attention on stage and in film. The artistic team included professional theatre artists from throughout the United States, while the cast was comprised of "actors from across ten states and eight Native [American nations]" (*Te Ata* World Premiere website). Some of these Native actors, such as Donna Couteau Brooks, who played Elder Te Ata, embodied the changes that have occurred in Native theatre over the recent decades. Brooks, whose professional career has long included performing as a Sac and Fox storyteller, was active in the early Native American theatre movement when she performed with Spiderwoman Theater; she had arrived at *Te Ata* rehearsals after working on *Grandchildren of the Buffalo Soldiers*, a play by the Assiniboine playwright, William S. Yellow Robe, Jr. *Grandchildren* had just gained the distinction of becoming the first Native American play in the United States to obtain a "fully-mounted professional collaborative touring production by regional theaters" when Trinity Rep and Penumbra Theatre Company joined to produce it ("Trinity Rep," website).

During *Te Ata*'s week-long run in August 2006, over 3,000 theatregoers traveled from 30 states to Oklahoma to witness a story about a journey in the opposite direction: a Chickasaw actor's crossing from Indian Territory onto the international stage (*Te Ata* World Premiere website). The production was an historic moment for both Native American and general theatrical history: for the first time, a play served as the site where State and Native governments came together to celebrate common roots; for the first time, a professional theatrical production became the chosen vehicle for a Native nation to express its identity. The World Premiere of JudyLee Oliva's *Te Ata* transformed from a mainstream production of a Native American play into a touchstone for Native theatre, not only staging the possibilities for Native American theatre, but also presenting a metatheatrical origin story about how such moments in Native American theatre came to be.

NATIVE AMERICAN THEATRICAL PERFORMANCE IN THE FIRST HALF OF THE TWENTIETH CENTURY

Mary "Te Ata" Thompson Fisher's (1895–1995) career represents the many challenges and difficult decisions Native American performers faced at the turn of the twentieth century. What makes her story unique amongst those of Native American actors from her era is that Te Ata pursued her theatrical career through an academic path that led her to Broadway. Her love of acting developed in her university theatre classes at the Oklahoma College for Women (OCW),[2] where she became the first Native American student to graduate. Te Ata's theatre teacher, Francis Dinsmore Davis, nurtured Te Ata's acting abilities and gifts for traditional Native storytelling.[3] When Te Ata graduated from OCW, her senior recital was a one-woman performance composed of traditional stories she had learned from her father. JudyLee Oliva, who researched Te Ata's life before beginning work on her play, writes that Te Ata "had to borrow much of her 'Indian' props, including a drum, a bow and arrow, and a costume. None of the props nor the costume was authentic, but the presentation marked the beginning of her career" ("Te Ata – Chickasaw" 7).

Following her graduation from OCW, Te Ata performed in Chautauqua shows, including the Redpath circuit, while taking graduate classes in acting at Carnegie Tech in Pittsburgh. Her Chautauqua performances were a continuation and expansion of the 1919 senior recital, and they allowed Te Ata to build her credentials as a professional performer before venturing to New York City. Te Ata's first Broadway performance was in the 1922 production of *The Red Poppy* with Estelle Winwood and Bela Lugosi, and although she went on to secure jobs with other Broadway shows, she soon became dissatisfied with the stereotypical "exotic" roles in which she was cast. Oliva writes, "[I]t was becoming apparent to Te Ata that the commercial theatre was interested in her primarily because she was an Indian with a gifted voice and graceful presence and not because of her acting ability. She was an anomaly and a novelty" (ibid., 7, 10).

In response to her Broadway experiences, Te Ata decided to take control of her image. She refined her one-woman show, added dramatic adaptations of poetry on Indian themes, and continued to add traditional legends from other Native nations. Te Ata's aim was not only to make a living as an entertainer, but also to educate audiences about the diversity across Native America by presenting accurate information about Native cultures. To these ends, Te Ata spent many of her vacations traveling to Native communities and educating herself about the different cultures. In turn, during her performances, Te Ata attributed traditional legends to their appropriate Native nations and explained the significance of her props and clothing (ibid., 15).

Te Ata's shows, which incorporated two styles of performance (Native American storytelling and classical acting for the Shakespearean stage), allowed her to gain recognition on her own terms. She performed for all audiences, Native and non-Native, schoolchildren and international leaders, and won the support of Mrs. Franklin Delano Roosevelt, who, with the president, invited Te Ata to become the "first performer to entertain at the White House during FDR's administration" (ibid., 11). In addition to her many national performances, including two at Carnegie Hall and a special performance at the Roosevelts' home in Hyde Park for King George VI and Queen Elizabeth, Te Ata also performed internationally. During her first European tour in 1930, she traveled as a cultural ambassador with letters of introduction from Vice President Charles Curtis[4] (ibid.) Significantly, at a time when misrepresentations of Native Americans abounded, Te Ata was able to maintain a professional career that upheld the dignity of Native cultures. She continued that mission until the late 1980s, when she retired to her home state of Oklahoma,[5] which honored Te Ata with the title of "Oklahoma's First State Treasure."

Te Ata's decision to leave Broadway for a theatrical career that she could more actively control was in response to the limitations placed on Native American performers and Native representation by the entertainment industry during the first half of the 1900s. These stereotypical limitations created characters in a national story that white Americans and Canadians told themselves about the development of their countries. The previous decade had been one of systematic government-enforced removal, isolation, eradication, and assimilation of Native cultures, so that white citizens could obtain more land, wealth, and rights as the new countries grew. The conflict between Native Americans and the new national governments inspired misrepresentations of Native people through various forms of media. Performance venues, such as theatre, cinemas, dime museums, wild-west shows, and world's-fair exhibitions, capitalized on the exotic allure of the "vanishing race." In acts of imperialist nostalgia, Native people were honored as romantic, brave, and spiritual, but doomed to extinction because of their "non-progressive" world views. However, these Indians were also "crafty" and at any time could switch from noble creatures to savage killers, slaying white women and children. The savage Indian was quite popular, owing to the need for the new countries to feel secure about their gross mistreatment of Native peoples. The savage stereotype also assuaged white doubts, as Native nations threatened each country's myth of superiority whenever Native people fought successful battles for their lands against non-Native troops. These stereotypes of Noble/Savage for men or Princess (ready-to-die-for-her-love-of-the-white-man)/Squaw (sexually ravenous savage) for women, weave throughout American history and, in so doing, persist in media representations of Native peoples, even today.

Government treatment of Native Americans has not only shaped the way Native peoples have been represented through performance, but also shapes how we in theatre studies, today, view the work of Native Americans in theatre history. For example, the Native American performers from the early 1900s who are recorded in general theatre history surveys are most often performers in exhibits and kitschy venues. Moreover, Native American performers of this era are usually remembered not by name – unless they happened to be a "fallen" Native leader like Sitting Bull in Buffalo Bill's Wild West Show – but by their ethnicity only, "Buffalo Bill's Indians," "an Indian in a dime museum." Yet, surprisingly, at the turn of the century a number of Native Americans, like Te Ata, were performing in various "legitimate" theatrical venues. An example is Pauline "Tekahionwake" Johnson (1861–1913), a Mohawk woman who was Te Ata's counterpart in Canada. In college, Johnson aspired to become a professional actor; however, that dream shifted when she began publishing her writing. We now remember Johnson primarily as a writer, but she did use her theatre training to give dramatic readings to promote her writing during the first decade of her professional publishing career. These performances incorporated Victorian-style language and sophistication to proclaim her writing's political message "that Canada was still Indian land wrested unfairly from indigenous hands" (Malinowski (ed.), *Notable*, 211). Other performers, such as Tsianina Redfeather Blackstone, who was Cree, and Ada Navarrete, who was Mayan, were Native opera singers.

Only recently have the stories of these Native theatre professionals from the early twentieth century been finding their ways into theatre history. While some of these early performers are emerging out of a relative invisibility, other performers have been present in theatre history all along; it is their Native identity that has been written as invisible. The stories of two of these Native American theatre figures, actor William Penn Adair Rogers (1879–1935) and playwright Rollie Lynn Riggs (1899–1954), both members of the Cherokee Nation, are under revision by scholars in Native studies.

Will Rogers was born in Indian Territory and raised within the Cherokee community, where his father was active in Cherokee Nation governance. Rogers' family had been deprived of a large portion of their ranch lands owing to federal policies that freed up Native lands for white settlers. As a student, Rogers transferred from a predominantly Native American biracial school to a mostly white school, where he suffered from racial slurs and developed "a sensitivity to his Cherokee Indian heritage…that was evident in his militant reaction to any criticism of Indians or people of partial Indian ancestry" (Markowitz (ed.), *American*, 304-305).

Rogers' performance career spanned from 1902 to 1935, during which time he became one of the United States' most beloved celebrities, honored for his quintessential American charm. Over those years, he performed in wild-west shows; in vaudeville, in the Ziegfeld Frolic and Follies; in Broadway plays and musicals; on radio; and in seventeen motion pictures (three of which he wrote, produced, directed, and starred in); additionally, he wrote books and a syndicated newspaper column. When he died, "The *New York Times* dedicated four full pages to him…the nation's movie theatres were darkened; CBS and NBC television stations observed a half-hour of silence; and in New York, a squadron of planes, each towing a long black streamer, flew over the city in a final tribute to the hero and friend of aviation" (Malinowski (ed.), *Notable*, 369). Despite Rogers' huge celebrity status and nickname, "The Cherokee Kid," most studies about his career have underplayed his Native American heritage, claiming that his Cherokee persona was private and held separately from his public persona.

Daniel Heath Justice, a Native literary critic and member of the Cherokee Nation, argues otherwise in *Our Fire Survives the Storm: A Cherokee Literary History*. Taking issue with some biographers who have interpreted Rogers' claims of Cherokee heritage as quirky wisecracks within a larger non-Native act, and others who dismiss Rogers' Native identity because he was a biracial member of the "assimilated" Cherokee Nation,[6] Justice claims Rogers as a powerful Native voice in America's history: "as a light-skinned Cherokee well-loved in the United States, he was a stealthy minority with access to a forum and a platform inaccessible to other Indians of his day" (*Fire*, 124). Justice revises Rogers' personal and professional biography to reveal the performer's close ties to his Cherokee community and his public advocacy of Native issues. Reclaiming Rogers' trademark evenhanded, under-stated satire as a Native form of humor, Justice traces Rogers' critiques of American policies toward Native nations, including the history of America's founding, the Trail of Tears, broken treaties, imperialism in Alaska and Hawaii, and capitalism veiled by religion. This revised Rogers is one who is precisely *more* American *because of* his Native American heritage, which inspired him to use humor to point out the failings of society. Thus, Rogers' own version of American history is one of violence and unrest, as he told his radio listeners:

Our record with the Indians is going to go down in history. It is going to make us mighty proud of it in the future when our children of ten more generations read of what we did to them. Every man in our history that killed the most Indians has got a statue built for him. The only difference between the Roman gladiators and the Pilgrims was that the Romans used a lion to cut down their native population, and the Pilgrims had a gun. (qtd. in ibid., 129)

Such a perspective cannot be dismissed easily as a mere character gag to garner fame. As Justice rightly restores Rogers to Cherokee literary history, theatre studies is challenged to rewrite how we view this star of the American stage.

Perhaps the general public did not see Rogers' Native heritage because his persona did not match the stereotypes that the general population read as "Indian." The invisibility derived not from Rogers' presentation of self but rather the general public's inability to see a contemporary Native presence in America. Lynn Riggs, like Rogers, was also a biracial Cherokee from Oklahoma whose professional theatrical work, although part of American theatre history, has only recently been incorporated into the story of Native

American theatre history. Like Rogers, Riggs did not adhere to prevailing stereotypes of Native peoples, yet his theatrical work reveals close ties to his Oklahoma and Native identity. Riggs now holds the distinction of being the first professional playwright of Native American theatre.

Born on Cherokee Nation land in the town of Claremore, Indian Territory, Riggs began writing plays while attending the University of Oklahoma (Braunlich, "Chronology," xvii; Weaver, "Foreword," xi). His impressive career as a playwright led him to New York City, where many of Riggs' scripts were professionally produced by theatre companies that featured first-rate actors such as Stella Adler and Lee Strasberg (Weaver, "Foreword," xi). Often, his plays dramatize relationships between people and their natural environments, particularly how the people and land of Oklahoma responded in the aftermath of Indian Territory's transition into statehood.

In 1988, Phyllis Cole Braunlich wrote *Haunted by Home*, a well-researched biography about Riggs' successful theatrical career; though, she underplays the significance of Riggs' Cherokee identity and how it shaped his work. A decade later, though, Native American literary scholars began to revisit Riggs' work and now challenge notions that *The Cherokee Night* (1932) is the only one of his plays that addresses Native issues. Jace Weaver's 1997 *That the People Might Live: Native American Literatures and Native American Community* examines Riggs' body of work to reveal an author who "unquestionably felt a responsibility to that part of his [Cherokee] heritage" and who used his writing to oppose the accepted representations of cowboys and Indians popular in film and literature (*That the People*, 97). Weaver's analysis of Riggs' work makes a convincing case, claiming the plays *Russet Mantle*, *The Year of Pilár*, and *The Cream in the Well*, and screenplays *Laughing Boy* and *The Plainsman* as Native-themed works. Weaver even rereads Riggs' most famous play, *Green Grow the Lilacs* (1931) – the play upon which Rodgers and Hammerstein based their musical *Oklahoma!* – through a Native lens and argues that the drama portrays Native and non-Native relations in Indian Territory during the transition to statehood. Native theatre scholar Jaye T. Darby takes Weaver's perspective one step further in "Broadway (Un) Bound: Lynn Riggs' *The Cherokee Night*" and marks Riggs' play as "a major work in modern Native American theatre" ("Broadway," 9). Darby investigates how, through his construction of *The Cherokee Night*, Riggs developed a distinctly Native American style of dramaturgy, one that he refused to alter in order to please Broadway producers and create another theatrical hit. In "Platiality in Native American Drama" (chapter 4) we will look closely at the play to see how Riggs began to envision a uniquely Native American style of theatre, one that persists today.

NATIVE AMERICAN THEATRE FROM THE RED POWER
MOVEMENT FORWARD

Some Native American literary scholars have referred to Riggs' work as a "coded" expression of Native American identity.[7] However, when one compares the cultural context of the pre-civil rights era to the post-civil rights era, it is not surprising that early twentieth-century Native writers and performers often expressed their cultural identity in a manner that sometimes appears understated, or coded, by our contemporary standards. It was not until the large, political civil rights movements of the 1960s that people of many cultural backgrounds began publically celebrating and expressing their ethnicity. Throughout Native American communities of the 1960s, this expression of Native identities derived largely from the Red Power Movement, in which intertribal organizations and activities worked both to reclaim Native representations and to draw public attention to issues affecting Native Americans. One of the most famous and audacious examples of this was the eighteen-month occupation of Alcatraz Island in 1969 by Native American activists whose demonstrations successfully educated the general public about the federal government's treatment of Native peoples, while also visibly protesting US policies that had appropriated Native lands.

Not surprisingly, the experimental theatre movements of the 1960s combined with the political motivations of Native peoples to inspire what many today consider to be the beginnings of the Native American theatre movement in the United States and Canada. Although Native theatre companies started forming as early as 1956, when a Cherokee actor, playwright, and director named Arthur Smith Junaluska founded the American Indian Drama Company in New York City (Swisher and Benally, *Native*, 157), the events most credited for stimulating contemporary Native American theatre occurred as the late 1960s transitioned into the early 1970s. The founding of a school, the Institute of American Indian Arts (IAIA), and of a theatre company, the Native American Theater Ensemble (NATE), are the two events that created networks of Native American theatre artists who continue to shape Native drama today.

In 1962, IAIA was founded in Santa Fe, New Mexico, with the purpose of providing Native students a formal arts education influenced by traditional Native American creative practices. By 1969, IAIA's Native theatre program had organized under the artistic direction of Rolland Meinholtz and a manifesto of Native theatre, written by the Cherokee director of IAIA, Lloyd Kiva New (Darby, "Introduction," vii; New, "Credo," 3–4). We will read in the following chapter how New's Credo set the metaphorical stage for a conscious development of Native American dramaturgical expressions, which have continued to reverberate throughout the field of Native drama despite IAIA's own challenges of keeping its theatre program running. Oneida playwright and IAIA theatre alumnus Bruce King is perhaps the best example of how the school's philosophies inspired the growth of the Native American theatre movement. In addition to his playwriting, King has remained influential in developing Native theatre companies through his work with the Indian Time Theater Project in Chicago, Echo-Hawk Theatre Ensemble, Thunderbird Theatre at Haskell Indian Nations University, and two tours as a returning faculty member in IAIA's theatre program (Geiogamah, "Introduction," x; Bruce King, "About," 499).

Hanay Geiogamah, a Kiowa/Delaware playwright, director, producer, and academic who has actively shaped the development of Native theatre for almost four decades, emerged as a leader of Native drama in 1972, when Ellen Stewart, director of La Mama Experimental Theater Club, worked with him to obtain the grants and performers necessary to found a Native American theatre troupe (Huntsman, "Native," xii). From NATE's original sixteen-member theatre company, we can trace the careers of many Native theatre artists actively working today, including Aleut actor and educator Jane Lind, and Navajo playwright and actor Geraldine Keams. In addition to writing the first plays associated with NATE, *Body Indian* (1972), *Foghorn* (1973), and *49* (1975), Geiogamah continued working as a playwright and then branched into other areas of Native American performance. In 1987 he established the American Indian Dance Theatre, and in 1997 he joined with Jaye T. Darby to develop Project HOOP (Honoring Our Origins and People through Native Theatre, Education, and Community Development) through UCLA.

Meanwhile, in 1974, two long-running academic programs were founded. North of the US border in Canada's theatre center, the Native Theatre School opened in Toronto. Similar to the IAIA theatre program, the Native Theatre School aimed to create an educational environment that supported the development of Native actors, playwrights, and directors. Some of the most famous Native actors in film, Oneida actor Graham Green and Cayuga actor Gary Farmer, came through this influential school. Now known as the Centre for Indigenous Theatre, the program has been transformed into a full-time academic program, including a three-year conservatory curriculum for actors (Centre for Indigenous Theatre website). In Kansas at the Haskell Indian Nations University, Thunderbird Theatre was founded and then grew under the mentorship of Pat Melody, who directed the group from 1975 through her retirement in 2007. In addition to its tours and collaborative projects, the company boasts a strong connection to Bruce King, who has served as an artist in residence. The program next came under the direction of Creek playwright, director, and theatre scholar Julie Pierson-Little Thunder, who arrived in Kansas from her successful founding and artistic direction of the Native theatre company Thunder Road in Tulsa, Oklahoma. Meanwhile, Thunderbird Theatre alumni have also started their own company, the American Indian Repertory Theatre, which opened with *Weaving the Rain*, a play written by Kiowa actor and dramatist Diane Yeahquo Reyner.

The most famous professional Native American theatre company in the United States emerged in 1975, when three sisters of Kuna and Rappahannock descent, Lisa Mayo, Gloria Miguel, and Muriel Miguel, combined to form what is now the oldest continually performing women's theatre group in North America, Spiderwoman Theater. These three core members of the group have worked with artists of Native and non-Native heritage,[8] using a playful, improvisatory style of theatre to draw attention to serious issues affecting women. By 1981, with their signature production of *Sun, Moon, and Feather*, the group began to focus solely on issues relating to Native American representation, especially the portrayal of Native women. Spiderwoman has toured across the world, introducing audiences everywhere to the group's unique style of creating plays, which they call "storyweaving." In this process, the sisters build their plays with interweaving types of story (personal memories, family stories, traditional myths, contemporary songs, and historical events) that structure the dramatic action through overlapping moments of theme, sound, and image (Spiderwoman Theater, "About," 501). In addition to their work as a theatre company, the members of Spiderwoman Theater have inspired Native and non-Native theatre artists through their storyweaving workshops and artist residencies at universities, reservations, and conferences. Each woman also works actively as an independent artist, writing her own plays and acting in various professional theatre venues. The legacy of Spiderwoman Theater will continue well into the future, as playwright/performers such as Monique Mojica and Murielle Borst, daughters of Gloria Miguel and Muriel Miguel respectively, continue to shape the future of Native American theatre through their performances, publications, and development of theatre companies.[9]

Despite the early and persistent activities of Native American theatre artists in the United States, it was during the 1980s in Canada, where funding for the arts is more accessible, that a ground-swell of theatrical activity began to shape the ways the world sees Native drama. Ojibway playwright Drew Hayden Taylor describes the 1982 founding of the most influential of all Native theatre companies, Toronto's Native Earth Performing Arts, as a casual event: the company "was formed by a loose group of artistic friends, urban Indians who wanted to act. The company functioned as a collective…There was no overall structure to the company, no artistic director, no administrator, no core funding, just a room at the Toronto Native Friendship Centre and an occasional show" ("Alive," 64). From those humble beginnings, Native Earth Performing Arts has grown into an extraordinary professional theatre company, garnering seven Dora Mavor Moore Awards and two Floyd S. Chalmers Awards (Native Earth website). Its list of artistic directors over the years reads as a virtual *Who's Who* in Native American theatre, including Algonquin playwright Yvette Nolan, Plains Cree playwright Floyd Favel, Drew Hayden Taylor, Monique Mojica, and Cree playwright Tomson Highway. Highway's famous *The Rez Sisters* (1986) and its companion play *Dry Lips Oughta Move to Kapuskasing* (1989) drew international attention to Highway's writing and his artistic direction of Native Earth, bringing professional Native American theatre into the mainstream theatre world. *Dry Lips* quickly became anthologized in major theatre publications and was selected by the Mirvishes for a 1991 revival production at the Royal Alexandra Theatre, marking Highway as one of "the very small and select group of Canadian playwrights to be offered a major commercial production in Toronto" (Filewood, "Receiving," 38). When Highway left the artistic-director position at Native Earth Performing Arts in the early 1990s, the company continued to grow as it produced the works of other rising stars in Native theatre, such as Joseph Dandurand (Kwantlen), Darrell Dennis (Shuswap), Daniel David Moses (Delaware), and Marie Clements (Metis). In interesting ways, the work of many of these theatre artists broadened to influence the work of other Native theatre groups in Canada, such as De-Ba-Jeh-Mu-Jig Theatre Group based on the Wikwemikong Reserve on Manitoulin Island. Founded in 1984 by Shirley Cheechoo, a Cree playwright, performer, and director, De-Ba-Jeh-Mu-Jig focuses on creating plays that address issues relevant to Cree and Ojibway youth; often, these plays incorporate Native languages. Both Highway and Moses worked closely with the company, which continues to thrive.

In the United States, where funding for the arts is limited, some professional Native American companies began to forge creative partnerships with organizations that could help support Native theatre's growth into commercial markets. Native Voices, a theatre company devoted to the development of new Native American scripts for the commercial theatre, was founded in 1994 by Randy Reinholz (Choctaw) and Jean Bruce Scott at Illinois State University, where they both taught in the theatre department. The program began in response to Reinholz's attempts to find a Native play to produce at the university. When he was unable to locate one, he and Bruce Scott decided to create "a play festival in the fall...which consisted of a week of workshops, discussions, and staged readings on campus" (Reinholz and Scott, "Native Voices," 268). Their advertisements for the festival attracted over fifty play submissions. In the summer of 1996, the Native Voices workshop series partnered with the American Indian Community House to host Native Voices' festival of plays, which included early versions of Clements' *Urban Tattoo*, Oliva's *Te Ata*, and Vickie Ramirez's (Tuscarora) *Smoke*, a presentation by Chuka Lokoli Native Theatre Ensemble. In 1999, Native Voices found a permanent home when it joined with Los Angeles' Autry Museum of Western Heritage to create Native Voices at the Autry. The partnership yielded a permanent rehearsal space and a more supportive infrastructure for the Native play development organization, which now serves as a networking site for other Native performing arts programs and Native artists' organizations (such as the Native American Film and Television Alliance). Over its history, Native Voices has worked with many Native playwrights, readying their scripts for the physical stage; some of these playwrights have included William S. Yellow Robe, Jr., William Lang (Lenape), Diane Glancy (Cherokee), James Lujan (Taos Pueblo), and Arigon Starr (Kickapoo/Creek). Similar to Native Earth Performing Arts members, many of these playwrights have gone on to found other theatre companies. For example in 2001, Clements, who has worked with both Native Voices and Native Earth, founded Vancouver's urban ink productions, a theatre company devoted to the development and production of multi-media, multi-disciplinary theatrical productions by First Nations artists. Meanwhile, Native Voices at the Autry has continued forming collaborative relationships with other institutions that can help promote the visibility of Native American theatre.

In 1997, two academic institutions committed their resources to the dual mission of developing and promoting Native American theatre while providing educational resources about Native theatre to the general public. The Native American Women Playwrights Archive (NAWPA), located at Miami University in Oxford, Ohio, considers itself to be a living archive that adheres to the following mission:

[to] indentify playwrights in North and South America, collect, preserve, and make their work more widely known, encourage performances and continued creativity,

and help educate playwrights, theater companies, and audiences about Native American theater. Recognizing the difficulty all playwrights have publishing their work, we want NAWPA to play a positive role in the production of Native drama. (Howard, "Introduction," 1–2)

In addition to housing both plays by Native women dramatists and a significant collection of Spiderwoman Theater's theatrical ephemera, NAWPA hosts conferences where playwrights and scholars dialogue about the state of Native American theatre. NAWPA also regularly produces works by its member playwrights and in 2008 published some of the archive's plays in *Footpaths and Bridges: Voices from the Native American Women Playwrights Archive* (edited by Huston-Findley and Howard). The anthology features works by Spiderwoman Theater, Oliva, Clements, Jules Arita Koostachin (Attawapiskat Band Cree), Marcie Rendon (White Earth Anishinabe), Martha Kreipe de Montaño (Prairie Band Potawatomi), Denise Mosely (Cherokee), Victoria Nalani Kneubuhl (Hawaiian/ Samoan), and Vera Manuel (Shuswap-Kootenai).

While NAWPA's primary concern is promoting the work of existing playwrights, UCLA's Project HOOP strongly emphasizes creating new works that emerge out of the direct experiences of Native communities. The program's founder is Hanay Geiogamah, who paired his considerable Native theatre development experiences with the methodologies of Jaye T. Darby, who has a Ph.D. in education. Thus, the program is highly pedagogical and emphasizes experiential learning. Pairing its theatre scholars and practitioners with Native communities on reservations and in tribal colleges, Project HOOP teaches youth about all facets of theatrical production, as communities work to create plays that stem from residents' experiences. In addition to this grassroots development of theatre artists and plays, Project HOOP also extends the field of Native American drama into higher education through its series of publications about Native theatre, including three play anthologies: *Stories of Our Way* (1999), *Keepers of the Morning Star: An Anthology of Native Women's Theater* (2003), Bruce King's *Evening at the Warbonnet and Other Plays* (2006); and a collection of readings about the theatre movement, *American Indian Theater in Performance* (2000), edited by Geiogamah and Darby.

In 2005, the Smithsonian's National Museum of the American Indian (NMAI) launched its ambitious Native Theatre Program. Although performances of Native plays had been occurring already in New York at the museum's George Gustave Heye Center, the museum's flagship venue, NMAI on the National Mall in Washington D.C., did not open until September of 2004. Featuring five indoor and outdoor performance venues,

"NMAI aims to become the nation's premiere institution for showcasing Native American performing arts"; accordingly, the museum invites all Native theatre artists from the western hemisphere to consider NMAI as a potential venue for their plays (Scott, "National Museum," 135). NMAI's inclusive vision of producing Native plays from North, Central, and South America for Native and non-Native audiences of all ages in the nation's capital marks a truly international venture in the production of Native American drama. Since the program was launched under the guidance of Vincent P. Scott, NMAI on the National Mall has produced several Native plays, some that demonstrate how Native theatre networks collaborate. These plays include: *Sacajawea's Sisters* by Ojibwe/Oneida performer Thirza Defoe; the family-friendly musical *Gunakadeit: An Alaskan Sea Monster Story* by Tlingit writer Ishmael Hope; *When My Spirit Raised Its Hands: The Story of Elizabeth Peratrovich and Alaskan Civil Rights* by Tlingit playwright/performer Diane E. Benson; Native Voices' tours of Glancy's *Stone Heart* and Arigon Starr's *The Red Road*; and a touring leg of Yellow Robe's *Grandchildren of the Buffalo Soldiers*.

THE CHALLENGE OF NATIVE AMERICAN DRAMA

We are at a crossroads. From the turn of the twentieth century through today, there exists a significant history of Native American theatre. This story of Native theatrical activity extends into grassroots, community-based programs, such as the Inuit Tunooniq Theatre company in Northern Canada; the thirty-seven-year-old Hawaiian theatre company, Kumu Kahua, in Honolulu;[10] and theatre initiatives sponsored by Native nations, such as the Chickasaw Nation's construction of a high-tech performance center to house Chickasaw productions, including those created by its children's theatre and adult theatre troupe, The Living History Players. Increasingly, this story is also reaching large, multicultural audiences through the intertribal theatre organizations that have proliferated since the 1970s and through mainstream commercial productions of plays by Highway, Yellow Robe, Oliva, and others.

For those who cannot travel to Native American theatrical productions, the publication of highly visible Native American play anthologies, begin-ning with the Theatre Communications Group's (TCG) *Seventh Generation* in 1999, has increased exponentially to bring Native drama to an unlimited readership. Moreover, Native play scripts will soon become accessible to people of all income levels, as the new Alexander Street Press *North American Indian Drama* collection enters public libraries. The on-line series aims to

collect and publish the full texts of over 200 plays by Native American dramatists, and, through a sliding-scale subscription plan, Alexander Street Press hopes to make its series an affordable addition to any library or institution that desires it.

As this field of theatre reaches a growing, more generalized audience, the question of how to read these plays arises. Certainly, from the identity-based theatre companies of the early 1970s, to academic initiatives to create plays shaped by Native methodologies, to Riggs' early attempts to construct a Native American dramaturgical style, we see that this field of drama is different. Playwrights such as Taylor and Nolan have written about the difficulties facing the critical reception of their plays. Similar to the responses that plagued Riggs' *The Cherokee Night*, Taylor was told by a producer during one play review that "the structure went against everything he was taught in drama" ("Alive," 65). Nolan argues that, in addition to struggling with structural issues, mainstream theatre critics, producers, and viewers are sometimes befuddled by their own preconceptions regarding Native representation. In "Selling Myself" Nolan writes, "There was an expectation of what kind of story I would tell, as a Native writer. And the story this audience came to hear was about Indian as victim" (ibid., 99). In a NAWPA playwrights and scholars roundtable about different reactions to Native plays, a frustrated Rendon asked, "'Why don't the white people work harder to get it and work harder to bring in Native performers and educate audiences?'" (qtd. in Huston-Findley and Howard (eds.), *Footpaths and Bridges*, viii).

I agree with Rendon about the need to educate readers and viewers of Native American theatre so that all audiences can better comprehend these works, which do incorporate dramaturgical attributes that are unique to Native American plays. However, I see the challenge more broadly. Indeed, there are "red" and "white" conflicts that contribute to the misreading of Native plays, but the core dilemma is theoretical and institutionalized: Native drama's intersection with the general theatre, which possesses a far greater scope than white viewers. At this juncture, Native American drama presents general theatre studies with a powerful, alternative vision of how plays are constructed and of what the theatre is capable. With its distinctive portrayals of place, language, and motion, Native American dramaturgy both complements and extends the theories of the general theatre. Thus, to better understand Native American plays is to better appreciate the significance of the theatrical medium. In that hope, I devote the remainder of this book to developing a critical methodology for reading the unique aspects of Native American dramaturgy.

Developing a critical perspective for Native American drama

DRAMA FROM "INDIAN FORMS"

> We believe that an exciting American Indian theatre can be evolved out of the framework of Indian traditions. We think this evolution must come from the most sensitive approaches imaginable in order not to misuse or cheapen the original nature of Indian forms.
>
> Lloyd Kiva New (Cherokee), "Credo," 3

Lloyd Kiva New delivered his "Credo for American Indian Theatre" in 1969 from Santa Fe, New Mexico, the site of a new venture in Native American education and artistic expression. There, Native American artists, educators, and activists founded the IAIA to provide Native students with a formal fine-arts education articulated through a curriculum that emphasized the integration of Native traditions into contemporary works of art. New's mission not only challenged IAIA's theatre students, then, but his "Credo" has also continued to be invoked across the field of Native American drama. When the *Canadian Theatre Review* devoted a special 1991 issue to Native theatre, New's "Credo" appeared in Hanay Geiogamah's assessment of the state of Native American theatre in the United States. Geiogamah affirmed loyalty to New's mission and then predicted that, with its commitment to Native frameworks, Native theatre will one day "stand proudly among America's other theatres – ethnic, commercial, and educational" ("Indian Theatre," 12, 14). Six years later, New's "Credo" was invoked by Monique Mojica, who spoke at the inauguration of NAWPA and proclaimed to the playwrights and scholars in attendance, "We know that this Native 'way' is a persistent and natural occurrence in our work" ("ETHNOSTRESS"). Later, when Project HOOP produced the world's first academic reader designed specifically for studying Native American theatrical performance, New's "Credo" appeared again, this time in its entirety, as the first chapter of *American Indian Theater in Performance* (2000).

But what is this "framework of Indian traditions," and how do these traditions influence Native American plays to be different from non-Native plays? And, finally, why does New ask for such a dramatic structure and then provide a caveat to be mindful to not "misuse or cheapen the original nature of Indian forms" in the creation of theatrical works? These questions lie at the heart of understanding what Native American drama is, what this field of theatre does, and how these plays are different from those found in other theatrical subjects. To begin to approach New's "Credo" is to begin to define, loosely, what it means when we hear that something is a Native American play. Any researcher of Native theatre will affirm that many topics appear when one searches under the term "Native American drama." Search engines turn up everything from anthropological descriptions of sacred Native rituals, to performance studies' analyses of communal ceremonies, to reviews of outdoor summer dramas, to Native-themed plays written by non-Native playwrights. While these subjects can help inform the ways in which we read plays by Native American playwrights, who might structure plot to reflect a ceremonial event, or construct characters that recall Native stereotypes, these subjects are not the same as the dynamic, growing field of Native American drama. Loosely defined, Native American drama is a field of theatre that focuses on plays authored by members of the indigenous nations of the American Western Hemisphere, plays that are both *secular* and *intertribal*.

The term *secular* denotes that Native American plays are not tied to any specific Native American religion. The plays are not scripted religious ceremonies, as one might find in anthropology, nor do they convey sacred details that belong to private, religious observances of Native peoples. Instead, the playwrights in this field write for a secular audience, viewers who may or may not share the authors' various religious belief systems.

Despite the secular nature of Native American drama, many playwrights do include spiritual perspectives in their plays, and these views sometimes differ greatly from those expressed by many world religions, including Christianity. Some Native literary critics, such as Jace Weaver (Cherokee) in *That the People Might Live*, argue that the dominant distinguishing feature of Native American literature is the way in which Native authors infuse their writings with worldviews that are – at their core – "theological" in nature (*That the People*, 28). Thus, readers and viewers of Native American drama will notice intense moments when physical and spiritual worlds intertwine. An example comes from *molly has her say* by Abenaki playwright Margaret Bruchac, who presents three characters from different generations simultaneously existing and influencing one another: Molly

Marie, a contemporary graduate student; Molly Ockett, an eighteenth-century Pequawket Abenaki doctor; and Old Mali, an ancient Abenaki grandmother. When such spiritual perspectives are staged, readers and viewers of Native plays will also notice an aesthetic distance. Reflecting New's prerequisite to not misuse Native spirituality, Native playwrights often stage the significance of the spiritual moment but honor the sacred nature of the details by keeping those private. In Bruce King's *Threads: Ethel Nickle's Little Acre,* we understand how the medicine inside Grandpa Woods' moose-hide bag transforms the family without King's having to expose to viewers the sacred items inside that bag (*Threads,* 162–164). In JudyLee Oliva's *Te Ata,* we hear Elder Te Ata's story of the Corn Ceremony, but the dancers on stage present "a stylized version" that protects the integrity of the actual ceremony (*Te Ata,* 9). These secularly staged spiritual moments, which are pervasive throughout Native plays, present one of the many attributes that make Native American dramaturgy so unique.

Related to its secular scope, Native American drama is largely *intertribal,* meaning that Native plays rarely address issues important to a single Native American nation; rather, they present topics that are relevant to people across Native America. Native playwrights often create characters that portray the variety of Native nations. Marie Clements, who is Metis, can create a play with Dene Nation, Japanese, and white characters, as she does in *Burning Vision;* or Yvette Nolan, who is Algonquin, can write *Annie Mae's Movement,* a biographical account of Anna Mae Pictou Aquash, a member of the Micmac Nation. Likewise, when Native plays are produced, it is not uncommon for Native actors to play characters who come from nations that are different from their own. For example, when Native Earth Performing Arts premiered Tomson Highway's *The Rez Sisters* in 1986, Gloria Miguel, Muriel Miguel, and Monique Mojica, who are all of Kuna/Rappahannock descent, played three Cree/Ojibway women (Highway, *Rez,* x). Through this intertribal nature of Native American drama, readers and viewers experience the multiculturalism of Native America, an abundant diversity that has existed since long before colonization.

MANY NATIONS, A NATIONALIST LITERATURE

Throughout these opening pages, I have referred to the names of many Native nations, while I have simultaneously used the general term, Native American, an arbitrary label that refers to the many indigenous nations of the American Western Hemisphere.[1] Already, as we address terminology

and the intertribal nature of Native American drama, it is clear that this field of theatre represents a broad range of complex theatrical activity growing out of the rich variety of Native multicultural experiences. In the United States alone there are well over 500 federally recognized Native nations existing within the federal nation's constructed boundaries. Each of these Native nations represents a distinct culture with its own history, language, homelands, and religion. Therefore, as I continue to write, I will introduce Native authors with their Native nations through the standard shorthand, thus: N. Scott Momaday (Kiowa). This diversity across Native America becomes complicated. It multiplies exponentially when one accounts for Native nations that are not federally recognized; for individuals who are members of more than one Native nation, or whose Native nations straddle international federal boundaries – such as the US/Canadian border; and for Native Americans who possess other ethnic backgrounds, such as German or African American heritage. Other factors, such as whether a person grew up on a reservation or in the city, within their nation's cultural traditions or removed from those traditions, all create a multiplicity of Native experiences that shape playwrights' expressions. Despite such wide-ranging diversity, Native artists and literary critics of Native and non-Native descent acknowledge a field of Native American theatre that holds the many, disparate Native voices together.

The gathering of theatrical voices from various Native nations derives in part from the intertribal theatre initiatives that generated the early Native American theatre movement beginning in the 1970s. The other influence comes from within this body of literature, something many critics have defined as a Native nationalist impulse that permeates Native literatures, including drama. Native American literary scholars, including Paula Gunn Allen (Laguna Pueblo/Sioux), Simon Ortiz (Acoma Pueblo), Robert Allen Warrior (Osage), Craig Womack (Creek/Cherokee), Daniel Justice, and Jace Weaver, have contributed to a substantial body of critical works addressing the distinctive attributes of Native American literature, particularly fiction and poetry. In their co-authored book, *American Indian Literary Nationalism*, Weaver, Womack, and Warrior build upon the foundations of their independent critical publications to call for a nationalist approach to Native literatures. The approach has three components: first, it embraces the established pre-colonial history of Native written and oral literatures, reaching back to the ancient Mayan and Aztec hieroglyphs through the rich storytelling traditions of Native peoples; second, it recognizes the distinctive worldview that commonly arises in the writings "of indigenous peoples of the hemisphere"; and, third, it requires critical approaches that can read "Native American literary output as separate and distinct from other national literatures" while supporting Native literature's "distinct identity" that functions "to serve the interests of indigenes and their communities," particularly with regard to issues of Native sovereignty (Weaver, *That the People*, 26; "Splitting" 165).

The differences between Native literatures and other literatures are both political and epistemological. Politically, Native literatures address issues of Native sovereignty – the right of each Native nation to govern itself through its own systems of law, societal structure, religion, and cultural values. In "Towards a National Indian Literature," Ortiz claims that Native authors write with:

a responsibility to advocate for their people's self-government, sovereignty, and control of land and natural resources; and…look also at racism, political and economic oppression, sexism, supremacism, and the needless and wasteful exploitation of land and people, especially in the US, [this responsibility is such a strong focus] that Indian literature is developing a character of nationalism which indeed it should have. (Ortiz, "Towards," 259)

While some readers might find the emphasis on sovereignty a post-colonial exercise, many Native literary critics caution against using such limited foundations for reading Native American literature. Thomas King (Cherokee) argues that the post-colonial lens, at best, fashions Native writing and art into a reactionary tactic against colonialism, a perspective that denies that Native artists write from their own volition. At worst, claims King, "the idea of post-colonial writing effectively cuts us off from our traditions, traditions that were in place before colonialism ever became a question, traditions which have come down to us through our cultures in spite of colonization" ("Godzilla," 11–12). For individuals, Native sovereignty itself encompasses a traditional, Native worldview that Weaver has broadly defined as something both spiritual and communal, a "oneness," or interconnectedness, that disregards the western boundaries between life and death; past, present, and future; spiritual and mundane; human and non-human. This ability to "embrace the universe" allows Native peoples to envision themselves as part of a "wider community," a term that Weaver claims "includes all the created order, which is also characterized in kinship terms. No sharp distinction is drawn between the human and non-human persons that make up the community"; thus, the term "'all my relations' is an encouragement for us to accept the responsibilities we have within this universal family" (*That the People*, 39).

Native American literature and, by extension, Native American drama actively strive for the continued emancipation of Native communities while, simultaneously, modeling the very philosophies that shape those communities. Playwright Floyd Favel has called Native theatre "an upstream journey to the source of the river of our culture, country and ourselves" ("Artificial Tree," 72). Naturally, in order to read these plays, one must be prepared to read with a perspective that is sensitive to the ways in which Native epistemologies shape the dramaturgy. We must understand how Native plays both reflect Native cultures and, in a reciprocal way, give back to Native communities.

NATIVE AMERICAN DRAMA

What may be most recognizable to readers and viewers who are encountering Native American drama for the first time is the reoccurrence of topics that address the more overt political sovereignty issues discussed above: reclaiming identities, revising history, revisiting oral traditions, and healing Native communities. Reclamation of Native American representation is quite common in Native plays for two reasons: the general theatre's long history of constructing Native American stereotypes of Indian princesses, vanishing nobles, and bloodthirsty savages, and because the Native American theatre presents an ideal venue for deconstructing such images. *Indian Radio Days*, by Choctaw playwrights LeAnne Howe and Roxy Gordon, is a farce set in a bingo parlor, where audiences play as they watch the recording of a "radio show." During the show's "commercial breaks," a series of Native American stereotypes are satirized, including the Indian princess used to promote "Land of Flakes Butter," and the mascot of Washington D.C.'s baseball team: "Coming this Saturday on RSN/Racist Sports Network is a classic rivalry that's guaranteed to give you testosterone fits! The 'Skins will try to fend off the Immigrants, live from RFK Stadium" (Howe and Gordon, *Radio Days*, 123, 122). Spiderwoman Theater's *Winnetou's Snake Oil Show from Wigwam City* comically lambasts German author Karl May's series of Winnetou stories, princesses from wild-west shows, and hobbyists' representations of Native American spirituality. Spiderwoman ends the play on a serious note, telling those who have co-opted and commoditized elements of Native spiritual traditions to "step back, move aside, sit down, hold your breath, save your own culture. Discover your own spirituality" (*Winnetou*, 30).

In addition to reclaiming representation of Native peoples' individual identities, many Native American plays revise history to honor the various ways Native people have survived European colonization of the Americas and international efforts to eradicate Native American cultures. Oliva's *Call of the River* presents the stories of contemporary Oklahomans who are descendants of the over thirty Native nations who were force-marched to Indian Territory beginning in the 1830s under the Indian Removal Act (1830). Nolan's *Annie Mae's Movement* explores the controversies surrounding the violent murder of Anna Mae Pictou Aquash, a leading member of the 1970s' American Indian Movement (AIM), whose death raises questions about the abuse of power in both the FBI and AIM. *The Indolent Boys*, a play by the famous author N. Scott Momaday, retells the story of three boys who were found frozen to death after having run away from boarding school in 1891. The play not only theatricalizes a story so important in Kiowa history that it was recorded in "pictographic calendars of the Kiowas," but also educates the public about the painful legacies of Indian boarding schools, where Native American children in the United States and Canada were forced to live away from their families while receiving an education that forbade speaking Native languages, practicing Native religions, and retaining Native cultural traditions (Momaday, *Indolent*, 5). As one reads such plays, it is often helpful to ground oneself in Native American history and a basic understanding of laws pertaining to Native American–national government relationships, especially those regarding Native homelands, languages, spiritual practices, education, and identity.[2]

Contradicting the systematic, historical attempts to remove Native peoples from their cultures, many of the plays in this field of drama evolve directly out of Native oral traditions that infuse constructions of both characters and plots. Many of Joseph Bruchac's (Abenaki) children's plays emerge out of the figures and events found in Native American legends. Joseph Dandurand's (Kwantlen) characters Sister Coyote and Brother Raven in *Please Do Not Touch the Indians* possess the qualities of their trickster namesakes. In *A Windigo Tale*, Armand Garnet Ruffo (Ojibway) draws upon the mythical Windigo, a giant, emaciated, ravenous cannibal, as a metaphor for the genocidal nature of Indian boarding schools. Even the name of the group Spiderwoman Theater comes from the Hopi deity, Spiderwoman, "who taught the people how to weave and said, 'You must make a mistake in every tapestry so that my spirit may come and go at will'" (Spiderwoman Theater, "About," 501). The group's storyweaving method emerges out of the very nature of storytelling, which is about finding one's placement within a community and connecting to that community as personal stories reveal points of connection between individuals.

NATIVE AMERICAN DRAMATURGY

This close connection between Native American theatre and Native story-telling is part of what makes Native dramaturgy so unique. Native plays are not merely a European form of expression used to convey Native American identity-based concerns; rather, they are, as Favel states, a form of "cere-monial life" that has the potential to "revitalize and transform" commun-ities; "we can touch the spirit of the dance, and the souls of our ancestors which live in the fibres and sinews of our bodies and in the pauses and intervals" (*Artificial Tree*, 71). Likewise, Ortiz argues that such Native artistic expressions, despite their use of the English language or certain literary conventions, remain Native American in their "truest and most authentic sense" because of "the creative ability of Indian people [to] gather in many forms of the socio-political colonizing force which beset them and to make these forms *meaningful in their own terms*" ("Towards," 254; emphasis added). The creative qualities that make the dramatic form "meaningful" in uniquely Native American terms is what sets Native American drama apart from other fields of theatre; these qualities are also what can befuddle readers and viewers who approach Native plays with criticism that is not rooted in Native intellectual traditions.[3]

The distinctive dramaturgical elements of Native American plays are actively pushing the boundaries of generalized theatrical performance and criticism. Like storytelling, Native plays often utilize a non-linear, some-times cyclical, plot structure, or – as we will see in a reading of Lynn Riggs' *The Cherokee Night* – a plot structure that mirrors a particular Native ceremony. Sometimes, the traditions of Native storytelling break the fourth wall to implicate the audience and make the viewers' experiences and stories part of the entire drama, literally setting in motion the communal, recip-rocal nature of Native storytelling. Sometimes, conflict, in the western dramatic sense, is not overt, as Native plays often focus on the interior issues of characters; and, sometimes, the very characters are difficult to recognize because they represent all the relations, from mythological, to non-human, to the spirit world, to the land itself. Weaver contends that Native literature's rejection of "any split between sacred and secular spheres" gives Native writing its distinctive quality, a worldview that "remains essentially religious, involving the Native's deepest sense of self and undergirding tribal life, existence, and identity" (*That the People*, 28).[4] Likewise, Native plays often dramatize the liquid boundaries between past and present, present and future, life and the afterlife. Such earthly/ spiritual interconnections open dramaturgical possibilities such as trickster shape-shifting and the synthesis of distant eras, and, in so doing, Native dramaturgy capitalizes on the extreme possibilities of human potential.

In a roundtable discussion on Native theatrical productions, the members of NAWPA discussed how "the most common element of their work that has often been misunderstood by non-Native audiences, directors, and performers is the concept of a coexistent spiritual reality" (Howard, "Introduction," 9). I have seen this confusion many times at post-performance discussions of Native American plays. My favorite example occurred after a Spiderwoman Theater performance of *Rever-ber-berations*, when a well-meaning audience member asked Gloria Miguel to talk about the portrayal of "the living dead" in the play. The combination of such misconceptions and the ever-broadening Native American theatre, which is now reaching both Native and non-Native viewers and readers, makes clear the need for a critical methodology specifically fashioned to address the unique attributes pervasive within Native American drama.

A CRITICAL PERSPECTIVE

While there is an abundance of Native American literary criticism devoted to how Native ways of knowing shape Native fiction and poetry, few critical studies have applied these Native epistemologies to drama. The trend is beginning, however, as more Native playwrights and scholars of Native theatre call increasingly for theoretical approaches that can address this field of drama that is, as Monique Mojica and Ric Knowles describe, "rooted in aboriginal world views and sensibilities" ("Introduction to *Staging*," v). Such studies will not only diminish the dangers of replicating a theoretical kind of colonization that derives from reading Native theatrical works with only non-Native, largely western-based concepts, but will also open new ways of seeing how Native concepts function, both on the page and in lived time and space. The theatre, with its aesthetic dependence on space, language, and movement, offers an ideal venue to explore Native American critical discourses, which derive directly from concepts of place, storytelling, and motion. Because Native American cultural theories connect quite naturally to the realm of the performative, a critical investigation of Native American dramaturgy accomplishes two things: it allows us to better understand this distinct field of drama by exploring Native theories in action, and it opens new ways of critically envisioning a fuller potential of theatre in general.

What I propose in this book is the first full-length examination of how Native American intellectual traditions actively construct Native theatre.[5] As such, this study will certainly be followed by others, as Native and non-Native scholars continue to build conversations amongst Native American drama, Native literary theory, and general theatrical criticism. I begin this study from the perspective that Native American drama is a separate field of theatre with a distinctive dramaturgy calling for critical understanding based particularly upon Native ways of knowing. Because of this approach, I privilege Native voices as I seek points of contact between Native American intellectual traditions and existing theatre theories. My goal is to offer a theoretical model for reading and viewing Native American plays, a model that is capable of addressing the unique qualities of Native American dramaturgy and is also mindful of the complex performative roots within and across Native American plays.

The abiding question that guides my research asks: how do points of contact between Native American intellectual traditions and theatre theories lead to a theoretical model that can de-center western theatrical perspectives while remaining flexible enough to accommodate the vast differences inherent within Native American theatre? What I offer is a dramaturgical model that presents a network of distinctive Native American discourses that focus on place, speech, and movement. These discourses are more than significant sites where Native American and theatrical theories intersect: they also comprise strands of Native American theories that actively weave from one discourse to the next. These interconnections provide flexibility for analyzing Native American plays, which themselves often serve as creative manifestations of Native cultural discourses.

Explaining how Native American aesthetics frequently embody Native theories, Kimberley Blaeser (Anishinaabe) has used a spider's web as a visual metaphor: the symbol conveys a quality of interrelatedness with a built-in flexibility. She states, "The web whose structure [Leslie Marmon] Silko identifies as central to Pueblo expression illustrates this complexity, involving as it does a center as well as an elaborate interweaving of both 'radial' and 'lateral' strands. In function it also involves the relationship between the various elements of construction, the vibration of the web in response to contact – motion" (Blaeser, "Like 'Reeds'," 557). In a similar fashion, I imagine the web as a metaphor for the theoretical model I offer in this book. The radial strands are the discourses of place, speech, and movement, and the lateral strands represent the multiple Native concepts that are contained within these discourses, ideas that endlessly intersect and affect one another. The limitless interconnections of ideas, which pull on and affect one another, accommodate the dynamic relationships and vast differences in Native American philosophies and theatre.

As we progress through this theoretical model for analyzing Native American plays, concepts of motion will provide the key for understanding the dynamism of Native American philosophies and for preventing the kind of criticism that distills Native works into stagnant categories. The concepts of motion I most frequently use come from Gerald Vizenor's (Anishinaabe) theory of "survivance," which is the survival and resistance of Native American people. Central to Vizenor's theory is the idea that continual motion prohibits the process of defining. Manifestations of continual motion (evident in trickster figures, metamorphoses, and transformations) run through Native American theatre and are reinforced through the inherent motion of theatre's live performance. This particular point of connection between Native philosophies and theatrical perform-ance sets the metaphorical stage for us to witness the multiplicity of Native voices and experiences ranging across and within Native American drama.

In order to demonstrate how these discourses function within Native American dramaturgy, I will divide the book into a series of chapters that first present each discourse and its interconnected concepts. Then, I will demonstrate, through close readings of selected Native American plays, how each discourse works to create meaning within different plays. Nine plays will serve as the subjects of these readings. Obviously, these nine works cannot represent the whole of Native theatre, but such limitations are necessary if we are going to look deeply into how the discourses function in Native plays. As I offer the analytical reading of these nine plays, I am aware that there is always an inherent problem in setting such boundaries in Native American studies. As Mojica and Knowles admit, such actions parallel colonizing tactics of "defining Native people's lands and measuring their identities"; however, such arbitrary boundaries are necessitated by the medium of print ("Introduction to *Staging*", iii). Accordingly, the scope I have selected for this book focuses on Native American drama in English from the United States and Canada. While I believe that Native plays from Latin America would also provide enlightening discussions about how the discourses function within Native plays, I have chosen to limit my focus to playwrights from the two countries that have shared a similar, concurrent history of Native theatrical development, which I outlined in "A History of Native American Drama" (chapter 1).

With my selection of plays and playwrights, I hope to demonstrate a range of theatrical styles and diversity of perspectives that Native American playwrights bring to their writings. The playwrights represent Native theatrical activity occurring in both the professional theatre and grassroots communities. Representing Native nations from across the United States and Canada, these authors reflect various Native American experiences, urban and traditional, historical and present. Cherokee playwright Lynn Riggs is the oldest playwright represented. His work reflects Native American playwriting in the professional theatre during the 1930s, an era prior to the civil rights movement and the freedoms it created for individuals to express their ethnic heritages. Similar to Riggs, Kiowa and Delaware playwright Hanay Geiogamah traveled from Oklahoma to New York, but the theatrical venues where his most famous plays were staged in the 1970s were experimental and embraced an active, sometimes overtly political, expression of intertribal Native identity. Spiderwoman Theater's plays also incorporate elements from the Red Power era and the experimental theatre of the 1960s and 1970s, but their plays are more closely connected to their personal experiences as Kuna and Rappahannock women who hail from Brooklyn, New York. Their blended heritage itself, Kuna (from Panama) and Rappahannock (from Virginia), tells a story of Native American survival: how new Native identities with unusual geographies emerged to undermine the forces of colonization.[6]

Tomson Highway, a Cree playwright originally from northern Manitoba, is the eleventh of twelve children and was born in a tent on his father's trap-line "not 10 feet from the dog-sled" his family used to travel in ("Introduction," vi). Highway spoke Cree exclusively until he was sent into the Canadian Indian boarding-school system at the age of six. Now "urban by choice," Highway writes for the professional theatre, where he is the most internationally acclaimed Native American playwright (Highway, "On Native," 1). Vera Manuel is a Secwepemc/Ktunaxa playwright and poet from British Columbia whose main concern is healing her community. She explains, "'My whole life I've been really working closely with my people, with the struggles that I see my people going through, generational grief things that people are struggling with'"; accordingly, her plays use streamlined theatrical conventions that are accessible to theatre venues in communities (Manuel qtd. in Howard, "Introduction," 8). Diane Glancy, a Cherokee playwright who is quite well known for her novels and poetry, creates her plays from an experimental perspective, challenging dramatic conventions with an intensive literary focus, in a manner similar to the works of Adrienne Kennedy and Gertrude Stein.

Metis playwright Marie Clements of Vancouver pushes the theatre's visual and staging boundaries with her mixed-media productions that collage layers of imagery with the rich languages of Native mythology and spoken-word poetry. The staging of her multi-media productions, written from an urban Native perspective, requires professional theatrical venues.

JudyLee Oliva, a nationally recognized Chickasaw playwright with a Master of Fine Arts in directing and a doctorate in theatre, also writes plays that often require complex technical-theatre capabilities, although her plays do range over many theatrical styles, from the theatre of the absurd, to realism, to intricate episodic plots. Oliva states:

I think it's important to understand that as a writer I've been trained in western theatre; at the same time, I know what storytelling is[...]I just think that Native people, as well as other cultures, need to see that we can tell our stories in main- stream theatre. We don't just have to have a small little set and tell stories and play the flute. We can have an orchestra, and the play can be about Native people (qtd. in Stanlake, "Interview," 116).

Victoria Nalani Kneubuhl, who is Native Hawaiian and Samoan, brings together her specific focus on Native Hawaiian and Samoan communities with a vision for the mainstream, professional theatre. While some readers may question my choice to include Kneubuhl within this study, I offer the critical reading of her work, in part, to demonstrate the difficulties of defining the field of Native American drama. Kneubuhl's plays, which draw upon the culture and history of Pacific Islanders, are regularly included in Native American play anthologies; in collections, such as those at NAWPA; and at theatrical events, such as the annual Native Theater Festival hosted by New York's Public Theater.[7] Many of Kneubuhl's plays have been commissioned for specific Hawaiian events and venues, and while theatres such as Kuma Kuhua Theatre of Honolulu produce her plays, Kneubuhl's work is quite accessible to theatre companies outside of Hawaii and Samoa.

The nine plays I have selected from these playwrights represent the history of Native American dramaturgy from 1932, the year that Riggs attempted to create a distinctly Native American play with *The Cherokee Night*, to Highway's 2004 script of *Ernestine Shuswap Gets Her Trout*, a play co- commissioned by the Secwepemc Cultural Education Society and Western Canada Theatre in honor of the 1910 Laurier Memorial, a document from the tribal Chiefs of the Thompson River Valley in British Columbia to the Prime Minister of Canada (see page 115). I believe that these nine plays provide very clear examples of how each discourse can function in Native American drama, and I have chosen them both for their artistic quality and for the ways in which their authors meld particular intellectual traditions with dramaturgical designs. Accordingly, I situate each script within an analytical discussion of the particular discourse that it most closely exemplifies. Such pairings will offer readers the clearest examples of how the discourses work to create meaning in Native American plays. Despite my choice to pair plays with the discourses to which they most closely correspond, I would like to suggest that any of the nine plays represented in this study could be read effectively through any combination of the three discourses this book presents. Moreover, I contend that these three discourses with their interconnected concepts present a helpful analytical tool for approaching the dramaturgical attributes of almost any Native American play.

The remainder of this book is separated into six analytical chapters followed by a brief conclusion. The six internal chapters follow a general pattern of introducing a Native American dramaturgical discourse followed by an examination of that discourse in action. "Native American platial history" (chapter 3), "Native storytelling" (chapter 5), and "Representing uncontainable identities" (chapter 7) respectively introduce the three discourses of place, speech, and motion. I follow each introductory chapter with a critical chapter that traces how three different plays manifest the discourse through their dramaturgical structures. Through this arrangement, I seek to lead readers through a network of critical ideas circulating within Native American dramaturgy.

"Native American platial history" (chapter 3) investigates Native American philosophies of place, such as Jana Sequoya's (Chickasaw) theory of geocentric identity, Vine Deloria, Jr.'s (Dakota Sioux) theory of place-based religions, and Jeannette C. Armstrong's (Okanagan) theory of land speaking. These Native American platial theories are synthesized with theatrical spatial theories, such as Una Chaudhuri's theory of geopathology in *Staging Place: The Geopathology of Modern Drama*. In "Platiality in Native American Drama" (chapter 4), I will demonstrate how platial theories create dramaturgical structures in three plays: Riggs' *The Cherokee Night*, Oliva's *The Fire and the Rose*, and Kneubuhl's *The Story of Susanna*. *The Cherokee Night* follows a ceremonial plot structure that reveals how a group of youths with Cherokee lineage identify with and deny their heritage over a span of thirty-six years, from 1895 through 1931. Oliva's *The Fire and the Rose* bases its structure on T. S. Eliot's *Four Quartets*. The play presents the friendship of two women, one Native and one non-Native, whose personal and professional struggles extend from life into the realm of the afterlife. Kneubuhl's *The Story of Susanna* fuses two stories, one biblical and the other contemporary, to investigate feminist issues of violence against women and claiming voice. Although these three plays represent both early and contemporary Native American dramaturgy and incorporate three vastly different approaches to plot structure and subject matter, Native intellectual traditions of place figure prominently in them all.

"Native storytelling" (chapter 5) examines the connection between traditional storytelling and live performance. LeAnne Howe's theory of tribalography, or the ability for stories to create a rhetorical space in which people can thread their own stories and histories into the stories and histories of other people, grounds the theories presented in this chapter. It is read in relation to works by other Native American theorists, such as Elizabeth Woody (Yakama/Navajo), Diane Glancy, and Paula Gunn Allen, who critically investigate storying, the tendency of many Native languages to linguistically link concepts of thought, wind, breath, speech, creation, storytelling, history, and teaching. Both tribalography and storying relate well with theatrical theories about language, such as Helen Gilbert and Joanne Tompkins' post-colonial theories of revisionist history and Elin Diamond's investigation of feminist storytelling and Brechtian techniques. "Storying and tribalography in Native American drama" (chapter 6) demonstrates how both tribalography and storying open new theoretical perspectives in Native plays, such as Spiderwoman Theater's *Rever-ber-berations*, Manuel's *The Strength of Indian Women*, and Highway's *Ernestine Shuswap*. Characteristic of Spiderwoman's plays, *Rever-ber-berations* is a script that requires that the writers (Lisa Mayo, Gloria Miguel, and Muriel Miguel) enact it. The play is the most serious of Spiderwoman's works, as it intimately investigates how each of the three sisters came to embrace her mother's spirituality. Manuel's *Strength of Indian Women* is concerned with helping Native American communities heal through openly airing their stories of boarding-school abuses. The play uses a fairly realistic, domestic, climactic-plot structure to model for viewers the therapeutic benefits of talking about the ways that past boarding-school experiences continue to affect the health of Native American communities. *Ernestine Shuswap*, Highway's recently commissioned play, blends his professional theatre style with community activism. Written to commemorate the Laurier Memorial, *Ernestine Shuswap* capitalizes on Highway's signature trickster humor to help stage the construction of the historic document. The dramatic effect is hilarious and deeply disturbing, educational and eventually hopeful.

"Representing uncontainable identities" (chapter 7) introduces Vizenor's theory of survivance in order to investigate how Native American theoretical concepts of movement influence Native American dramaturgy. According to Vizenor's theory, Native American peoples' survival depends upon their ability to resist defined categories that can easily turn into stereotypical representations. This theory intersects with post-colonial readings that address portrayals of Native American identities and also sets the stage for readers to view the transformations and metamorphoses that regularly occur in Native American literature. The philosophy of survivance has roots in traditional Native American creation stories, emphasizing motion and change through Native concepts of chance, seasonal cycles, human/earth reciprocity, and trickster transformations. "Acts of survivance in Native American drama" (chapter 8) traces the discourse of movement through the metamorphosis-rich texts of Geiogamah's *Foghorn*, Glancy's *The Woman Who Was a Red Deer Dressed for the Deer Dance*, and Clements' *Urban Tattoo*. Originally staged by NATE in 1973, during the height of the Red Power Movement, *Foghorn* is one of the most political plays in Native American theatre. The episodic script uses biting satire to make a statement about the troubled history of colonization and the evolving relationship between Native peoples and the federal government. Glancy's *Red Deer* is an experimental play that focuses on fusions of monologue and dialogue, myth and reality, to portray dissonances and fissures in the conversations between a traditional Cherokee grandmother and her troubled granddaughter. Clements' *Urban Tattoo* is a one-woman play that Clements both wrote and performed, although the script would not lose meaning if another actor were to present it. Representative of Clements' work, the play fuses performance traditions of acting, spoken word, song, mythology, and dance; it also incorporates both a physical set and a virtual set of projections and film. The play tells the survival story of Rosemarie, a young woman who leaves her Native community to work in the city, where her identity comes under attack.

The last chapter, "Interconnected theories and the future of Native American drama," reviews the discourses and discusses how the concepts contained within them often work in concert with one another. Emphasizing the points of connection across the discourses enables people to envision the inherent complexity of Native American dramaturgy, the multiple ways in which Native plays work to make meaning from a diversity of Native experiences. The chapter concludes by indicating the potential for Native American theatre's unique and intricate dramaturgical networks to expand existing theoretical methodologies within the general discipline of theatre studies.

CHAPTER 3

Native American platial history

> The multifaceted battle to appropriate Native land, supplant Native Religion, and undermine Native traditional structures is the mise-en-scène of American Indian intellectual work of the past one hundred years.
>
> Robert Allen Warrior (Osage), *Tribal Secrets*, 87

To speak creditably about the ways Native American theories of place infuse Native literature, it is necessary to have a rudimentary knowledge of American history from a perspective of those whose ancestors first belonged to these lands. History, like theatre, is open to interpretation, and the stories of history that are most valued by a national government usually become the stories that are canonized as the country's "official" history taught within the public-school system. In "The Demography of Native North America," Lenore Stiffarm (Gros Ventre) and Phil Lane, Jr. (Yankton Sioux/Chickasaw) take a revisionist-history approach to the well-known story about how North America was first settled by colonists laying the groundwork for the future United States.

Basing their study on estimates of pre-European contact populations, Stiffarm and Lane construct a very different version of this "land of the pilgrim's pride." Rather than telling a romantic story of Europeans discovering a sparsely inhabited, virgin wilderness from which they carved a civilization, this account of American history tells of a continent rich with millions of indigenous inhabitants who belonged to hundreds of distinct Native nations, many structured in agriculturally based communities that regularly traded with other Native nations in well-established trading towns. According to this version of America's founding, the effectiveness of the hungry and weary settlers to cultivate a "wild" land did not happen by divine assistance, but through force. European settlers built their towns upon the pre-established Native American towns. Even the US capital was built on top of a Conoy Indian trading town, Naconchtanke (Weatherford, *Indian Givers*, 231).

Stiffarm and Lane argue that a faulty pre-contact population estimate by the anthropologist James Mooney helps to continue the silencing of Native American versions of history. In the 1920s, Mooney claimed that 1,152,590 Native people existed in North America in the year 1500. He derived this number from "counts of Indians recorded by the original New England colonists," estimates that were highly problematic owing to the imported epidemics that had swiftly devastated indigenous populations. Mooney then further reduced these numbers by half because he found the colonists' counts to be "exaggerated"' (Stiffarm and Lane, "Demography," 24). As time passed, scholars quoted Mooney's estimate, and then quoted each other quoting Mooney's estimate, until the figure of 1 million pre-contact Native Americans was regarded as fact.

Significantly, contemporaries of Mooney, such as Herbert Spinden, arrived at higher population numbers. Using burial-mound archeology as the basis for his study, Spinden estimated that "fifty to seventy-five-million Native people had lived in the Americas (*circa* 1200)...[and that] the population of the Ohio River Valley alone had been as great as Mooney's estimate for the entirety of North America"[2] (ibid., 25). Stiffarm and Lane cite other scholars' estimates of pre-contact populations, such as Emmanuel H. Domenech's (1860) estimate of 16 to 17 million in North America; Woodrow Borah, Leslie Simpson, and Sherburn Cook's (1964) estimate of 100 million in the hemisphere; and Kirkpatrick Sale's (1990) estimate of 15 million Native Americans in North America (ibid., 25–27).

What is at stake in continuing to cite and teach Mooney's estimate of 1,152,590 Native Americans? And how is that number connected to the issue of place? First, larger numbers would challenge the myth of how America was settled. A population of 1 to 2 million North American inhabitants supports the legend that this continent had vast, uninhabited virgin lands just waiting to be settled. The low population number also supports the myth that Native peoples were disordered, nomadic wanderers, with communities too small to achieve stability or longevity. Moreover, these small numbers lighten the burden of guilt associated with the European invasion: if only 1 to 2 million people lived on America's soil, then the epidemics of smallpox, whooping cough, measles, and scarlet fever must have done little to diminish the indigenous populations of North America.

Conversely, when one accepts a much larger population estimate, one also must acknowledge that agricultural communities played a large part in sustaining the population, a concept supported by the fact that four-sevenths (by conservative estimates) to two-thirds (by liberal estimates) of today's American agriculture are plants that were domesticated and cultivated by pre-contact Native American communities (ibid., 30). To recognize a population of 15 million is to acknowledge that Native nations were organized, self-sufficient, stable, and healthy. It is to accept that the colonists' settling of America occurred not by discovery but through ugly, brutal conquest, an interruption to the citizenry that had already cultivated these lands long ago. Such ideas interrogate the very laws Euro-Americans used to justify their "natural rights" to the land.

In 1823, Supreme Court Chief Justice John Marshall ruled in the *Johnson* v. *McIntosh* case that "the U.S. holds 'inherent and preeminent rights' over Indian lands" (ibid., 28). This decision created legal precedents for future land disputes between Native American peoples and the United States.[3] Marshall derived his decision from the British Doctrine of Discovery and Rights of Conquest, which developed out of the medieval concept of "Norman Yoke." Stiffarm and Lane (ibid., 28) explain:

In simplest terms, the concept [Norman Yoke] as it was eventually articulated in John Locke's philosophy of Natural Law,[4] held that any "Christian" (read: European) happening upon "waste land" – most particularly land that was vacant or virtually vacant of human inhabitants – assumed not only a "natural right," but indeed *an obligation* to put such land to "productive use." Having thus performed "God's will" by "cultivating" and thereby "conquering" the former "wilderness," its "discoverer" can be said to own it.[5]

For the Doctrine of Discovery and Rights of Conquest to pertain to American soil, it was imperative for the United States to deny the existence of a large Native American population with diverse, dynamic communities that had already cultivated the wilderness and put the land to "productive use." By constructing a romanticized myth about an untamed continent inhabited sparsely by "savages" who were "too primitive" to develop the land's natural resources, the US government justified its legal claim – albeit through its own laws – to the land. When viewed through the context of US legal justifications for land rights, Mooney's population estimates can be viewed as both a product and instrument of America's mythic founding. Mooney's population of 1,152,590 Native Americans was produced from the same ideology that Marshall used to grant the United States "inherent and preeminent rights" over Native American homelands. As an instrument of the American myth, Mooney's estimate helps to silence alternative versions of American history.

Marshall's 1823 decision continued the United States' willful ignorance of Native American peoples by providing one answer to the nation's "Indian Question," which asked: how might Americans deal with the Native populations that must be displaced from their traditional lands so that Euro-Americans can gain control of the land and its resources? All various answers to the "Indian Question" concentrated on the continued eradication of Native American peoples. Often this erasure took the form of genocide, as in the "Indian Wars" (1816–1890s),[6] during which the United States aimed to "exterminate" all Native Americans who refused to relinquish traditional lands demanded by the federal government. Coinciding with the Indian Wars were the years of "Indian Removal" or "Relocation," which lasted roughly from 1816 to 1850.[7] Following the War of 1812, the US government entered into a series of treaties with Native nations that exchanged Native lands east of the Mississippi River for money and new lands west of the Mississippi River. William T. Hagan explains, "There was ample evidence to indicate that these treaties were of the usual pattern. Bribery was common with chiefs succumbing to a variety of enticements" (*American Indians*, 80).[8] Frank Pommersheim, Chief Justice for the Cheyenne River Sioux Tribal Court of Appeals and Associate Justice for the Mississippi Band of Choctaw Supreme Court, argues that while the exchange of land made little financial sense, what was at stake for Native peoples was an autonomous way of life in a *guaranteed homeland*. Pommersheim explains:

> Treaties represent a bargained-for exchange, and it is important to understand what the exchange was. The Indians usually agreed to make peace and cede land – often vast amounts of it – to the federal government in exchange for a cessation of hostilities, the provision of some services, and most important, the *establishment and recognition of a homeland* free from the incursion of both the state and non-Indian settlers. (*Braid of Feathers*, 17; emphasis added)

In the exchange of irreplaceable traditional homelands, Native peoples negotiated for something even more priceless: lands within which tribal nations could live according to their own traditions without further displacement. However, as Manifest Destiny moved westward, the United States' promises of lands protected, or "reserved," for Native Americans were soon broken.

The General Allotment Act of 1887 worked to fracture Native American communities and traditions in much the same way as westward expansion had divided the lands of Native America. Again, the conduit of this policy was land. The objective of the General Allotment Act was twofold: first, it aimed to transfer more Native American lands to non-Native peoples; second, it worked to further weaken Native communities by dissolving their cultural networks from within the tribally held lands. The General

Allotment Act, which was legally in effect until 1934, undermined Native American traditional concepts of communal land ownership by dividing the reserved lands into portions that were then allotted to individuals. The act "authorized the Bureau of Indian Affairs (BIA) to allot 160 acres of tribal land to each head of household and forty acres to each minor" (ibid., 19). "Heads of households" were defined as males, which meant that this method of land allocation often undermined the role of Native American women, who within matrilineal societies were traditionally recognized as the heads of families. Not only did the act value men above women, it valued partially white Native people above those who did not have European heritage. Stiffarm and Lane ("Demography," 40–41) state:

all full-bloods were tightly restricted to small land parcels and, as legally defined "incompetents," expressly denied control over them for a minimum of twenty-five years. Mixed-bloods, on the other hand, were often allotted much larger parcels, often in better areas, and with immediate full control over their property.[9] Such processes...served to foster deep divisions within most native societies over the years.

The devastation caused by the General Allotment Act did not end with its attempts to destabilize Native American traditions and communities: it also overturned the previous treaty agreements protecting "reserved" lands. Through parceling off sections of land to individual Native people, the federal government was left with a "surplus" of formerly reserved lands. The government opened the surplus for non-Native homesteading. The Oklahoma land-run of 1889 is one example of how the General Allotment Act opened Native American lands to non-Native settlers.[10] During the years of the General Allotment Act's operation, the 138 million acres of lands reserved for Native Americans shrank to 52 million acres. The once-protected lands of tribal nations became checkered with non-Native people who further interfered with Native American traditions, institutions, and communities. This disruption aided the goal of the act: to eliminate Native cultures through assimilation. Pommersheim states, "President Theodore Roosevelt most forcefully described this Act as 'a mighty pulverizing engine to break up the tribal mass. It acts directly upon the family and the individual'"[11] (*Braid of Feathers*, 19).

The objective to "break up the tribal mass" by attacking "the family and the individual" became easier after the General Allotment Act. The ability of members of tribal nations to self-govern was hindered by the growing influence of federal government policies and compulsory Christianity. Christian organizations planted themselves upon the surplus reservation lands and, in collaboration with the BIA, attempted to eradicate Native American spiritual identity. Pommersheim (ibid., 21) states:

The missionaries in particular wreaked havoc with their religious and educational programs, particularly the boarding school program which took Indian children away from their families for substantial periods of time and specifically forbade the speaking of tribal languages in school. It is not difficult to perceive the strain and pressure placed on traditional culture under these circumstances. This is even more apparent when these policies were joined to BIA directives outlawing traditional religious practices…As a result, the core of the culture was driven underground in a shadow existence.

Through the boarding-school system, which transplanted children – ages five to twenty-one – from their homelands to schools often hundreds of miles away, the federal government attempted to halt the transmission of Native American cultures from parents and elders to their children. On various fronts, boarding schools assaulted the children's sense of belonging to their distinct tribal nations. Boarding schools often combined children from different Native American cultures in an attempt to discourage communication amongst the children, who spoke different languages and had different customs according to their cultures. This practice also attempted to expunge, from the children's hearts, their unique identities. Under the boarding-school system, children were all labeled as a homogeneous group, "Indians," rather than by the names of their individual Native nations. Individualized identity was further erased through rules that forced children to speak only English, forbad the practice of Native religions, and required students to cut their hair and wear the clothing provided by the schools. Most boarding schools provided no seasonal breaks for children and, instead, worked the children through the summers in order to help pay for school expenses. In "American Indian Education in the United States: Indoctrination for Subordination to Colonialism," Jorge Noriega (Mestizo) states that:

It was not unusual, under these conditions, for a child to be taken at age six or seven and to never see his or her home and family again until age seventeen or eighteen. At this point, they were often *sent* back, but in a condition largely devoid of conceptions of both their own cultures and their intended roles within them. ("American Indian," 381)

The attendance of Native American children in government-sanctioned Indian schools was made compulsory from the 1887 General Allotment Act until the 1934 Indian Reorganization Act, which then favored less expensive, government-supported day schools. Nevertheless, many Indian boarding schools continued to be in existence through the 1970s.[12]

By uprooting children from their homes and families, the federal government appeared to succeed at "killing the Indian"[13] within the children. Indeed, the government's tactics were powerful, but they were not defeating. Hanay Geiogamah states, "It was not until the late 1940s and early 1950s that cultural traditions and performances would reawaken within tribal life and slowly begin to generate creative energy and vision for a new phase of Indian people's journey" ("New American Indian," 159). This journey, in many ways, builds upon reclaiming relationships to place: the individual's place within one's tribal nation, the history of Native peoples on the continent, and the right to practice Native religions upon sacred places. It is not without significance that the 1978 American Indian Religious Freedom Act bridges the concept of place with religious practices. As Hagan states, the act "declared that the United States would 'protect and preserve for American Indians their inherent right of freedom to believe, express, and exercise the traditional religions'." And this would include "'*access to sites*, use and possession of sacred objects, and the freedom to worship through ceremonials and traditional rites'" (*American Indians*, 208; emphasis added).[14]

This connection between Native American peoples and the lands integral to their cultures is a through-line which one can use not only to retrace the histories of distinct Native nations, but also to understand the complex concepts shaping the various aesthetic works of Native artists today. When Robert Allen Warrior writes that the relationship between Native American communities and place is such a crucial component of knowledge that it drives Native American scholarship, his terminology in such phrases as "sup*plant* Native religion" and "under*mine* Native traditional social structures" points to how Native American authors are using concepts of place in the construction of their theoretical and artistic works (*Tribal Secrets*, 87; emphasis added). In theatre, this emphasis on people's relationships with the land creates a distinctive dramaturgical attribute that emphasizes a complicated networking of ideas relating to place. This is not to say that all Native playwrights approach place in the same way. On the contrary, Native playwrights approach place with an infinite array of considerations, perspectives, and experiences. Nevertheless, due to the relationships Native nations have historically maintained with their homelands, and the way in which the acquisition of those lands was the dominant aim of colonization, issues of place figure prominently throughout Native American theatrical literature, as Native American perspectives of place shape concepts of language, community, religion, and politics.

CHAPTER 4

Platiality in Native American drama

[One] of the results of over three centuries of contact has been the
nearly complete severing of this cultural taproot connecting Indian
people to the land. Impaired but not eradicated, this root is being
rediscovered and tended with renewed vigor and stewardship.

Pommersheim, *Braid of Feathers*, 14

There is a stated belief that the magic of words holds things together
and provides stability for the people. Native Theater was established
on that hope. It is a gathering of stories in a setting in order to connect
with the land, to find placement for the words even if that land is
somewhere in the human heart.

Diane Glancy (Cherokee), "Native American Theater"

Place figures so predominantly in Native American plays that one could
argue that it carries the same value as characters do and often functions just
as actively. Speaking of what inspires many Native American dramatists to
write, Tomson Highway explains that Native theatre is an art form that
reminds all people to honor the deep culture and meanings residing in the
land. He states, "we…ultimately want to be heard so the dreamlife of this
particular people, this particular landscape, can achieve some degree of
exposure among general audiences. They just may learn, we keep hoping,
something new and something terribly relevant and beautiful about that
particular landscape they too have become inhabitants of" (Highway, "On
Native," 3). Staging this awareness of the land's profound meanings is one of
the Native theatre's strongest dramaturgical attributes.

Accordingly, many Native playwrights speak, as Highway does, about
the important roles that place enacts in Native dramaturgy. Delaware
playwright Daniel David Moses recalls how Ben Cardinal's (Cree) play
Generic Warriors and No Name Indians won him over when it staged the
connections that multiple generations of people can make through place.
He states, "Native writers write differently from non-Native writers, I saw
the reason I have fallen in love with the play had to do with recognizing the

way it structured reality and the landscape it grew from" (Moses, "Handful," 143). Concepts of place inform the dramatic structure of Native plays, such as Patti Flather and Leonard Linklater's (Vuntut Gwich'in) *Sixty Below*, where "the spirit world and the landscape are one"; and Drew Hayden Taylor's *Girl Who Loved Her Horses*, in which the play's tranquil pacing is periodically "ruptured by the insistent intrusion of the numinous" earth (D'Aeath, "Introduction to *Sixty Below*," 431; Mojica and Knowles, "Introduction to *Girl*," 313). In other works, such as Daystar's (Pembina Chippewa) dance-drama *No Home but the Heart*, place creates both the dramatic structure and the protagonist's superobjective, to trace her way back to her ancestors and homelands. In a more lighthearted discussion of place, Highway's introduction to the popular *Rez Sisters* claims that his ambition "in life is to make 'the rez' cool, to show and celebrate what funky folk Canada's Indian people really are" ("Introduction," iv). Native American dramatists' broad emphasis on the relevance of place makes platial discourse a significant element of Native dramaturgy, an element to which readers and viewers of Native plays must pay close attention. In these Native American plays, concepts of character, belonging, spirituality, time, and language all emanate from interrelated concepts of place.

Platial theory provides a significant point of connection between theatrical criticism and Native American literary theory. Investigating theatrical theories alone is to never know the full power of place, how deeply Native concepts of place-focused language, community, and belief systems can enrich our understandings of platiality. Similarly, Native American literary theories that do not explore how concepts of place are enacted upon the Native stage miss envisioning the full power of palatial theories, as they infuse an art form that depends upon the dynamics of lived time and space. Native American plays offer a uniquely visceral venue for us to explore the potential of theories of place.

Recent theatrical scholarship has focused a great amount of attention on platial theories, but only recently has this scholarship begun to look at Native American plays.[1] Una Chaudhuri's aforementioned *Staging Place* provides an important example of theatrical platial theory that uses a theoretical discourse of place to develop a critical theory intended for the analysis of both mainstream and marginal drama from the nineteenth century forward (*Staging Place*, xiii). While Chaudhuri's platial methodology deals with what she calls the "painful politics of location," her theory does not develop platial concepts that are particular to Native American dramaturgy (ibid., 56). Largely, Chaudhuri's theory of place is concerned with issues of identity in modern and contemporary drama, particularly those issues that hinge upon "a negotiation with – and on occasion a heroic overcoming of – the power of place" (ibid.). This theory of place focuses predominantly on the realm of the metaphor of home.

Conversely, the relationship between place and a person's existence in Native American literature extends the metaphor of home into a very literal understanding of place, specifically land. The difference between figurative and literal connections between people and homelands is the primary difference between Native and non-Native theories of place; thus, in Native American theatre, it is important to differentiate between space and place. In *Space and Place: The Perspective of Experience*, geographer Yi-Fu Tuan pinpoints the distinction by explaining, "In experience, the meaning of space often merges with that of place. 'Space' is more abstract than 'place.' What begins as undifferentiated space becomes place as we get to know it better and endow it with value" (*Space and Place*, 6). Place is what results when people experience a location, physically, and come to understand that location through both body and mind. Philosopher Edward Casey emphasizes the necessity of embodied experiences upon landscapes in his definition of place. He states, "Body and landscape present themselves as coeval epicenters around which particular places pivot and radiate. They are, at the very least, the bounds of places...Between the two boundaries [of body and landscape] – and very much as a function of their differential interplay – implacement occurs. *Place is what takes place between body and landscape*" (*Getting Back*, 29, emphasis added). The notion that places, specific landscapes, are endowed with value, which can only be fully realized through a physical interaction with the land, underpins many Native American writings about the relationship between people and places. For example, N. Scott Momaday's *The Way to Rainy Mountain*, an autobiographical account of the author's journey retracing the Kiowa migration from Western Montana to Oklahoma, ends with the recommendation:

Once in his life a man ought to concentrate his mind upon the remembered earth, I believe. He ought to give himself up to a particular landscape in his experience, to look at it from as many angles as he can, to wonder about it, to dwell upon it. He ought to imagine that he touches it with his hands at every season and listens to the sounds that are made upon it. He ought to imagine the creatures there and all the faintest motions of the wind. He ought to recollect the glare of noon and all the colors of dawn and dusk. (*Rainy Mountain*, 83)

Momaday's advice emphasizes intimate relationships between humans and specific landscapes that, although emotional and mental, must be forged through lived experience. Literal, embodied exchanges between people and lands that result in "implacement," or a deeper knowledge of one's values and culture(s), is what moves me to speak of Native American concepts of land as *place*, over the more generic sense of *space*. As Helen Gilbert and Joanne Tompkins suggest regarding indigenous theatre, Native American plays often counter dramaturgies that relegate landscape to scenery, mood, and given circumstances; thus, they "can effectively dismantle the myth of *terra nullius* by revealing the land as an object of discursive and territorial contention, as well as an 'accumulative text' that records in multiple inscriptions the spatial forms and fantasies of both settler and indigenous cultures" (*Post-Colonial Drama*, 156). In Native dramaturgy, places, like characters, not only record cultural history, but also dynamically participate in the play's present actions through relationships forged between human beings and the land. Accordingly, when discussing Native American dramatic enactments of place, I will refer to them as "platial," borrowing from Chaudhuri's term "platiality," which she defines as "a recognition of the signifying power and political potential of *specific places*" (*Staging Place*, 5).

As I discussed in the previous chapter, this literal sense of place is developed out of the complicated histories between Native American peoples and lands. Chickasaw writer Jana Sequoya explains in her essay "How (!) Is an Indian?" that:

> The conditions of being Indian have changed...and many of those changes are directly related to differing degrees of access to land and resources among Native American peoples, as well as to corresponding restrictions on traditional religious and economic practices which depend on such access. Real...answers to the question of "how" is an Indian, then, must depend in part on whether one is Indian in the city or the country; whether in the ways of tradition or of modernization; whether drawing more on old or on new cultural influences. ("How (!)," 455)

With this link between literal place and identity, Native concepts of place extend the existing theatrical models of platial theory. In Native American dramaturgy, home is a physical place which has a network of meaningful information rooted within it. Moreover, dramatic articulations of Native American platial philosophies do not exist in a vacuum; rather, they are a continuation of a philosophy that appears across many genres of Native American literature. Robert Allen Warrior maintains that issues of place are a crucial component of Native American intellectual traditions, while Pommersheim stresses the importance of place not just in legal activity but also in literature. He states that the connection between Native peoples and the land "is so prevalent that it has been noted as a recurrent theme in contemporary Indian literature. The theme involves the loss of the old guardian spirits of place and the process by which they might be made to speak again – how the land may become numinous once more and speak to its dwellers" (*Braid of Feathers*, 14). Because Native American platial theories have a rich history of shaping Native art and scholarship, they offer an ideal way to approach Native theatre in a manner that builds upon generalized theatrical theories while honoring the distinctive attributes of Native dramaturgy. To demonstrate how platial discourse both informs Native American dramaturgy and extends theatrical theories of place, this chapter investigates three Native plays that function strongly as an aesthetic manifestation of Native American platial theories. I begin the exploration of platiality in Native dramaturgy with an analysis of Lynn Riggs' *The Cherokee Night*,[2] the author's attempt to create a distinctly Native form of drama. I read Riggs' 1932 drama in tandem with two contemporary Native plays that also draw upon interweaving concepts within Native platial discourse: JudyLee Oliva's *The Fire and the Rose*[3] and Victoria Nalani Kneubuhl's *The Story of Susanna*.[4] Within all three plays, platial concepts structure the dramatic meanings within the plays and also provide insight into the plays' staging.

Riggs' *The Cherokee Night* dramatically records the difficulties that Native people faced when they attempted to rekindle a relationship with their numinous homelands while living within a general society that actively worked to eradicate Native traditions. Set between the years 1895 and 1931, the play focuses on a group of mixed-blood Cherokee youths who come of age during the turbulent period created by laws seeking to divide tribal communities when Indian Territory transitioned to Oklahoma statehood in 1907. The many conflicts that Riggs presents are violent, haunting, and so disturbing that recent scholars, in a kind of rediscovery of Riggs, differ wildly in their estimations of *The Cherokee Night*. Cherokee scholar Daniel Justice reads the play through principals of balance between the Cherokee "red, 'Chickamauga consciousness'" associated with the war governance that led the nation during times of strife, and the "white 'Beloved Path'" that led the Cherokee Nation during times of peace (*Fire*, 30). He concludes that Riggs' *The Cherokee Night* exposes a playwright "struggling with the legacies of his people and his homeland, seeking to walk the Beloved Path but ultimately failing to find the balance the Path demands" (ibid., 92–93). In *Red on Red: Native American Literary Separatism*, Craig Womack is drawn to Riggs' contradictory views of a bucolic Oklahoma and a horrific

Oklahoma. Womack argues that this tension gives way to hopelessness in *The Cherokee Night*, a "portrayal of doomed and tragic Cherokees [that] has everything to do with [Riggs'] closeted condition" as a "Native gay guy" from Oklahoma (*Red*, 19). Jace Weaver, another Cherokee theorist and close colleague of Womack's, also notes the pervasive despair in the play, but he leaves room for hope in the characters' futures: "Only before statehood, before the loss of political, territorial sovereignty, was there any hope for wholeness. Now the hope rests in memory, in not forgetting one's Indianness and in moving ahead along an uncertain path" (*That the People*, 103). Jaye T. Darby adopts Weaver's focus on the Cherokee communal values in the play and proclaims that, despite the play's pessimistic tones, *The Cherokee Night* itself is an artistic triumph, "a major work in modern Native American theatre," because Riggs risked "a critical failure by Broadway standards" in order to develop a play that is "a carefully crafted assertion of Native performance elements and communal values in deliberate opposition to mainstream American dramatic conventions and individualistic ideology of the 1920s and 1930s" ("Broadway," 9).

I believe that a platial reading of *The Cherokee Night* within the context of those Cherokee communal values that Darby and Weaver uphold reveals a play that not only confronts directly the harsh prejudices against and within Oklahoma–Native communities at the turn of the twentieth century, but also functions as a ceremonial return to a Cherokee ethos of sacred place and community. Riggs accomplishes this through a unique dramatic structure that relies upon Cherokee concepts of place, specifically those associated with clan placement upon Cherokee ceremonial grounds. From his construction of characters, to setting, themes, language, and dramatic structure, Riggs deliberately constructs a play that reflects Cherokee epistemologies that are part of Native American platial discourse. This conscious blend of Native theories with theatrical aesthetics allows us to see *The Cherokee Night* as the first major Native American play to use a distinctly Native form of dramaturgy.

There is no doubt amongst scholars that Riggs viewed *The Cherokee Night* as his best and most profound theatrical work. As early as 1928, Riggs had begun to envision a play that he said he had "'contemplated for some time, a dramatic study of the descendants of the Cherokee Indians in Oklahoma, to be called *The Cherokee Night*'" (Riggs qtd. in Braunlich, *Haunted*, 77). The play he would create disregarded the conventions of realism, for which Riggs and such contemporaries of his as Tennessee Williams were well known. Instead of focusing its dramatic action on a protagonist, *The Cherokee Night* opens with seven characters, whose lives we loosely follow through the remainder of the drama. Some of these seven characters we never see again; others we revisit in later scenes that only sometimes allow the character from Scene One to be the new scene's central focus. In all, there are seven scenes, which Riggs titles and presents achronologically: Scene One "Sixty-Seven Arrowheads" (1915); Scene Two "The Hatchet" (1927); Scene Three "Liniment" (1931); Scene Four "The Place Where the Nigger Was Found" (1906); Scene Five "The High Mountain" (1913); Scene Six "The White Turkey" (1919); and Scene Seven "The Cherokee Night" (1895). These seven scenes represent the seven clans of the Cherokee Nation, and the number seven itself alludes to the play's ceremonial nature, one that is communicated through an idea of placement. The Cherokee Nation official website explains:

Certain numbers play an important role in the ceremonies of the Cherokee. The numbers four and seven repeatedly occur in myths, stories, and ceremonies. Four represents all the familiar forces, also represented in the cardinal directions…east, west, north and south…The number seven represents the seven clans of the Cherokee, [which] are also associated with directions. In addition to the four cardinal directions, three others exist. Up (the Upper World), down (the Lower World) and center (where we live, and where "you" always are). ("Traditional Cherokee")

The other strong element of place in *The Cherokee Night* is the omnipresent visual image of Claremore Mound, the site of the last major battle between the Cherokee Nation and the Osage Nation in Oklahoma. Scenes One and Seven both occur a little above the base of Claremore Mound; the remainder of the scenes occur away from the mound, which waxes and wanes in the background to depict how close or far the characters are from this sacred site associated with Native burial grounds. The symbolism of Claremore Mound, coupled with the dramatic tensions between Cherokee communal values and American individualist values, constructs the meaning of *The Cherokee Night*'s scenes.

Oliva's *The Fire and the Rose* is a play about space, namely turning space into place through the interchange between bodies and land. The play tells the story of two friends: Joannie, a poet of Chickasaw descent, and Bernie, a non-Native woman who teaches literature at a private, Catholic university. Both women search for meaning in their existence; however, each does so in a different way. Bernie faces crises in her marriage and Christian faith. Meanwhile, Joannie, who by the end of the first scene of the play has died an early death from ovarian cancer, wrestles with a less traditional and more complicated search for the meaning of her pre- and post-death existence.

Joannie's widowed husband, Miles, approaches Bernie with his wife's last wish: for Bernie to edit Joannie's book of poetry before its target December 1999 publication. During the process of editing her friend's last words, Bernie is "visited" four times by Joannie, who struggles – even after death – with questions about life and spirituality. Much of Joannie's battle is rooted in reclaiming the Chickasaw heritage that her family had denied after her grandmother's death. Joannie's post-death existence is driven by a counter-clockwise movement through time in order to reconnect to a place of meaning. Her journey echoes many of the metaphysical musings within T. S. Eliot's *Four Quartets*, a collection of poems in which Eliot questions relationships between life and the afterlife, and acts of reckoning between humans and the divine. Oliva takes her play's title, *The Fire and the Rose*, from the final lines of *Four Quartets*, which she quotes on her play's opening page:

> And all shall be well and
> All manner of thing shall be well
> When the tongues of flame are in-folded
> Into the crowned knot of fire
> And the fire and the rose are one.
>
> (Eliot, "Little Gidding," 5. 42–46)

Thus, the plot plays off of Eliot while it simultaneously works, according to its own methods, to provide Joannie and Bernie with answers to difficult questions regarding the meanings of their lives.

The Story of Susanna is a more politically charged play that interrogates both biblical mythos and western notions of gendered space in order to invert power structures and reclaim both space and myth for women. Susanna, the play's central character, exists in two worlds. In the first one, she is the biblical Susanna from the Book of Daniel. Daniel, Chapter 13 tells the story of "Susanna's Virtue."[5] According to the story, Susanna was saved by Daniel's defense of her when two judges, in an effort to disguise their attempted rape of her, falsely condemned Susanna for infidelity toward her husband.[6] In the second world of the play, Susanna is a contemporary girl who grows into a woman. Act One depicts the contemporary Susanna's introduction to the societal conventions of gendered roles and dating. In Act Two, the contemporary Susanna is living at Threshold, a transitional home for women who are acclimatizing to society after having undergone traumatic events. Susanna is there recovering from a car wreck that killed her abusive boyfriend, Lee. In this act, Kneubuhl also introduces the stories of other women: Molly Lightfoot, a Native American woman who is at the home recovering from a gunshot wound caused by a man who accuses her of stalking his family; Hazel, a penniless woman who arrived at the home after her lover threw her over a balcony for attempting to steal his diamond cufflinks; Marina, an ex-actress who is there recovering from a shooting incident that left her brain-damaged and killed her daughter; and Adele, the social worker who runs the home. By infusing these politicized stories of gender, class, and ethnicity with Native theories of place, Kneubuhl constructs a complex plot that leads not only to the women's healing but also to the transformation of the biblical story weaving throughout the play.

Through detailed stage directions, Riggs, Oliva, and Kneubuhl describe theatrical conventions that support the non-linear plots of *The Cherokee Night*, *The Fire and the Rose*, and *The Story of Susanna*. These descriptions provide instructions for how each play should look, how individual scenes should transition from and relate to one another, and how the staging of each production should work to inscribe stage space with meaning. Riggs' stage directions focus heavily on symbolic images that create a philosophical frame for understanding *The Cherokee Night*. Scene One begins with a visual and aural prologue that focuses the audience's attention on the Cherokee Nation's displacement and certain platial symbols that represent the health of the Cherokee Nation. It is worth reading the opening stage directions closely to ascertain how Riggs envisions concepts of place throughout the play.

Strangely, the first image is of a teepee, associated with Native Plains cultures, not the Native nations from the East. However, this teepee is more metaphorical than practical. Riggs states: "*from a place of darkness a gigantic teepee thrusts itself up into the light – white and glistening... The shining buffalo skin sides, once stretched and taut, shedding both rain and sun, lie slack on the poles as if the inner structure had withdrawn a little, had crept inward toward a center, inching along the earth*" (*Cherokee*, 112). The teepee represents a nomadic home, perhaps associated with the upheaval deriving from the Trail of Tears and its aftermath, or perhaps borrowing a pan-Indian symbol for all audience members to read. What is unusual about the teepee is that this home appears weakened but not entirely empty. While the teepee's fire has gone out, "*somewhere inside is the muffled thud of a drum and the sound of deep voices*" (ibid.). In future scenes, whenever the characters become aware of personal ties to their Cherokee ancestors, the drumming will grow, as if it comes from deep within Claremore Mound. On the surface of the teepee are seven pictographs telling "*the story of a man's life.*" Many of these relate to aspects of Cherokee life: a deer hunt; "*a mountain with a summit of flame*"; "*a road* [that] *branches out in seven directions*"; a waterfall; and lastly, in a scene of great transition, "*across a deep chasm a warrior leaps, and in his hands are curious fetishes carved from granite*" (ibid.). Many of these images relate to specific aspects of Cherokee traditions and also foreshadow future scenes in the play. The final image of the man with fetishes directly pertains to the first scene, "Sixty-Seven Arrowheads," in which an old man named Talbert, who has been digging up arrowheads from Claremore Mound, tells the six Cherokee youths, "I'll go on and on till I drop, I'll dig up the whole mountain, I'll find thousands and thousands! I'll give 'em all to the Cherokees. When they touch 'em, they'll remember. *The feel of flint in their hands!* Take 'em, you! Take 'em!" (ibid., 129). Flint is connected to warfare as well as to the beginnings of ceremonial action, when a sacred fire is lit and maintained (Cherokee Nation website, "Cherokee Stomp Dance").

Quickly, Riggs exchanges the image of the teepee and its voices for the image of Claremore Mound and the voices of the three Cherokee couples who are picnicking there. He describes the scene as:

twilight of a summer day in 1915. A shale cliff capped with limestone and about six feet high runs across the back, uneroded by the years. Behind it, the hill mounts steadily to the summit…A gnarled cedar tree clings to the edge a little distance back and sways against the still sky. From its high stance, it looks two ways – forward down the flinty slope, and backward down another cliff and the unseen riverbed hundreds of feet below. (ibid., 112)

The uneroded mound symbolizes how the land's embedded powers remain potent, despite the changing conditions of the humans who live upon it; while the cedar tree, one of the most revered plants used in traditional Cherokee ceremonies, also connotes spiritual survival (Cherokee Nation website, "Traditional Cherokee"). Darby writes that the tree's "placement suggests a spiritual landscape marked by endurance and vulnerability" ("Broadway," 14). Though the cedar is weathered and bent, it persists, keeping a personified watchfulness over the Cherokee future, symbolized by the youth upon the hill, and the nation's past, symbolized by the path leading backward to the riverbed. To reinforce this endurance of Cherokee spirituality, the modern-day scene of the youth incorporates elements of hope. They sit under a starry sky where "*a fire burns. Three couples – boys and girls – sit about it, eating their picnic supper. They are all part Cherokee Indian, some a quarter, some a sixteenth or a thirty-second; one of them is a half-breed. The fire crackles, its light playing over them mysteriously*" (Riggs, *Cherokee*, 112). From the starlit sky to the paired youth, the scene prepares viewers to anticipate something more, something that connects to the sacred fire and the description of the youths' Cherokee heritage.

Riggs' emphasis on the characters' blood quantum has inspired some critics to infer that the playwright equated lower percentages of Cherokee blood with an inability to connect to Cherokee ways of knowing. However, for Riggs and other Oklahoman-Natives of his era, discussions of blood quantum had very real consequences regarding land rights and the ways in which non-Native governments viewed Native identity. Justice writes, "Blood quantum and ethnicity, and the moral character that accompanies both in Riggs' Cherokee world, are consistently embedded within a concept of land that is central to the well-being of both individuals and cultures – concerns that were central to Riggs' own outland traumas" (*Fire*, 100). While I agree that *The Cherokee Night*'s characters locate their Native identities in their relationships and access to the land, I believe something more complex than the equation of Cherokee morality with higher Cherokee blood quantum occurs in Riggs' drama. Riggs himself was bicultural, yet he still identified himself as Cherokee. Moreover, as we will see, some of the characters who have lower levels of Cherokee blood do indeed have strong connections to their Native roots. Riggs' common mention of blood quantum, I believe, allows readers and viewers to see the complexities within both Native America and Oklahoma during the early days of statehood. As Weaver reminds us, "turn-of-the-century Indian Territory was racially mixed, with Natives, whites, and African Americans all interacting," and most of Riggs' plays attempt to stage the Oklahoma that he experienced ("Foreword," xiii). Blood quantum was part of that Oklahoma, which Riggs' characters present as they use their degrees of Cherokee blood to assign value to themselves and others, sometimes in ways that associate great worth to Cherokee blood and other times in ways that locate one's value in "passing" as non-Native. Such complexities within Native America were new to audiences of the 1930s. Riggs' Cherokee characters, with their discussions of blood quantum and traditional beliefs, even looked different from the Indians who populated films and plays. Riggs "gave detailed instructions about the costumes; Native Americans dressed exactly like white settlers of this time, with the possible exception of preferring beaded moccasins to leather shoes" (Weaver, "Introduction," 107).

In addition to Riggs' concerns about the presentation of Native characters, he was similarly deliberate about how to stage Claremore Mound and a Cherokee Oklahoma. As he completed the script, Riggs embarked on a series of traveling lectures about his playwriting. Interestingly, he journeyed in regions that retraced the Cherokee Nation's removal from eastern homelands in North Carolina to Claremore, Oklahoma. In these lectures, Riggs proclaimed, "'I say unblushingly that unless the drama does something for the soul of man it isn't justifying itself'" (qtd. in Braunlich, *Haunted*, 109). He told reporters that "he felt as if he were only *beginning* to write," as he focused more on the realism of the human spirit, rather than the realism of movies (ibid.; emphasis added). In May of 1931, this quest to stage reality led him home to Claremore, where he took the photographs that he would use in staging *The Cherokee Night*, landscapes capturing Claremore Mound, Nowatta, Bartlesville, and the nearby woods (ibid.). The alteration of slides that projected these natural landscapes became the means by which Riggs created seamless transitions between his disparate scenes.

In *The Fire and the Rose*, Oliva also relies on fluid transitions. Through detailed stage directions, she describes theatrical conventions that support *The Fire and the Rose*'s non-realistic plot, inscribe the stage space with meaning, and stage Joannie and Bernie's extraordinary friendship. Although the play is set during the year between October of 1998 and 1999, Oliva's stage directions clearly state that "*time has no meaning in some of the scenes as the action moves both in and out of reality*" (*Fire*, iii). The fluid nature of time permits the play's action to move non-linearly, so that Joannie, even after death, can visit Bernie. To support this convention of time, Oliva situates the play's dramatic action within a visual world of dissolving boundaries. Her stage directions state:

The setting is a vague landscape with a variety of levels, like shifts of sand. The various vistas are inspired by Glass Sculptor, Dale Chihuly. Each scene should flow into the next without blackouts or time lapses. There is a feeling, always present, of one of the elements – earth, wind, fire, and water. No set pieces are realistic except for the desk and piano which remain on stage throughout. (ibid.)[7]

By freeing the set design from realistic staging conventions that work to affix permanent definitions to stage space, Oliva's staging accentuates the liminal nature of theatrical space, allowing for the play of locations, time, and existence. Emphasizing a sense of placelessness, the presentational set mirrors the dramatic action, in which individual scenes blend into one another through characters' overlapped lines, subtle segues in musical composition, or similar sounds morphing from one into another. The four elements allude to a shared theme in the construction of *Four Quartets* and *The Fire and the Rose*. In *Four Quartets*, Eliot incorporates a physical element into each of his poems: "Burnt Norton," air; "East Coker," earth; "The Dry Salvages," water; and "Little Gidding," fire. In *The Fire and the Rose*, Oliva uses a specific element to thematically underlie each of the four post-death conversations shared between Joannie and Bernie: first, earth; second, fire; third, air; and fourth, water. Oliva's use of the elements does more than reflect *Four Quartets*, it demonstrates how, in Joannie's world, place is a presence that human beings experience through the interchange between the five senses and the earth's natural elements. In each of the four conversations, the natural element gives the stage space a particular sense of place upon which Joannie obtains and articulates new understandings of herself, her Chickasaw culture, and current existence. Through these visits, Joannie's journey leads her to a reckoning with the presence of place and its inherent network of meanings.

Although also non-realistic, Kneubuhl's *The Story of Susanna* uses theatrical conventions in yet a different way. Her dramatic structure alludes to the performances of classical Greek theatre, as Kneubuhl begins her play with a prologue performed by masked dancers. Music underscores the dancers' stylized pantomime version of the biblical story of Daniel and Susanna. Simultaneously, two additional masked performers recite the biblical story in a kind of call and response, each speaker chanting every other line. These first moments place the biblical text within a mythological framework by relying upon the same types of convention that classical Greek playwrights used to investigate the relationships between religious stories and social structures.

Kneubuhl's set description continues to borrow from classical Greek theatrical conventions by marking private and public spaces on the stage. She calls for a bare stage composed of three separate levels, each containing its own pool of light. The stage directions state:

Three intersecting offset circles. The Upper Circle is center back and the smallest circle. The Middle Circle is two steps lower, larger, and extends forward and stage right. Two steps down, the Lower Circle, delineated at stage level, is the largest circle and extends forward and stage left. The use of these areas changes between acts and within the acts themselves. The circles are supplemented by minimal movable props. (Kneubuhl, *Susanna*, 296)

Except for the prologue and certain designated scenes with Daniel, all of the play's action occurs within these three areas.

Act One designates the three spaces in the following manner. Mythical scenes between Daniel and Susanna take place in the upper circle, which is also the highest circle. The two lower spaces belong to the contemporary Susanna and her friends. The middle circle is a kind of private space in which Susanna and her adolescent friends struggle to make sense of their gendered roles. In this middle-sized pool of light, the girls practice applying make-up and reciting "I love you" to imaginary lovers. Here, the adolescents ponder when it is right to have sex and whether or not it hurts. The space also contains private scenes between Susanna and her first boyfriend, Lee. It is here that Susanna confronts Lee's expectations of their gender-powered relationship, one that he enforces with abuse. The lowest circle is largest, literally and figuratively, as it designates a public space in the contemporary Susanna's world. This circle is where school dances and parties take place. In Act One, Kneubuhl uses these platial designations to juxtapose the mythical and contemporary scenes. Daniel remains in the upper circle for Act One's mythical scenes, while the actress who plays Susanna merely steps from the upper circle into one of the two lower circles when the dramatic action switches from mythical to contemporary time. Likewise, Susanna's contemporary friends and boyfriend step between the contemporary-private (middle) and contemporary-public (lower) circles. Significantly, Susanna is the only character who can traverse all three spheres. The character's freedom of movement enables Kneubuhl to draw connections between the mythical and contemporary stories of Susanna.

In Act Two, Kneubuhl slightly restructures the use of space to signify how both Susannas lose their connections to the spiritual world. The mythical Daniel rarely appears in Act Two. When he does, he often has no direct interaction with Susanna. Thus, the small upper-level circle no longer contains the mythical world of Susanna and Daniel. Instead, this circle designates the contemporary Susanna's most private space, her bedroom in the transitional home. With no space remaining for the mythical world, Daniel is forced to skirt the peripheries of Kneubuhl's three pools of light. The central, somewhat larger circle contains scenes in which the women at Threshold work through psychological issues. In group sessions, each participant attempts to reshape her identity by untangling her personal story from the accounts of those who have abused her. It is here that each woman recounts the events that led her to Threshold. This is also the space in which Molly Lightfoot and Adele battle over the truth, when Molly challenges the charges of the man whose false accusations condemned her to Threshold. Like Act One, Act Two's lower circle remains the most public area of the stage. The large circle contains scenes where the women of Threshold interact in a more social manner. Here, they visit with one another while they perform housekeeping tasks that keep the home running. Occasionally, the space signifies the outdoors, both Threshold's grounds and the remembered homelands of Molly's community. In this lower circle, Molly reclaims the story of America's history for Native Americans.

As we move into a critical examination of how issues of place are inscribed within Native American dramaturgy, I propose a framework focused upon three interrelated concepts contained within Native platial discourse. I will call these three branches of thought *rootedness, worlds of existence*, and *language as landscape*. The concept of *rootedness* is concerned with Sequoya's discussion of a "geocentric sense of identity" ("How (!)," 459). Rootedness draws a direct correlation between the formation of one's identity and her relationship with a literal, geographic, place. *Worlds of existence* is concerned with the way in which individuals connect to the sacred through specific relationships with significant geographic places. The concept of *language as landscape* alludes to the idea that language arises from a community's relationship with its homeland. Although I would argue that these Native platial concepts permeate the field of Native American drama, I will limit our in-depth exploration of these intellectual traditions to readings of these three, specific plays that overtly stage Native platial discourse.

ROOTEDNESS: GEOCENTRIC IDENTITY

In *Staging Place*, Chaudhuri coins the term "geopathology," which she defines as "the problem of place" (*Staging Place*, 55). While Chaudhuri neither intends nor attempts to develop concepts that are particular to Native plays, her framework does lay the groundwork upon which theatre studies can begin to approach the unique platial aspects of Native American dramaturgy. Chaudhuri theorizes that the problem arises out of a contradictory relationship between characters and their homes: a character needs a home in order to construct an identity; yet, that home can also serve as a type of prison. According to this paradox, characters must undergo a somewhat painful displacement through which they can achieve a new construction of identity that does not rely upon the stasis of place. Although these issues of belonging and displacement also arise in Native American literature, the solution to conflict often lies not in a rupture with home, but in a renewal of a geocentric identity, growing out of the dynamic relationships between individuals and their homelands. The difference between general theatrical studies' platial theories and Native American platial theories resides in different conceptions of land and the types of relationship that such beliefs inspire.

However scholars may feel about Riggs' *The Cherokee Night*, they are in agreement that Riggs wrote from what Justice calls "a geocentric connectedness...a consciousness and conscience rooted in the land" of the Cherokee Nation of Oklahoma (*Fire*, 93). Riggs' writing career repeatedly returned to Oklahomans, the interior "stories of flawed human beings and their relationship to place," even as he chose to live his adult years in New York and New Mexico (Weaver, "Foreword," xii). Riggs' strong nostalgia for Oklahoma is so pronounced in his personal correspondence that Braunlich titles her biography of him *Haunted by Home*, an apt description for an author whose writing reveals a doubled sense of reverence and profound loss associated with Indian Territory, the second home of the Cherokee Nation to be expropriated, this time to make ready for Oklahoma. "[S]patial orientation of Native peoples is crucial," Weaver states; so much so that "[w]hen Natives are removed from their traditional lands, they are robbed of more than territory; they are deprived of numinous landscapes that are central to their faith and their identity, lands populated by their relations, ancestors, animals and beings both physical and mythological. *A kind of psychic homicide is committed*" (*That the People*, 38; emphasis added). *The Cherokee Night* stages characters that are living with haunting reminders of a dual "psychic homicide," the Trail of Tears and the more recent federal policies aimed at taking Cherokee homelands. Accordingly, the play begins as a ghost story.

Scene One, "Sixty-Seven Arrowheads," opens at twilight, as the group of six sit around a campfire finishing their dinner. The young people know each other from childhood, although they have gone different directions with their own lives. Riggs describes them as: Viney Jones, a young know-it-all teacher with brown hair; Hutch Moree, a large, blond man who stutters and works as an oil teamster; Audeal Coombs, a beautician with wavy blonde hair; Art Osburn, a dark-skinned, angry young man; Bee Newcomb, a dark brunette, both "*vivid and strange-looking*," who works as a waitress and prostitute; and Gar Breeden, an athlete who has lost his college scholarship. Gar and Bee share the same father, a part-Cherokee outlaw named Edgar Spench. Riggs states that Gar is half Cherokee, while Bee's heritage is one-quarter. Blood quantum enters the conversation when Bee leads the group in mocking Gar for his being absorbed in thought: "Look at old Tight-Mouth! Heap Big Chief! Hey, Gar, wake up! [...] Two or three year ago he talked as much as anyone. *Now* look at him! Him don't eat, him don't talk. Him think. Him name Chief Squat-in-the-Grass" (Riggs, *Cherokee*, 115). Although Bee accentuates the cultural difference between the others and Gar, even going so far as to use stereotypically broken English to characterize his Indianness, Gar uses the topic of Cherokee blood to see the group as a whole community, to remind them of their history and the land where they sit:

GAR: (*With some fire.*) Well, you're all of you part Cherokee, like me! (*Lapsing again into quietness, looking away.*) We're settin' on the graves of a lot of dead ones – in case you've forgot.

BEE: (*Softly.*) Here?
GAR: Here.

They are silent for a moment, awed a little, something forgotten coming to life in them. (ibid., 118)

The action of eating and playing on the graves of their ancestors is irreverent, and although the others try to dismiss the strange feelings evoked by Gar's words, something unsettling has crept into their evening, setting the stage for more intense connections between the youth, the land, and their ancestors.

A seventh person, Old Man Talbert, startles the group after Art finds him digging near the Osage Chief Claremont's grave. Talbert is an elder of sorts, but like Riggs' other Cherokee characters, he is a troubling figure. Defensive for being accused of grave-robbing, Talbert first threatens the group, until Gar attempts to calm him asking, "Mr. Talbert, don't you know me? [...] I'm Gar Breeden. You ort to recollect me [...] Once I ask at yore house for water, and you give me a drink from the well, years ago. And you give me sump'n else too [...] You give me a eagle feather. Don't you remember? (ibid., 124). When Gar reminds Talbert who the other youths are, "all raised around here, same as me," Talbert's feigned loss of memory turns into a condemnation of the group (ibid.). He tells them, "I've seen too much of you, anyway! Clutter up the world – all of you – that's whut you do! Good fer nuthin' [...] You're no use to anybody. You're lost. You might as well be dead" (ibid., 125). (See figure 1.)

At first, it's easy to dismiss Talbert, as most of the youths do, but then he confesses the burden he carries, a haunting that stems from the place where these seven have met. As Talbert tells his story, Riggs weaves together a narrative about land, belonging, ancestry, and forgetfulness. The story begins by paralleling the evening the youths have just shared. Talbert tells them, "Ten year ago this summer. A night jist like this. Stars. I come up here by myself to smoke and laze. I built a far – just like that. There I set" (ibid., 126). The connections – the same place, the same stars, the same fire – are underscored by the same sounds that started the play. Riggs writes that the group "*stands, still afraid, but hypnotized, rooted, unable to move. A mysterious drumbeat rises in the silence, growing slowly in volume through the rest of the scene*" (ibid.). Talbert says that the evening, which had begun in reminiscence of his childhood, turned into a sacred moment when winds began to blow through tops of pines, another species of tree revered in traditional Cherokee ceremonies (Cherokee Nation, "Traditional Cherokee"). In that

1. Talbert intrudes on the picnic, *The Cherokee Night*, 1932.

place, Talbert witnessed the nineteenth-century Battle of Claremore Mound. He was not an invisible witness, however. He received a mission from a warrior who told Talbert, directly, that he has seen "'*Us* – the Cherokees – in our full pride, our last glory! This is the way we are, the way we was meant to be'" (Riggs, *Cherokee*, 127). The warrior's language is both inclusive, bringing Talbert – and now the youths – into the story, and also present, evoking a timeless connection amongst the generations. As Talbert repeats the warrior's language, his words shift from prose to the heightened language of poetry, which ceremonially recounts the battle and then offers the warning:

> But this was moons ago;
> We, too, are dead.
> We have no bodies,
> We are homeless ghosts,
> We are made of air.

Who made us that, Jim Talbert? Our children – our children's children! They've forgot who we was, who *they* are! You too, Jim Talbert, like all the rest.

Are you sunk already to the white man's way – with your soft voice and your flabby arm?
Have you forgot the use of the tomahawk and the bow?

Not only in war – in quiet times – the way we lived:
Have you forgot the smoky fire, the well-filled bowl?
Do you speak with the River God, the Long Person no more – no more with the
    vast Horned-Snake, the giant Terrapin, with Nuta, the Sun?[8]

> Are you a tree struck by lightnin'?
> Are you a deer with a wounded side?
> All of you – all our people – have come to the same place!

>> The grass is withered.
>> Where the river was is red sand.
>> Fire eats the timber.
>> Night – *night* – has come to our people!"   (ibid., 127–128)

This ceremonial language, full of Cherokee sacred elements and mythological figures, attempts to call the youths back to their heritage, to the
knowledge of their ancestors and lifeways that might flow again like the
revered rivers.

From the visionary experience, Talbert has found his way to "prove my
right to be a Cherokee like my fathers before me! Even though I lived in a
frame house, and paid taxes, and et my grub out of a tin can – I knowed
whut I could do not to be lost. I found the way before too late. That's whut I
was doin' – *there!* – when you saw me!" (ibid., 128). Like the last figure in
Riggs' teepee apparition, Talbert had decided to dig up all the arrowheads
on Claremore Mound in order to carry them to the current Cherokee
descendants, who might touch them and revive their cultural values. The
picnickers are alarmed. Art and Viney react violently, while Bee attempts to
shock the old man's sensibilities by claiming that she is a whore. Her
bravado gives ways to tears, however, as the drumbeat increases and everyone witnesses a connection between the spiritual and contemporary worlds.
Talbert calls:

They've come back like before! See the hair shine! Come down, come down! Show
yerselves! Yer people have forgot who you are. They're withered like leaves. Come
down! (*The* GROUP *stands, transfixed, rooted, afraid to move. Exultantly.*) You hear
me! I see you. You're coming! I knowed you would! Light on yer warbonnets! Yer
feet step soft. Yer teeth glitter. *This* way! *This* way!

    *The lights have begun to go down, all except a glow on the summit of the hill. It begins
to move slowly downward. The stars have gone out. The glow creeps down the hillside
strangely. The throbbing drum goes on into the darkness.* (ibid., 130)

All seven people share a profound sense of Cherokee community in this
moment. Riggs writes that they are "exultant," proud, and elated to witness

the coming of their ancestors in this sacred place. Riggs underscores the importance of this moment with his use of sound and lighting, which allows his audience to associate the glow and drumming with the visceral connections made between the characters and their Native heritage. This scene establishes Claremore Mound as the central metaphor that symbolizes Cherokee heritage; consequently, as we watch each achronological scene unfold, we relate it back to this communal moment.

The initial scene also establishes one more important dramatic convention for *The Cherokee Night*. It begins the association between individual scenes and Cherokee clans. Despite all of his flaws, Talbert functions as a kind of elder, attempting to restore something that has been broken in the spirits of the Cherokee youths. As such, the scene relates to the Blue Clan, or *Anisahoni*, which is believed to be the oldest of the Cherokee clans and historically "produced many people who were able to make special medicines for the children" (Cherokee Nation website, "Cherokee Clans"). The following two scenes show how three of the youths, Bee, Art, and Viney, ultimately fail to internalize the lessons of kinship begun at Claremore Mound.

Scene Two, "The Hatchet," occurs twelve years later in the Rogers County Jail. As the drumbeats of Scene One segue into sounds of rain on the jail's metal roof, the view of Claremore Mound transitions; it looms as a witness "*in the darkness, dim and silent, dwarfing the scene*" (Riggs, *Cherokee*, 131). Bee has been hired to trick Art into confessing to the murder of his wife, a Native woman named Clara. While she first views the task as an easy way to earn some money, Bee's set-up job soon unravels to reveal elements of internalized racism and overwhelming isolation. She tells Art that she doesn't care if he killed "that old Indian womern [sic] [...] Kill a dozen, you cain't make *me* mad. Competition's fierce" (ibid., 136). From viewing other Native women as mere competition for prostitution to wondering how she could live in the same town with her childhood friends and yet never see them, Bee's statements expose a woman devoid of a sense of community. Her loneliness breaks only when Art's confession expresses levels of rage and hate that Bee finds empathetic: "Hate! Everybody! Me, too! Like me! [...] I won't give you away – I thought it was the money – [...] Listen, that's the way I feel – All the men I'd kill! I can see how you felt" (ibid., 139). This moment of realizing their similar pain is also the very moment that Bee betrays Art to the county sheriff. Bee has failed to protect Art, just as Art's rage led him to slaughter his wife. Art's confession will allow the county to hang him for murder, a reality that Bee mourns, crying, "Leave me here. Slam the bolts to! What's the dif? I'm dead. Bury me" (ibid., 141). The scene represents a war turned inward, as members of the Cherokee community turn against one another through both murder and the literal selling of one another and themselves. Bee understands this, as the sheriff congratulates her, saying that "The county shore owes you a lot," to which she responds, "The county owes me plenty" (ibid., 142). In times of war, the Wolf Clan, *Aniwaya*, would provide a war chief, because "Wolves are known as pro-tectors," but Bee's and Art's actions represent the antithesis of this tradition, as both attack their own community from within (Cherokee Nation website, "Cherokee Clans").

Scene Three, "Liniment," is also associated with a Cherokee clan, the Wild Potato Clan, *Anigotegewi*, "known to be 'keepers of the land,' and gatherers," especially of wild potatoes, a staple of Cherokee diets before the Trail of Tears (ibid.). Interestingly, the scene represents both failure and hope, as Viney returns home to Claremore in 1931, after a ten-year absence and during the era of the Great Depression and Dust Bowl. Viney now lives in a Quapaw, Oklahoma mansion with her husband, the town's mayor; while her sister, Sarah Pickard, a Cherokee Christian, lives in a shack that she cannot afford to heat. Maisie, Sarah's seventeen-year-old daughter, cares for Sarah, who suffers from crippling arthritis. Sarah's greatest pain, how-ever, comes from having sold off her Cherokee land allotment in order to survive the Depression. As a dim Claremore Mound towers above the shack, we are reminded of the connections between Cherokee ancestry, community, and the land, values that Sarah retains and teaches to Maisie. In contrast, Viney's rejection of the Cherokee ways becomes clear when Sarah asks what happened to Hutch:

VINEY: I don't know and I don't care [...] That dumb Indian, that's all he was! [...] He didn't have any *change* in him, he was stuck some way. He was broody and sullen, he couldn't seem to get hold of himself, like a lot of part Indian's around here.

SARAH: And what about you, Viney? [...] You're more Cherokee than Hutch.

VINEY: Well, I'm thankful to say it doesn't show [...] Being a part Indian? What would it get me? Do you think I want to be ignorant and hungry and crazy in my head half the time like a lot of 'em around here? Do you think I want to be looked down on because I can't do anything, can't get along like other people? Do you think I want to make the kind of mess of my life *you* have – and live in a filthy hole like this the rest of my days –? (Riggs, *Cherokee*, 151)

Viney's choice to pass as non-Native allows Riggs to display some of the racist ideas society openly expressed about the Native people of his generation. Through the socio-economic context of the scene, however, Riggs undercuts these stereotypes by relating Sarah's condition to a regional trauma that affected Native and non-Native people alike. Although Sarah, like most of Riggs' characters, has her own prejudices, her indictment of Viney upholds a sense of Cherokee community rooted in concepts of place. As she accuses her sister of having "turned your back on what you ought to a-been proud of," the staging conventions shift to allow Sarah's response to transform into a ceremonial moment that links Sarah directly to the Cherokee homelands and the words of her ancestors.

In his discussion of the significance of homelands in Native American cultures, Pommersheim delineates some of the major cultural philosophies that stem from platial discourse. He states, "The importance of the land is severalfold. Beyond the obvious fact that the land provides subsistence, it is the source of spiritual origins and sustaining myth, which in turn provide a landscape of cultural and emotional meaning. The land often determines the values of the human landscape" (Pommersheim, *Braid of Feathers*, 14). In *The Fire and the Rose*, Oliva also reflects on these intricate relationships between people, land, spirituality, and meaning. Significantly, Oliva frames these human–place relationships differently for her two main characters. Rootedness drives Joannie's quest for meaning, which is embedded in a metaphorical and literal return to home, whereas Bernie's journey follows Chaudhuri's aforementioned pattern of severing from place.

Joannie's geopathology derives from three levels of displacement: literal, figurative, and literal-historical. These levels of displacement serve as a barrier to her ability to cultivate a geocentric identity. Joannie's early death serves as literal displacement. This literal displacement from the earth complicates her two other levels of displacement. The second level is figurative. Joannie comes from a family that has Chickasaw lineage but allowed its Native American heritage to be forgotten after the death of Joannie's maternal grandmother. Because the death of her grandmother cut off her access to inherited traditional knowledge, Joannie is disconnected from a figurative discourse of home, community, and – by extension – identity. It is important to note the differences between the staging of Joannie and Grandmother. Significantly, despite her death, Joannie not only returns to the earth during her four post-death conversations with Bernie, but she also returns in corporeal form. Bernie can see, touch, hear, and feel Joannie. Thus, during these four visits, Joannie is able to have an embodied experience with place. In contrast, Grandmother, who also resides in a post-death existence (and shares space on stage), remains unseen by Bernie and, throughout most of the play, by Joannie as well. This staging choice dramatically portrays the fissure between Joannie and her grand-mother's wisdom; it also communicates to the audience that Grandmother appears in a spiritual, rather than physical, form. Joannie's figurative displacement connects to the third, literal-historical level of displacement. Joannie and her family are from Oklahoma, the terminating point of the Trail of Tears. Ironically, these two final levels of displacement, figurative and literal-historical, are eventually conquered through the first, Joannie's death, which frees Joannie to physically journey back into her own ancestral past to heal her rupture with place.

Scene Three stages Joannie's first post-death appearance to Bernie and quickly associates Joannie's return with a dramatic portrayal of the numi-nous earth. In accordance with the play's style, Scene Two, which occurs in the living characters' daily life, and Scene Three, a visitation scene, blend seamlessly into one another. Moreover, as each visitation scene in the play occurs the focus on its natural element intensifies, allowing the visitation scene to take on unique, localized aspects that contrast the scenes occurring between living characters. The subtle amplification of natural elements throughout each of the visitation scenes allows the less-defined space of *The Fire and the Rose*'s world to transition into an embodied experience and place of meaning for Joannie.

In Scene Two, Miles and Bernie are sipping coffee while taking a walk along the beach after Joannie's funeral. Here, Miles presents Bernie with a folder of Joannie's writings. He states:

Lots of writing, some are poems, others just thoughts that she wrote. Some she recorded on a tape recorder when she couldn't write. Some she just recited to me as she rested [...] In the other folders are the pieces that she had already decided to include. But...what you have...are her last thoughts, her last rhymes [...] Bernie, these are her last ideas about...last [...] She wants you to edit them and then send them with the others...she spoke to her editor and cleared it. They want to shoot for a December 1999 publication. (Oliva, *Fire*, 12)

Bernie is uncertain about the responsibility of such a task. When Miles leaves her alone to think through the situation, Bernie buries their coffee mugs in the sand, looks up to the sky and states, "I am missing you, Joannie Wilson Kozak. (*She waits, almost as if for an answer, silence*) And I am pissing mad about missing...you!' (ibid., 14). Immediately, Scene Two gives way to Scene Three. Oliva's stage directions read:

GRANDMOTHER lets out a shrill Indian trill and exits, just as JOANNIE enters echoing the trill. She rides in on a bright red scooter, dressed in pedal pushers, plaid shirt and sneakers. She now has two braids. As she rides, she lets out whoops and hollers that sound more like an Indian massacre then the normal yells and chants of a child on a scooter. While JOANNIE rides over the entire stage, GRANDMOTHER enters with a bag full of Starbucks coffee mugs which she drops in a heap, exits. BERNIE runs at the sight of the mugs seemingly appearing from nowhere, and runs smack into JOANNIE. (ibid., 14–15)

This moment does more than dramatically stage Joannie's physical return to Bernie: it provides concrete examples of Native platiality in action. Joannie's existence and the earth are connected in a powerful way. Like the mugs, Joannie's body does not rest peacefully in the ground. Echoing the screams of her ancestors fighting for their lands, Joannie explodes out of the realm of the afterlife. Simultaneously, via Grandmother, the earth expresses displeasure at being a receptacle for Bernie's empty mugs. Important connotations weave through the moment. Oliva juxtaposes the image of the nation's land overwhelmed by consumer waste with an earlier memory of when its original inhabitants were violently stripped away. As the earth reclaims volition, Joannie whizzes from death into the world of the living to exclaim, "I'm not a ghost" (ibid., 16).

Joannie tells Bernie that she has chosen to live now the childhood that was denied her during life. This claim parallels the action with which Eliot begins his first section of *Four Quartets*. "Burnt Norton" opens with a soul's return to "our first world" of idyllic innocence, childhood, and serenity, represented by a rose garden (Eliot, "Burnt Norton," 1.24). Joannie attempts to explain to a bewildered Bernie the significance of her return to the living world:

JOANNIE: "We had the experience but missed the meaning."
BERNIE: What? What?
JOANNIE: [...] You know that line better than I do. You introduced it to me. You
made me a fan of his [...] I read T. S. Eliot at your insistence. We're building –
"sudden illumination"; what we're talking about – you and me, conversations: death, faith, love, life – all the things we talked about before.
(Oliva, *Fire*, 19–20)

Joannie's references to experiences, missed meanings, and sudden illumination come from "The Dry Salvages" (2. 37–38, 44–51) where Eliot writes:

It seems, as one becomes older,
That the past has another pattern, and ceases to be a mere sequence –
[...]
                    but the sudden illumination –
We had the experience but missed the meaning,
And approach to the meaning restores the experience
In a different form, beyond any meaning,

We can assign to happiness. I have said before
That the past experience revived in the meaning
Is not the experience of one life only
But of many generations –.

Through revisiting her past experiences, Joannie's quest for meaning will create a new form of understanding that was not fully attainable during her lifetime. Joannie tells Bernie that the best place to begin their quests for meaning "is at the end and with what you don't know" (Oliva, *Fire*, 20). Joannie's healing depends upon her ability to transcend layers of time backward – from her own life, to her grandmother's life, to the Chickasaw Nation prior to removal from its ancestral home. By retracing first her own steps, then those of her ancestors, Joannie will not only build sudden illumination but will also "revive" the meaning of her personal experiences within the context of the "many generations" of her ancestors.

The specific aspects of Joannie's quest – her embodied return to the earth, building a castle with Bernie out of the Starbucks mugs that have erupted from the earth, and stressing the importance of returning to earth to gain meaning through physical experiences – parallel Casey's description of the imperative relationship between human beings and landscapes. He writes:

Whether guided by landmarks or by one's own pathmarks, I rely on my body as the primary agent in the landscape. Landmarks call for perception (typically, but not exclusively, visual), while the trailsigns of my own trajectory are the concrete precipitates of my bodily movements on the land. In the latter case, my body marks its way through an otherwise unmarked landscape. To retrace the steps of one's own making is to remark one's own marks, and thus find one's way. (Casey, *Getting Back*, 26)

Of course, finding one's way contains a double meaning. It is a physical act of bringing one's body to a familiar location and a mental act of recognition through physical presence in place. Not only is the subject upon the landscape active, the land itself plays a reciprocal role. Conjoining body and landscape expresses an equivalent value of both people and place in the construction of meaning; likewise, in Native American stagings of platiality, this equality allows place to obtain a dramatic presence that can act with character-like volition.

The places with which Joannie must reunite extend beyond her former lived experiences, because Joannie's specific form of displacement occurs within her Native country. This literal-historical form of displacement continually works to estrange Joannie from her homeland – even as she is located within the places of her past – because the rupture between the Chickasaw Nation and its lands occurred at home, on American soil. Chaudhuri's investigation of platiality comes closest to these unique complexities of Native American displacement in her analysis of the literal displacement experienced by immigrants to new countries. She states that this literal rupture takes "social instability as its basic norm" and "traces the difficulty [of] constituting identities on the slippery ground of immigrant experience," where the immigrant works to attain self-definition within the new, often contradictory, country (Chaudhuri, *Staging Place*, 173). The solution Chaudhuri poses to the immigrant's conflict is plurality, "a demonstration of the possibility of entertaining two or more cultural contexts simultaneously, of inhabiting two or more homes simultaneously" (ibid., 212).

Although Joannie shares the immigrant's literal rupture with place, the solution to her geopathology cannot be found in mere pluralism. A plural identity, stemming from the colonization of her home, is precisely part of the problem. In "Voice of the Land: Giving the Good Word," poet and prose writer Elizabeth Woody explains the difficulty of negotiating a place-centered identity after the effects of European conquest. She states:

One's identity as an indigenous person – an Indian – is a hard and difficult awareness when you look at Indian extermination and removal, much of which was subsidized by the u.s. [sic] government for the purpose of westward expansion. And when you really look, you soon realize that this happened in order to ensure that non-Indian newcomers would take root in a way that meant that enormous amounts of people, forests, and animals in this rich homeland would be dispossessed or destroyed. (Woody, "Voice," 152)

Woody's statement exposes the conflicts of Joannie's plural identity. For Joannie to accept plurality, she must negotiate not only different cultures, but also the contradictions of place and history. She must negotiate: being a citizen of the very country that displaced her people; recovering a geocentric identity after her ancestors were forced off their lands; and learning about her Chickasaw community in the aftermath of governmental policies that attempted to erase tribal languages, traditional knowledge, spiritual practices, and Native pride.

In Scene Four, "Farewell to an American Icon," Miles recalls how plurality betrayed his wife. Linking Joannie's spirit to the land, Miles tells his friends about the time Joannie lost the chance to represent the state of

Oklahoma, when a low score on her talent entry dropped her to first runner-up in the Miss Oklahoma pageant. He states:

For her talent she did what she called a "traditional buckskin" dance, to a recording of Indian drums and flute. Then over that she recorded her voice reciting one of her poems. The judges told her that it wasn't real talent. She had the Indians mad at her because it wasn't traditional, with the poetry, and she had the white people telling her it wasn't a "traditional" enough dance for a pageant. (Oliva, *Fire*, 23)

Joannie's plurality worked against her in a doubled manner. Despite her identity as an American and an indigenous woman, both Native Americans and non-Natives rejected her for failing to adhere to a singular, definable identity.

When she appears for their second conversation, Joannie restages her performance of personal, Chickasaw identity. She arrives wearing the buckskin dress, carrying an Indian shawl with swaying fringe, and dancing the Traditional Women's Buckskin Dance. In response to Bernie's initial surprise at seeing Joannie looking so "Indian," Joannie shares a piece of information that she has gleaned: "Bernie, we can reclaim the past. I'm doing it now" (ibid., 37). Significantly, Joannie's use of the word "reclaim" signifies not only a metaphorical act of reclaiming one's traditions, but also a more literal sense of reclaiming Native American homelands, those distinct places that shape the traditions and values of Pommersheim's "human landscape."

Bernie's journey follows a different path. The pattern of her character's development presents a forward migration, as she continually breaks with place, seeking freedom of space and discovering through separations the meaning of her existence. In the play's exposition, one learns that Bernie has moved from Missouri to a beachfront bungalow in Seattle. However, despite Bernie's affinity for her new home, it imprisons her. Bernie and her husband, Tony, are undergoing a marriage crisis played out according to each partner's relationship to place. Bernie has recently thrown out many of Tony's belongings, stating, "You can't spread out here like you can in the Midwest – the ocean gets in the way. I like it. It's cozy" (ibid., 5). Yet, her husband calls their bungalow "claustrophobic" and overpriced. Eventually, Bernie and Tony's platial conflict motivates Bernie to enact a rupture with home.

Through contrasting Bernie and Joannie's respective desires for space and place, Oliva conditions her audiences to envision Native American dramaturgical expressions of platiality. The concept of rootedness – that humans experience meaning through implacement, a reciprocal relationship between humans and landscape – is framed by Oliva's choice to stage the post-death Joannie as an embodied person returned to earth in order to reclaim both her history and identity. As Joannie retraces her steps, mapping places out of the space inhabited by the other characters, Oliva theatricalizes the power of place through Native platial concepts that reflect the specificity of place, pushing theatrical readings of platiality toward a more particular focus on human–land connections. Oliva continues to reveal examples of platial specificity as she stages the added relationships between land, spirituality, and language.

Similar to the youths of *The Cherokee Night* and Joannie in *The Fire and the Rose*, Kneubuhl's *The Story of Susanna* focuses upon a woman who must reclaim a geocentric identity. In this play, Susanna attempts to construct cultural and emotional meaning while navigating through the mixed messages that contemporary American society tells young women about their worth. Kneubuhl depicts Susanna's journey through a plot structure that first connects Native platial theories to aspects of women's spirituality and then infuses those shared values into a biblical story staged with classical notions of gendered space. The result is a play that challenges conventional notions of space, biblical myth, and the land's value.

When speaking about her work, Kneubuhl places the importance of her own homeland as a central motivating force. In her introduction to *The Story of Susanna*, Kneubuhl states:

I hope my work has encouraged both adult and young audiences to appreciate our island home and the unique community in which we live. Having lived nearly all of my life in either Hawaii or American Samoa, I feel an unbroken connection between my self, my work and the Pacific. My sense of who I am and the visionary focus which has guided my writing are inextricably woven together with my experiences of island life. I have been fortunate as an artist in having a rich wellspring from which to draw. (Kneubuhl, "Author's," 292-293)

This "unbroken connection" between one's self and homeland not only inspires Kneubuhl's work, it also weaves a foundation for the play's structure both on the page and on the stage. To situate the importance of place in *The Story of Susanna*, Kneubuhl begins the play with a retelling of the story's biblical version in which the land's presence and significance, though not the story's most crucial element, cannot be denied. Kneubuhl's two masked actors begin the story, stating:

PLAYER 1: This is the story of Susanna as it comes to us from the Greek Bible and the Vulgate.
PLAYER 2: There once lived a man in Babylon whose name was Joakim.

PLAYER 1: Joakim was rich, and he had a fine house, and adjoining his house was a fine garden.

PLAYER 2: He married a wife named Susanna, the daughter of Hilkiah.

PLAYER 1: And Susanna was pious and beautiful and well raised in the law of Moses.

PLAYER 2: Two of the elders of the people were appointed judges, and came constantly to Joakim's house.

PLAYER 1: And all who had cases to be decided came there.

PLAYER 2: And it happened that when the people left at midday –

PLAYER 1: Susanna would go into her husband's garden.

PLAYER 2: So the two elders saw her every day.

PLAYER 1: And they conceived a passion for her.

PLAYER 2: They were smitten with her.

PLAYER 1: Their thoughts were perverted.

PLAYER 2: And they could not look up to heaven –

PLAYER 1: or consider justice in giving judgment –

PLAYER 2: so great was their desire for her

PLAYER 1: And they said one to another:

PLAYER 1 AND PLAYER 2: (*to each other*): "Let us agree to try to find her alone."

PLAYER 2: And it happened one day that Susanna went to the garden…

(Kneubuhl, *Susanna*, 297–298)

After narrowing down the location of the incident – in Babylon, on Joakim's property, in the garden – the story's action begins. The elders attack Susanna when she is alone in the garden. Once the men make their sexual advances, Susanna refuses them. In retaliation, they claim to have caught Susanna committing adultery with a man in her garden. They publicly unveil, judge, and condemn Susanna to death. However, God responds to Susanna's prayers for help and sends Daniel to rescue her. Daniel exposes the elders' deceit by asking each of them separately, "'Now you, if you saw this woman, under which tree did she lie with the young man?'" (ibid., 299). When one elder claims that the event occurred under a small mastic tree, and the other a mighty oak, Daniel sentences the two elders to death. Thus, in essence, place – specifically two of the garden trees – saves Susanna from her death sentence. Yet, despite the story's initial focus on Susanna, it is Daniel who "from that day onward […] had a great reputation in the eyes of the people" (ibid.).

By selecting this particular Bible story, Kneubuhl establishes many of the issues that will emerge throughout her play. The story inherently depicts a strong sense of gendered space, namely the private sphere of women versus the public nature of men. Susanna stays within her home until the house and garden are empty. Then she comes out of hiding.[9] She is veiled. She never speaks, nor is she asked to tell her own story of what had happened. On the other hand, the men act socially. They hold judicial, political gatherings. They expose Susanna by unveiling her in public. They not only have the power to speak, but their words are also taken seriously.

Through her unique staging conventions in *The Story of Susanna*, Kneubuhl capitalizes upon these notions of gendered space. Her three circles reflect classical Greek staging practices that worked to physically depict dramatic tensions, which often stemmed from the political binary oppositions of female/male, private/public, home/social, chthonic/Olympian, and nature/ political.[10] In both Acts One and Two, Kneubuhl mirrors the classical Greek horizontal division between upstage (private) and downstage (public) space. In the ancient Greek theatre, the skene literally blocked the private area, usually the inside of a home (woman's space), from view. The actions in *The Story of Susanna* mark the middle circle as private (hidden) space and the lower circle as public (seen) space. Kneubuhl's staging also plays with the vertical axis of classical Greek theatre. The vertical axis emanated from the Greek theatre's thymele, or altar, where either sacrifices were burned for the Olympian gods above or libations were poured into the earth for the chthonic deities below.[11] Human beings lived in the land between the sky/high/bright/democratic/masculine gods and the earth/low/ dark/communal/female deities. This notion of space is articulated in many world religions, including Christianity, which place the heavens above, hell below, and humans in the middle. Kneubuhl collapses these hierarchical notions of space into her staging by making the highest circle represent biblical mythos in Act One. At the end of Act Two, however, she uses the downstage, and physically lowest, circle to represent a new kind of sacred space, the garden of Threshold, where the women gather for a planting ceremony. Significantly, even Kneubuhl's choice to name the home "Threshold" reflects feminist readings of the values of space in classical Greek theatre. Scolnicov theorizes, "From a spatial point of view, the world of men and the world of women meet on the threshold [the skene's door-way]. Thus, the very shape a [classical Greek] play gives its theatrical space is indicative of views on the nature and relationship between the sexes and on the position of women in society" (*Woman's*, 6).

Kneubuhl's staging conventions emphasize the vertical axis in order to play with the delineations of space contained within the Bible's version of the story of Susanna and Daniel. Despite the biblical story's overarching notions of public/private gendered space, it also contains elements that complicate such clear-cut delineations of space. In the biblical story, the garden, like the house, belongs to Joakim. It is a public location where the men hear cases and cast judgment, yet it is also the hidden, private place in which the elders attempt to rape Susanna. Because the house and garden are both designated for Joakim's social interactions, Susanna has no place of refuge. Disconnected from any sense of homeland, she appears as one of Joakim's possessions, contained within the confining spheres of her husband's garden, his property, the laws of Moses, and Babylon.

Kneubuhl recognizes the biblical depiction of Susanna's placement and begins deconstructing the story by emphasizing connections between Susanna and the garden. In *The Story of Susanna*, Susanna not only reclaims the garden, but also the garden transforms into a metaphor for Susanna. As Kneubuhl's mythical Susanna begins to piece together the fragments of her own story, she states:

There are places on this earth, Daniel, places of freedom and solitude. There are worlds we make, gardens for the performance of miracles. There are scenes we pass through, scenes in which we know ourselves, by being part of something great and fragile and full of wonder, and that garden was *mine*. They [the elders] snapped things off that were meant to bloom. They trampled things that, for the first time ever, had a chance to grow. And who? Who has ever answered for that? (Kneubuhl, *Susanna*, 304)

The garden is the place whence Susanna derives her identity. By being rooted in the garden, Susanna connects to a "fragile" place "full of wonder," a human–land relationship that allows Susanna to know herself. Her sense of being is so connected to the garden that she relates the elder's sexual abuse of her to their invasion and devastation of the garden itself. This paradoxical understanding of the land as being both an origin for one's identity and a place of loss is discussed by Pommersheim in his explanation of the complicated relationship between Native American peoples and their lands. He states:

The reservation is home. It is a place where the land lives and stalks people; a place where the land looks after people and makes them live right; a place where the earth provides solace and nurture. Yet, paradoxically, it is also a place where the land has been wounded; a place where the sacred hoop has been broken; a place stained with violence and suffering. And this painful truth also stalks the people and their Mother. (Pommersheim, *Braid of Feathers*, 15)

The notion of Native homelands that both nurture and haunt their inhabitants is the major point of connection between Pommersheim's statement and Kneubuhl's playwriting.[12] In *The Story of Susanna*, the mythical Susanna's journey reflects the idea that a sense of wholeness derives from place, and yet wholeness is challenged when one's homelands have been invaded and "stained with violence." As Act One unfolds, Kneubuhl's mythical Susanna increasingly struggles to overcome the violence done to her garden and herself. In response, she begins to withdraw from the play's action.

The mythical Susanna's choice to disassociate herself from her own story, her friendship with Daniel, and her garden occurs in tandem with the journey of the contemporary Susanna's attempts to construct her feminine identity according to societal norms. Act One depicts several scenes in which the contemporary Susanna becomes increasingly aware of how women conform to societal expectations. For example, Scene Five occurs in the middle circle as Susanna and her girlfriends ready themselves for a dance. Here, Kneubuhl parodies the notion of women using makeup in order to "look natural." The contemporary Susanna cites the rules of makeup as she applies it: "Makeup should be applied with the greatest care and look as natural as possible" (Kneubuhl, *Susanna*, 308). As the lesson continues, the "naturalness" of the makeup exposes the construction of the ideal woman:

Blush should highlight your cheekbones and give your face a flushed, excited look... Use eye shadow to create dramatic effects and to give yourself that aura of mystery... Start the eyeliner under your eye so that it begins at the center of your pupil and take the line out to the edge. This will make your eyes look bigger, doe-like and more inviting...Lips, the lips are very important. Outline them with a darker pencil and fill them in with color. Full, they should look full. (ibid., 309–310)

Once she has applied all of her makeup, the contemporary Susanna seems unable to recognize her own reflection. In the ultimate act of disassociating with nature, she disconnects from herself, stating, "I'm looking at my reflection, but it's like I've left my body and I'm looking at an empty thing" (ibid., 312).

By the end of Act One, the contemporary Susanna has followed the societal expectations of women's behavior directly into an abusive relationship with Lee, a young heroine addict. Rather than having secured a geocentric identity, Susanna roots her sense of cultural and emotional meaning in her boyfriend. Her pledge of commitment to him is phrased in the language of place: "you're my whole universe" (ibid., 317). While the contemporary Susanna roots herself in Lee, the action is mirrored by the mythical Susanna's collapse. In the upper circle, the mythical Susanna likens her body to a land sliced by an icy glacier:

Imagine if you will, being frozen alive while the bright sun shines above you like a shimmering disc. You feel a cold, icy sharpness moving down the rivers of your veins, moving like the steady ocean tides toward the heart, the heart which just sits there beating like it has all the time in the world. The beautiful heart with all of its irregular contours – round, smooth, dense, deep, so full of life, is the shape, yes, the perfect shape for a glacier. (ibid., 320)

The mythical Susanna enacts her surrender to icy silence by stepping out of upper circle and not returning to this mythical area. Only Daniel remains in the upper circle pledging that he will wait for her. Although both the mythical and contemporary Susannas end Act One as women severed from their geocentric identities, Kneubuhl indites that the ties to the land are strong. The apparent defeat of the women is merely a winter. Alone in the upper circle, Daniel states, "There is a certain cycle in the seasons when we must put everything away, when we bury things, pack them down underground and smooth over the top like no one's ever been there. Then there is nothing to do but wait" (ibid., 323). In the uncertain ending of Act One, Daniel and the audience wait to see if either Susanna can recover herself.

WORLDS OF EXISTENCE: THE SACREDNESS OF PLACES

In *The Cherokee Night, The Story of Susanna*, and *The Fire and the Rose*, Native American theories of place go beyond merely nurturing a healthy sense of self: these theories also tie the characters to larger systems of meaning. Through what Pommersheim calls "the cultural taproot," the characters in Native American plays who find placement in a direct relationship with the land also connect to a series of relationships emanating from place. Knowing one's right relationship with place extends into knowing one's right relationship within a community, and knowing one's right relationship within the spiritual world. As in many Native American plays, the plays of Riggs, Oliva, and Kneubuhl provide artistic demonstrations of Native American concepts that broaden theatrical frameworks through an emphasis on Native philosophies stressing the sacred notion of place.

In *The Cherokee Night*, Sarah exhibits the interconnections between self, place, community, and the spiritual world when she confronts Viney during a moment that shifts from realism to ritual. Riggs states, "*The lights begin to go down strangely. A fantastic glow from the stove creeps into the room, blotting out its realistic outline, its encompassing walls, throwing SARAH's shadow, huge and dark, on the wall*" (Riggs, *Cherokee*, 152). The lighting change aligns Sarah's shadow with the looming Claremore Mound, almost as if the woman and the land were one. The glowing refers back to the moment that Viney had witnessed the ancestors' descent, back in 1915, on Claremore

Mound. Sarah's language, reminiscent of Talbert's in Scene One, shifts to poetry. Riggs likens her to an oracle, who first pronounces a fierce warning:

> You'll come to a close tight place in the hills, between rocks.
> The rocks'll close together!
> They'll squeeze you dry.
> Your flesh'll fall from you like feathers,
> Your bones'll crumble.
>
> You can't turn back.
> You'll *want* to turn back! [...]
>
> One thing you can't do, you with your table full of meat
>   and furs around your neck:
> You can't take a path you ain't meant to.
> It'll take you to the jaws of wild animals,
> It'll guide you west, to the rivers of quicksand,
> It'll take you to jagged cliffs,
> It'll lead you to death!   (ibid.)

Although Sarah has all but disowned her sister, whom she condemns for possessing the worst qualities of both Native and white people, she then offers one more poetic pronouncement. It is an invocation to remember their mother's wisdom, knowledge rooted in being keepers of the land. She states:

The way to be is to be humble, and remember the life that's in you. Our Maw told us once the way we was meant to live. "Remember it," she said. "Remember it and your days'll be food and drink. They'll be a river in the desert, they'll be waving grass and deer feeding."
Quietly, like a prayer.

> "The man'll plow the ground," Maw said.
> "And he'll plant and cultivate.
> The woman'll have her garden and her house.

There'll be pork and corn dodgers, molasses from the cane patch, beans on the vine.
There'll be berries and fruit – blackberries, strawberries, plums.
The woods'll be thick with squirrels.
The woman'll go down to the branch with her apron full of corn and a pan of ashes
    to make hominy.

> The nights'll come.
> Children'll be born.
> The gods of the earth things – the gods of the stone and the tree and all natural
>   things
> Will live by their side.
> And the God of the Christians, too,
> Will keep them from sin."

Crying out, as the vision and the memory have become slowly too powerful, too painful.
>Maw! Maw! Where are you?
>Where has the good life gone to?
>It's got fur away and dim. It's not plain any more.
>I can't follow.
>I tried! I tried – ! [...]
>I failed.   (ibid., 153)

Sarah's geocentric language exhibits her connections to her ancestral knowledge, even though her poverty and the selling of her land allotment lead her to believe she has somehow failed her culture. Riggs contrasts Sarah's self-judgment with the real failure of Viney, who throws 50 cents at her sister's feet before abandoning her for good. Maisie, the child raised with her grandmother's knowledge, tries to cheer her mother by playing a hymn on the family's one possession, an old organ that had belonged to the grandmother. Although Maisie's hope is naive and her song bitter-sweet, the lyrics of "My Faith Looks Up to Thee" both reflect the grandmother's Cherokee Christian perspective and increase the play's focus on issues of spirituality.

The following scene, "The Place Where the Nigger Was Found," goes back in time to 1906 in order to stage the characters' early awareness of both the spiritual connections with place and the complicated world of racial relations in which they live. Gar, Art, and Hutch are all boys searching the woods near Claremore for the place where an African American was murdered during a card game the previous night. As hunters, the boys try to read the landscape for signs, reflecting aspects of the Deer Clan, *Aniawi*, "historically known as fast runners and hunters" and also "messengers on an earthly level, delivering messages from village to village, or person to person" (Cherokee Nation website, "Cherokee Clans"). With the image of Claremore Mound sharply in the distance, Gar exhibits the same sensitivity to place that he possesses in Scene One and teaches his companions to "Listen [...] Use your head. Be still [...] Plain as day. 'F you'd listen to yerself a little, you'd know sump'n" (Riggs, *Cherokee*, 159).

While they share the experience of listening to and feeling the natural world, the boys are also quite cruel. Hutch picks on Gar for not having any parents and having been raised by Mr. Ferber, a German man who wants Gar to go to college. When Hutch claims, "Somebody told me them old Creek Indians married niggers. Us Cherokees wouldn't do that," Art tries to ostracize him with a contemptuous, "You ain't a Cherokee" (ibid., 162). Hutch's retort is a claim both for Cherokee blood and land: "I am! I'm a sixteenth. I got land, I guess" (ibid.). The talk of ethnic differences elicits all manner of racial slurs ignorant of the complicated history of black freedmen who came to Oklahoma on the Trail of Tears with Native people who had once enslaved them. The boys even play into stereotypes of Indianness that eventually reveal Art's disturbed psyche. Art begins to "*run in a wide circle, hypnotized, around the central pile of leaves, scooped up like a mound of a grave. As he runs, he stops quickly, picking up a heavy short club*" (ibid., 163). He begins an "incantation" about how he would "hack" a black man if he saw one. The ritual is disturbing, turning human beings into prey and portraying an utter lack of respect for life and the place of a man's murder. Soon all the boys play Indian: "*They begin slapping rapidly their own open mouths, from which pours the high queer interrupted conventionalized Indian cry, fearful and disturbing in the shaken gloom. ART's savage cry goes on and on*" (ibid., 164). Strangely, the real begins to answer the boys' simulations, as the ancestors start to teach the difference between playing and being. Riggs writes, "*At the top of Claremore Mound a drum begins. Suddenly, as if by plan, the running figures stop dead still, close together* [...] *The drum rises and reverberates in the silence. Like a great and quickened heartbeat*" (ibid.). Art thrusts his hands into the leaves. As he withdraws, blood streaks his palms. He recoils "*In ecstasy and horror*" and states, "Got blood on my hands!" (ibid.).

Art's cry foreshadows the killer he is to become, but it also judges historic wrongs that occurred before the Trail of Tears, when wealthy Cherokee families in Georgia owned slaves, a social convention that helped mark Cherokee people as "civilized" in America's eyes. The boys run in fear, but their actions have awakened spirits from the earth. Riggs writes:

The drum stops, cut off short. Silence. The sun becomes brighter, more dazzling [...] *Then slowly, rising from the warmed and fertile earth, a giant NEGRO, naked to the waist, lifts himself into the sun from behind the thick underbrush. His black body glistens. He stares off toward the fleeing boys, stretches himself, comes forward a step from the sun into shadow, in a movement real and ghostly, as if he were two presences: the murderer undismayed by his crime, and the very emanation of the dead man himself* [...] *one hand moves itself forward to a blackberry spray, in an uncalculated reflex, gathers two berries and lifts them idly to his mouth. Then he yawns. Then the sun dies. All below becomes dark.*

A light goes up, glows on the summit of Claremore Mound. An Indian, slim, aristocratic, minute in the distance, stands up against the sky. A drum is beating – harsh and troubled. It is like a fevered and aching disquiet at the pit of the world. (ibid., 165)

While many discuss this scene in relation to Riggs' homosexuality, the scene's imagery must ultimately work on a dramaturgical level. The attractive male figures restore a timeless dignity to the races the boys have spoken of so prejudicially. In this land, both men are also connected: they each come from the earth; they stand against the sun and sky. Although they are physically separated, the men's pairing represents a kind of equivalence, reflecting a shared condition, a shared history of oppression. Riggs' *"fevered and aching disquiet at the pit of the world"* reveals a land haunted by the way human beings have turned upon one another.

Riggs' own letters exhibit the way Oklahoma's land and history often haunted him. In 1928, he wrote to his advisor, Barrett Clark:

I can't even begin to suggest something in Oklahoma I shall never be free of: that heavy unbroken, unyielding crusted day – morning bound to night – like a stretched tympanum overhead, under which one hungers dully, is lonely, weakly rebellious, and can think only clearly about the grave, and the slope to the grave.

It seems to me more and more that I am haunted and driven by pictures and pictures – ominous, gray, violent, unserene –…So it begins to grow on me that only in that borderland of life, that disjointed, slightly unfocussed arena can we touch the pains of truth. And wouldn't it be good to be felled by those feet, to be a good Christian in those unholy and playful jaws? (qtd. in Braunlich, *Haunted*, 76)

Gar, in many ways, is *The Cherokee Night*'s most haunted figure. His experiences closely mirror the frustrations that Riggs recorded when he felt most estranged from Oklahoma. Trying to live within his Cherokee heritage, but haunted by his parents' deaths that denied him a traditional upbringing, Gar is a character who hungers for a cultural and spiritual homecoming.

Scene Five, "The High Mountain," represents Gar's lowest moment. It occurs in 1913, two years before the opening scene on Claremore Mound and seven years after the scene in the woods. As the scene begins the second act of *The Cherokee Night*, its staging elements strangely reflect Scene One. This scene occurs on another hill, Eagle Bluff, which also has *"a gnarled and twisted tree…on a sheer edge of a cliff,"* but the community here is white, and the spiritual moment for which they gather is a church service (Riggs, *Cherokee*, 166). Claremore Mound is still present, although *"on the distant horizon, small, indistinct against the sky"* (ibid.). The congregants are a backwards bunch, dressed in ragged, outdated pioneer clothing. Their charismatic worship service borrows an ecstatic form of place-based language; however, the people's religion, like their subsistence, is inauthentic, stolen. Their mountaintop village looks down upon the seat of the Cherokee Nation, Tahlequah, Oklahoma, a town the sect regularly raids without remorse: "Ain't we one of the Lost Tribes of Israel? Ain't we God's favorites? Them ole Cherokees ort to be proud to furnish God's People a cow or a sack of corn or half a hog onct [sic] in a while. Do 'em good" (ibid., 167).

Gar, abandoning a disappointing journey to Tahlequah, climbs Eagle Bluff, where the congregation mistakes him for a spy and tries to shoot him. Gar tells Jonas, their spiritual leader, that he has run away from home and is on a kind of spiritual quest for belonging. Although Gar has been associated with birds in Scene One, when he reminds Talbert about the eagle feather, and again in Scene Four, when he proves Art wrong by identifying a chicken hawk, it is this scene on Eagle Bluff that most clearly connects him to the Bird Clan, *Anitsisqua*. The Cherokee Nation official website explains:

Members of the Bird Clan were historically known as messengers. The belief that birds are messengers between earth and heaven, or People and the Creator, gave the members of this clan the responsibility of caring for the birds…Our earned Eagle feathers were originally presented by the members of this clan, as they were the only ones able to collect them. (Cherokee Nation website, "Cherokee Clans")

Gar's gifts for interpreting the spiritual world explain his ability to first sense spiritual moments and then teach others how to listen to the world around them. But in 1913, after being thrown out of college, Gar feels lost. He confesses to Jonas:

They's [sic] no place for me anywhere, see! Mr. Ferber wanted me to be educated, like him. He's my gurardeen. He sent me to A. and M. I played football, made the track team. Didn't study. Didn't want to study. I got kicked out. I didn't belong there. Don't belong in Claremore. No place for me anywhere! Come down to Tahlequah yesterday to see if – to see – I thought this bein' the head of – Listen, I'm half Cherokee. I thought they could help me out here, I thought they – Old men sittin' in the square! No Tribe to go to, no Council to help me out of the kind of trouble I'm in. Nuthin' to count on – ! (Riggs, *Cherokee*, 180)

Although Gar has gone to Tahlequah, he has given up his quest for belonging without speaking to anyone. It seems as if Gar went to the seat of the Cherokee Nation looking for a stereotypical tribal council, which led him to overlook the elders in his midst, something he does not miss again when he meets Talbert. Jonas builds upon Gar's feelings of abandonment; and as the preacher's language invokes the mythology of the vanishing Indian, Gar, on this "borderland," touches "the pains of truth."

In devilish tones, alluding to Satan's temptation of Christ in the desert, Jonas tells Gar:

You're alone, then. Lost! No one to help […] There's no help from the Cherokees. They're dying out. They're hardly a Tribe any more. They have no order of life you could live. Their ways are going. Their customs change. That part of you can never be fulfilled. What's left? You must look to heaven! Like us! (*A terrific intensity and power, almost hypnotic, has gathered in his voice. The lights everywhere begin to go down, except a concentrated glow on GAR and the fanatic old man. GAR begins to feel the strangeness. The valley and the colored fields have disappeared. Claremore Mound's faint outline no longer stands up on the horizon)* [...] Our eyes on the hereafter! Our feet in the Now! We walk here on the mountaintop away from the world and its wickedness. We lay up treasures in heaven. Listen to me! (ibid., 181)

Jonas' words articulate Gar's deepest fears, so much so that Gar's connection to Claremore Mound literally disappears; still, something in Jonas' words betrays Gar's very sense of self. It is one thing for Gar to lament that no Cherokee will help him; it is quite another for a white man to tell Gar that he and his people are dying. Jonas' language morphs into simulated strains of nature-centered liturgy, "We touch the rocks. We lift a hand as a tree lifts its branches. We are part of wild, growing things" (ibid., 181). From this frenzied sermon, Jonas launches into his proposition. He offers Gar dominion over Eagle Bluff and its congregation.

Gar's response presents a tonal shift in *The Cherokee Night*. Although his language is rough, Gar condemns the appropriation of place-based spirituality and claims vital life for Cherokee people: "What you offer me is crazy! They were right about you down below [in Tahlequah]. You touch the rocks, yes! You are exalted and stirred, O God yes! Let me go!" (ibid., 183). Instead, Jonas and his church members chain Gar to a post, where they plan to leave him to die. As they return to their worship service, Gar begins to claim his life, yelling, "I won't die this way! [...] You won't kill me! You won't kill me. You can't kill me! I'm going to live. Live! And I'll burn your goddamned tabernacle to the ground!" (ibid., 186). Of course, we do know that Gar lives. He returns home to Claremore, where, in 1915, he recognizes the power of the ancestors residing in the land and works to mediate between his friends and the ancestors coming toward them. As Scene Four ends, a group of men from Tahlequah are ascending Eagle Bluff, and while we do not know how things ultimately are resolved, we can infer that the Cherokee men from Tahlequah are the ones who free Gar, allowing him a homecoming in the Cherokee community. The play's last two scenes increase the focus on Cherokee homecomings, each expressed through ceremonial forms of language.

In *The Fire and the Rose*, Oliva articulates the concept of the sacredness of places, contrasting Joannie's place-based spiritual knowledge with the kind of Christian spirituality that Bernie practices. These two different views of spirituality coincide with the women's separate paths. As Joannie backtracks through her three levels of displacement, she simultaneously retraces her family's lost traditions in order to return to a sacred place of meaning that also holds the key to her current state of existence. In *God is Red*, author, professor, lawyer, and philosopher Vine Deloria, Jr. builds his argument around a central concept, which he terms "the sacredness of places" (*God is Red*, 2). According to Deloria, the spiritual connection between sacred places and Native American communities resides in the specific relationship between a particular physical location and the people connected to that land. He states:

The vast majority of Indian tribal religions...have a sacred center at a particular place, be it a river, a mountain, a plateau, valley, or other natural feature. This center enables the people to look out along the four dimensions and locate their lands, to relate all historical events within the confines of this particular land, and to accept responsibility for it. Regardless of what subsequently happens to the people, the sacred lands remain as permanent fixtures in their cultural or religious understanding. Thus, many tribes now living in Oklahoma, but formerly from the eastern United States, still hold in their hearts the sacred locations of their history, and small groups travel to obscure locations in secret to continue tribal ceremonial life. (ibid., 67)

Being a descendant of the members of the Chickasaw Nation who had been forced to march from their homelands to Indian Territory, Joannie's personal, cultural, and religious understanding depends upon a reckoning with the sacred places of her own history. This need shapes the direction of her search for a spiritual home. Conversely, although Bernie also seeks spiritual guidance, the forward motion of her journey takes on an apocalyptic shape. Thus, while Joannie and Bernie attempt to fulfill a similar need, they do so in two separate worlds of existence: one specific, tangible, and tied to a living relationship with the past and its sacred places; the other, unknown, ephemeral, and suspended in an unknown future space.

As the play progresses, religious questions fill the stage. The strife between Bernie and Tony becomes entangled with religion, and both characters look to the Christian god for answers. They read the Bible in search of direction and attend a church-affiliated marriage counselor. When their attempts fail, both characters distance themselves from one another. Tony secludes himself at his piano composing jazz renditions of church hymns, while Bernie questions the interconnectedness between her faith, her marriage, and her identity.

Oliva sets Joannie's second visit within the element of fire, which physically stages thematic associations amongst Joannie's childhood memories of the fire pit at summer camp, the Chihuly exhibit Joannie and Bernie once visited together, and aspects of Joannie's Chickasaw identity. The stage directions call for a more intense shift into this second visitation scene, defining the campfire as a more specific location than previous scenes in the play. Powwow music, which grows in volume, underscores the transition into the second visit. Oliva calls for the lights to "*shift as if in the middle of an absurd campfire. There is a faint suggestion of Chihuly's red neon tepees and water spears*" (Oliva, *Fire*, 36). During the second visit, Joannie attempts to free her friend by leading her through a rite of passage. Joannie explains, "Eliot wrote, 'Ring the bell backwards.' I've been doing that but in your case I'm not sure that's the sound you need to hear…You have to walk away from the knowledge of your experiences and learn another way" (ibid., 40). The challenge that Joannie makes to Bernie is to move beyond the rules that imprison her, and the symbolic representation of that challenge – a spontaneous book-burning of societal rules – appropriates Christian ritual language of creation and communion for radical ends:

BEARNIE: Joannie, I don't know how. I've always learned the rules. Played by the rules. Obeyed the laws…
JOANNIE: Okay, so we burn them. Torch conformity. A bonfire of rhetorical backlash. Come on. This is your chance.
BEARNIE: No, there would be chaos.
JOANNIE: No, before the ordered universe, there was chaos. And ever since then we have ruled and lawed ourselves right back into disorder. Maybe we should start over and find another way. It will be an "exercise" as you say to your students – an exercise in – burning Bernadette's bondage.
She rises and gets BERNIE up. She takes [her] *shawl, wraps the papers and feather* [from her powwow regalia] *inside.*
Torching litany! Striking a match to the statutes.
Hands the shawl to BERNIE.
I want you to have these things. In remembrance of me. And what we are about to do. (ibid., 41)

Joannie's gift to Bernie signifies a reciprocal, spiritual bond between the two friends that is forged through Joannie's material sacrifice and Bernie's acceptance to remember her through ceremonial actions. Paradoxically, although reminiscent of communion, a Christian rite often perceived as a static recreation of Jesus Christ's Last Supper, the ritual to which Joannie invites Bernie is designed to defy fixed guidelines of behavior and knowledge. Piano music underscores the scene with a less and less recognizable rendition of the hymn "Trust and Obey." At first, Bernie enjoys burning the symbolic books; however, she confronts a spiritual crisis when Joannie attempts to throw the Bible into the bonfire. Bernie "*Clings to the Bible fiercely*" as Joannie questions, "If we burn this […] does that mean you lose your faith? You lose whatever this book and the words and the history taught you?" (ibid., 44, 43).

The conflict between the women represents a clash between Christianity and traditional Native American religious practices; moreover, the contrast between these two spiritual ways of knowing is rooted in issues of place. Deloria asserts that the major difference between Native American religions and Christianity is that they are based, respectively, on differing values of space and time. He states:

American Indians hold their lands – places – as having the highest possible meaning, and all their statements are made with this reference point in mind. Immigrants review the movement of their ancestors across the continent as a steady progression of basically good events and experiences, thereby placing history – time – in the best possible light. When one group is concerned with the philosophical problem of space and the other with the philosophical problem of time, then the statements of either group do not make much sense when transferred from one context to the other without the proper consideration of what is taking place. (Vine Deloria, Jr., *God is Red*, 62–63)

Building upon these two perspectives, Deloria goes on to explain that because place-based religions value the personal experiences that occur between people and their sacred places, religious traditions can change through time in order to meet the changing needs of both people and land. Conversely, he argues, world religions supplant the power of place by focusing on linear time. According to this time-based model, stories of historical religious events shape the beliefs and behavior of present-day people in order that they may be judged righteous in the climactic future. Privileging time allows the religion to become "universal," rather than local, because it can focus on timeless "truths" – such as Bernie's laws – rather than on dynamic relationships with place. Critical of world religions, Deloria argues "that ecological, political, and spiritual crises of the twentieth century are the result of the misguided attempt to separate humanity from the rest of creation while maintaining a relationship to a god who acts in experienced history" (Warrior, *Tribal Secrets*, 71). Bernie represents such a spiritual crisis, as she clings to her Bible, a time-centered book that literally "takes the place" of local, place-centered religious experiences.

By shifting from a place-centered communal knowledge to a time-centered universal knowledge, Christianity places much importance upon the apocalypse. In *The Fire and the Rose*, the measuring of linear time preoccupies the play's non-Native characters as they near the millennium's end. Interestingly, the approaching millennium evokes the fear of the end of time, which – for the non-Native characters – is synonymous with the end of the earth and human existence. When Bernie and Tony host a small get-together to create a millennium time capsule, the topic of time dominates the characters' conversations. Ironically, the time capsule itself represents the need to locate a meaningful existence in place, as the characters attempt to preserve a moment of their lives through a literal burial of the time capsule.

The items placed in the time capsule represent the unnatural and arbitrary methods people use to construct and measure a meaningful existence: gauges that measure individual worth, business cards that replace identity with phone and fax numbers, and keys that represent the boundaries erected amongst people. As the game progresses, an uneasy, apocalyptic feeling prevails. Tony predicts that, owing to technology's increasing ability to control the earth, rainbows will be gone in the next millennium. He states, "there'll be no tokens of covenant" (Oliva, *Fire*, 31). His fear articulates Chaudhuri's geopathetic reading of contemporary plays that locate "ill-location" in "the recognition that no heroism or departure can redeem the wasteland to which the world has been reduced by the forces of modernity" (Chaudhuri, *Staging Place*, 251). While allowing non-Native characters to lament such ecological devastation, *The Fire and the Rose* counters the anxieties with presentations of the numinous earth during the scenes shared between Joannie and Bernie. Nevertheless, Bernie shares Tony's apprehension concerning the loss of covenant and Christianity's failure to extend its religious promises through time. The playing style of the scene shifts to reflect Bernie's perception. The music underscoring the scene gains volume and grows distorted, as bright lights "engulf" the stage (Oliva, *Fire*, 31). Bernie transitions into a dreamlike state and asserts, "There is no assurance. I mean insurance. Governments can't regulate it; people can't afford it and God can't endorse it" (ibid.).

As Bernie experiences instability from confronting her disillusionment with God, she anxiously searches for one of Joannie's poems while stating, "Where are you – Joannie. Grandfath…No GrandMOTHER. Footprints on my Grandmother's Grave. A sonnet. That was the name of your poem" (ibid., 32). Bernie's words allude to archetypal figures shifting from time (Grandfather Time) to place (Grandmother Earth). In the tension between the powers of time and place, Bernie worries that she is losing her ability to make sense of life. She picks up a paperback copy of *Four Quartets* and ponders, "'They can tell you, being dead: the communication of the dead is tongued with fire beyond the language of the living.' All these years I thought I knew what that meant. *She puts the book down and picks one page*" (ibid., 34). Next, she reads Joannie's poem, "Dancing on My

Grandmother's Grave," which draws the presence of Joannie and her Grandmother, who enter the stage dancing in a large circle, while the setting changes to represent the campfire. Bernie and Joannie are unaware of Grandmother as they begin to visit. Although Bernie's experiences continue to adhere to linear time, she confesses that her quest for meaning is developing strong parallels to Joannie's. She states:

BERNIE: There's a short little poem that I found of yours, scribbled on the margin. I don't think it was finished. It didn't have a title. It keeps running through my head. "We look for a place/Some place to belong/To land in, a home/A hand, a hug, base-someplace." "We look...
BERNIE AND JOANNIE: "for a place/Someplace to belong/To land in, a home/A hand, a hug, base-someplace."
JOANNIE: Fairly parochial writing.
   [...]
BERNIE: Agreed, but it sums up my existence now, parochial or not.   (ibid., 38)

As Bernie shares Joannie's embodied explorations, she obtains an understanding that perhaps she, too, lacks a sense of purpose due to her own placelessness. Joannie's lack of rootedness is so pervasive that its effects permeate all aspects of her life, identity, spirituality, and death. Bernie's placelessness similarly affects her spirituality, yet remains within the bounds of a Christian worldview.

Oliva's choice to stage and validate Native localized religious perspectives and Christian frameworks for her respective characters displays a complicated overlapping of platial issues. Platiality is fluid, affecting all people whatever their ethnicities, while it is also particular to Native American people. In respect to spirituality, Native American platiality emphasizes the direct relationship between people and specific lands. In localized religions, the power of land overrides the power of time. Specific landscapes can connect people from various eras, from disparate worlds of existence: Joannie can defy death to return to the earth, and Grandmother's spirit can inhabit specific locations of Joannie's past experiences. In such places, the land serves as a site for the communication of spiritual knowledge; consequently, in Native American dramaturgy, language also becomes an important platial concept, drawing together issues of identity, spirituality, and place.

Kneubuhl's *The Story of Susanna* also confronts the spiritual conflict between the Judeo-Christian focus upon rules and the traditional Native American spiritual focus upon one's relationship with the land. By questioning elements of time-centered religions and emphasizing the elements of localized place-centered belief systems, Kneubuhl's play begins to deconstruct the "universal" authority of world religions. The staging of place-centered philosophies frees the plot from conventions of linear time, allowing place – specifically the mythical Susanna's garden and the contemporary Susanna's institutional home – to connect two apparently different times. Kneubuhl's initial juxtaposed relationship between the scenes depicting separate eras eventually gives way to scenes in which mythical time and contemporary time move simultaneously.

Kneubuhl parallels the biblical and contemporary Susannas' relationships to place during the transition from Act One to Act Two. Act One ends with the mythical Susanna's entering into a winter's dormancy, while Act Two begins with the contemporary Susanna's entering the women's transitional home. The home's name, "Threshold," alludes to the home's purpose, a place where the women step from old into new ways of life, and it alludes also to the natural world, the season of winter's inactivity separating the death of autumn and the renewal of spring. As the mythical Susanna figuratively enters the earth for a season of rest, her rebirth becomes the responsibility of the contemporary Susanna, whose choices have the potential to restore the women's geocentric identities through a reckoning with the sacredness of place.

On the mythical level of *The Story of Susanna*, Kneubuhl presents the conflict between Susanna and the laws of Moses under which she was raised and punished. Reflecting Deloria's description of conflicts between world religions and local religion, Kneubuhl's mythical Susanna expresses her desire to be freed from law and reunited with nature. In Act One, Scene Eight she states:

Once, Daniel, I had a dream. I dreamed I was not raised in the law, a pious woman, Hilkiah's daughter, but instead, a nomad's child, those wanderers from the south. In the dream, I am a nomad's child in my sunrinsed clothes, insulting Babylon with insolent lips that twitch and laugh at the laws of Moses. Wanderers have no need of laws, for we keep secrets instead, secrets grown from bones, from the marrow of bones and secrets from the voices of songs. Somewhere we meet, and I sing you away, away from the judges, away from the kings of Babylon, away from the dragons and lions. I sing you only: the wide floating islands of the desert, a sea woven from the sky, and I make you a shimmering garden, on the shoreline of my dreams. (Kneubuhl, *Susanna*, 316)

Susanna's dream incorporates many theories stemming from Native American platial discourse. The vision begins by differentiating between two belief systems: one tied to Hebrew law, the other to the land. Then, the dream conveys how cultural and spiritual meaning is taught in localized religions. In her dream, Susanna is a daughter of nomads who live in a direct relationship with the land. No longer Hilkiah's daughter, she can reject the roles placed upon her through Hebrew law. Knowledge now comes to her through the bones of her ancestors. The transference of spiritual knowledge from the bones of ancestors to a living descendant derives from two sources simultaneously: family (ancestors) and the earth (where the bones are buried). Furthermore, this knowledge is personal (being from the family), localized (being from the earth), and powerful. Once the daughter of nomads learns the songs of her ancestors' bones and sings them herself, she has a spiritual power greater than the law. It is a power strong enough to sing Daniel out of the biblical books of judges' laws and into his own reckoning with place.

The conflict for the mythical Susanna is that the biblical laws have imprisoned her. The Book of Daniel has recorded another person's version of Susanna's life and her garden. Before she can overcome the laws that define and confine her, Susanna must heal both her emotional wounds and the damage done to her garden home during its invasion. Pommersheim speaks of this need for abused lands to be restored into what he calls "sacred texts." He states, "The land needs to be retained, restored, and redefined… Its spiritual role – long atrophied – must be revivified. Its healing role – long obscured – must be revitalized. The land must hold the people and give direction to their aspirations and yearnings" (Pommersheim, *Braid of Feathers*, 34). Framed by the play's action, the biblical story of Susanna works to erase the sacred text of place when the Bible defines the garden as Joakim's, omits Susanna's voice, converts her personal story into a demonstration of laws, and discounts the damage the invading elders have done to Susanna and the garden.

In the play's contemporary world, Susanna faces a crisis of ideology as she becomes closer to Lee. In a rare moment when *The Story of Susanna*'s worlds of myth and contemporary society overlap, Lee enters the middle circle, as Susanna steps from the upper circle of myth into the middle circle of private life. Knowing that she has been interacting with another personal and "imaginary" world, Lee chastises Susanna. He attempts to sever Susanna's former knowledge of self with a new ideology as he tells her, "I'm real. I'm part of reality. You want to live in the real world don't you?" and then commands Susanna to "forget all that other stuff" (Kneubuhl, *Susanna*, 321). To mirror the connection between the mythical Susanna, whose heart has been frozen by glaciers, and the contemporary Susanna, who agrees to surrender her own reality to Lee's, Kneubuhl's stage directions state that "*Susanna, looking at Lee, freezes in a sculptured pose*" (ibid.). Once both

Susannas are stripped of their connections to the sacred text of place, Kneubuhl's mythical Susanna opens Act Two by giving Daniel her dreams and visions (symbolized by a small wooden box) before exiting the stage and action of the play (ibid., 328).

Although the mythical Susanna exits Act Two's action, the world of myth continues to intermingle with contemporary society through the character of Daniel, who, in the new stage configuration, skirts the edges of Kneubuhl's circles and occasionally enters the light to speak for Susanna. Since Daniel's descriptions of Susanna's struggles can no longer be differentiated as having belonged to the Susanna of myth or the Susanna in Threshold, his statements interweave the worlds of myth and contemporary society. When the contemporary Susanna sleeps in her Threshold bedroom, now designated in the upper circle that belonged to the world of myth in Act One, Daniel enters the light and speaks:

Here are some things she wanted me to tell you: awake or asleep, it all comes back when you least expect it. The things that happened once come back. Your mind is very strong and can fight with the scenes that try to run like movies over and over, showing the same reel, but your body, your body is so vulnerable, and there is no way to protect it from the fear imprinted on every cell [...] Awake or asleep, it all comes back and every breath is a prayer for survival. (ibid., 343)

As Daniel's lines blur the dreams of both Susannas, the worlds of myth and reality coexist; they begin to mirror and affect one another, a concept that derives from Native platial concepts that recognize the simultaneous presence of different worlds of existence. The phenomenon is a function of place as sacred text. Pommersheim explains:

As part of the sacred text, the land…is *not* primarily a book of answers but rather a principle symbol – perhaps *the* principle symbol of and thus a central occasion of recalling and heeding – the fundamental aspirations of the tradition. It summons the heart and the spirit to difficult labor. In this sense, the sacred text constantly *disturbs*: it serves a prophetic function in the life of the community…The "sacred text" itself guarantees nothing, but it does hold the necessary potential to mediate the past of the tradition with its present predicament. (*Braid of Feathers*, 35)

By connecting the Susanna of myth and the Susanna of Threshold, the power of place allows the events of the past to mediate and guide Susanna's choices in the present. Through the sacredness of place, contemporary Susanna recalls a mythical knowledge that allows her to heed the experiences of the past. Such ancient knowledge disturbs her present course of action and reunites Susanna with past traditions.

The traditions to which Susanna returns uphold the sacredness of place and restore the connections between women, nature, and creation. This philosophical move allows Kneubuhl to emphasize both Native philosophies of place and a feminist reclaiming of the Bible's story of Susanna. In *The Sacred Hoop: Recovering the Feminine in American Indian Traditions*, Paula Gunn Allen focuses upon the connections between Native American women, the earth, and spirituality by referring to creation myths. She states:

There is a spirit that pervades everything, that is capable of powerful song and radiant movement, and that moves in and out of the mind...Old Spider Woman is one name for this quintessential spirit, and Serpent Woman is another. Corn Woman is one aspect of her, and Earth Woman is another, and what they together have made is called Creation, Earth, creatures, plants, and light. At the center of all is Woman, and no thing is sacred...without her blessing, her thinking. (Allen, *Sacred*, 13)

By rooting the experiences of the contemporary Susanna within the mythical Susanna and her garden and infusing the biblical narrative with Native American platial theories, Kneubuhl works to prepare her audience to envision a different version of the biblical Susanna. Her version upholds not only the sacredness of place, but also the feminine spirit of creation inhabiting the worlds of myth and reality.

Wiles' analysis of classical Greek theatre recognizes the blending of spiritual realms and lived reality when he explains that "The chorus opens up a different kind of dramatic space, and establishes a different kind of relationship between the human and divine" (*Tragedy*, 11). Kneubuhl establishes this human/divine interaction in her play's prologue with the masked chorus-like figures; then she continues it as the story of Daniel and Susanna mingles with the contemporary characters. Interestingly, Wiles asserts that through the chorus in classical Greek theatre, "both [human and divine] worlds are coexistent in theatrical space, and *each informs the other*" (ibid., 9; emphasis added). *The Story of Susanna* capitalizes upon the reciprocity between these two worlds. Not only can the past disrupt the present, but the present can alter the past. As their Act One dialogue delves into a discussion of the Bible, Daniel tells Susanna:

This is what they wrote down about me: "And the Lord stirred the Holy Spirit of a young man named Daniel." But I didn't need a holy spirit to see what was happening. It was so easy to unravel their [the elders'] story, so simple to prove them wrong – corroborating evidence, witnesses examined separately, and then they proceeded to make sure I was never forgotten. I was the chosen one. They always get it wrong, don't they? They picked me to put in their canon, to put in the holy book of Daniel. But I know, I have always known, it's *your* story. (Kneubuhl, *Susanna*, 312)

This small shift in ownership of *The Story of Susanna* destabilizes the fixed nature of the Bible's account and works to prepare the audience to accept another version of reality in which the contemporary Susanna's actions will reclaim and rewrite the story of the biblical Susanna.

In the penultimate scene of the play, the worlds of myth and contemporary society begin to mix not only thematically but also spatially. Daniel appears on stage and speaks of the mythical Susanna's moment of crisis, in which she recognized that there was no meaning to be found in her religious world and that only her own decisions could shape her fate (ibid., 364). Interspersed with Daniel's spoken lines, the climax of the contemporary Susanna's story takes place in the upper circle. In this moment, Susanna confronts and admits the truth that she was responsible for causing the car wreck that killed her boyfriend. She states, "I meant it for both of us...but it only took him. I killed him" (ibid., 365). The recognition, which occurs simultaneously for both Susannas, is marked by Daniel's mythical sharing of stage space with contemporary action. As Kneubuhl uses the crisis to physically blend the worlds of mythical and contemporary existence, she also directs the audience to the final strand of platial discourse that will allow both Susannas to cultivate a geocentric identity. To heal this relationship with place and to restore the spiritual power of the damaged garden, Susanna must find her voice to reclaim her own story.

LANGUAGE AS LANDSCAPE: MOTHER TONGUE/MOTHER EARTH

In Native American platial theories, language stems from the earth. Language, in part, facilitates the reciprocal relationship between people and their places of origin. For example, in many Pueblo philosophies, as demonstrated earlier by Allen, it was the language of the creation deities that formed the earth and its inhabitants. Place holds people and teaches them this language. People, in turn, complete the reciprocal relationship with place and its creators by using language in a sacred way to honor the earth. The sacred uses of language are found in ceremony, in song, and in traditional stories (or myths). To have this understanding of the power of language allows a person to connect to place and to attain cultural, spiritual, and emotional knowledge. Significantly, the healing of Riggs' Cherokee characters, Joannie, and Susanna depends upon a reckoning with place through language.

In *The Cherokee Night* we see this sacred use of language when Talbert tells the story of the ancestors, when Sarah recounts her mother's teachings, and when Gar proclaims that no one will steal his spirituality or take his life. The last two scenes of *The Cherokee Night* provide the clearest examples of how a ceremonial use of language heals the rupture between individuals, their homelands, and their community (both living and spiritual). Scene Six, "The White Turkey," stages Hutch's homecoming. The scene is set in 1919 at the Whiteturkey farmhouse, the family home of Kate, Hutch's Osage girlfriend, and of her brother, Clabe. The house is dilapidated and the farmland around it withered. Riggs describes the drab landscape as punctuated by "*a Stutz Bearcat, 1919 model, of startling red color*" (Riggs, *Cherokee*, 187). Hutch, now returned from World War I, where he saved Clabe's life in battle, lives here with Kate; "*Claremore Mound is a thin far silhouette against the sky*" (ibid.).

The scene concentrates on questions of sickness and healing. As such, with its dominant colors of red and white, Scene Five is aligned with the Paint Clan, *Aniwodi*, whose members "were historically known as a prominent medicine people. Medicine is often 'painted' on after harvesting, mixing and performing other aspects of the ceremony" (Cherokee Nation website, "Cherokee Clans"). Hutch, whose fair hair, large frame, and stuttering have always made him feel like an outsider, is now apparently "fixed" from his speech impediment by Kate, who keeps him as a possession, along with her three cars and the airplane she plans to purchase. Although Kate and Clabe have become wildly rich from Osage oil, their spiritual illness is as apparent as the barren landscape that surrounds their family home. Kate expresses a disregard for Native communities and lands when she meets George, Hutch's older brother, who has come looking for him. She shrugs off George's questions about why she and Clabe have let their family's land allotments go to ruin, replying, "Who wants to farm?" (Riggs, *Cherokee*, 190). George reminds Kate that her father had been a farmer, to which she responds, "Yeah, but he's dead. And I'm rich" (ibid.). In her materialistic frame of reference, Native heritage is only good for what it gets a person. "It's hard luck to be born part Cherokee instead of full-blood Osage," Kate quips. "[Hutch] might as well be white trash for all the good bein' Indian does him" (ibid.).

As they wait for Hutch to come out of the farmhouse, George tries to relate to Kate by asking her if she knows the legend of how her name, Whiteturkey, came to be. His story of a red canoe and a talking white turkey elicits Kate's disdain: "Of all the bunk! Turkeys don't talk" (ibid., 192). George decides to save his words for Hutch, but the brothers' reunion is not easy. Both Kate and Hutch are fearful of George's language. Hutch tells George to "Get the hell out of here! [...] I don't want to hear," while Kate warns, "He don't stutter any more [...] I cured him of that. It's more'n you could do, for all your education! You not gonna get him back! I c'n tell you that, right now! You'd have him tied up in knots" (ibid., 194). George persists. First, he condemns his brother's sense of being physically "fixed," while living a selfish, corrupt lifestyle. Then, George reminds Hutch of the Cherokee–Osage historic warring, before accusing him of prostituting his manhood for Osage money. Finally, George reminds Hutch of his responsibilities to his land, community, and self:

I'll go [...] Listen, I'm at the hotel tomorrow. Come and see me. They're making that new road from Claremore north through Vinita and up to the Kansas line. It would be a good job for you, get you away from this – all this. Your teams are in the pasture, idle. They ought to be working. You ought to be working. (ibid., 197)

Although we don't see Hutch's final decision, we know that George's language has begun to heal the rupture between Hutch and his sense of family, Cherokee community, and responsibilities to land. As George's "medicine" overwhelms Kate's, Hutch's stutter returns, reflecting the burden of responsibility he now acknowledges.

The play's final scene, "The Cherokee Night," is also its first scene, chronologically. Set in 1895, Scene Seven returns us to the play's beginning setting, except that a cabin now occupies the picnic site and the landscape is outlined in snow. The scene begins in darkness. Riggs writes that, first, "*a drumbeat rises, grows tremendous in volume*"; then, Claremore Mound appears at the same time as "*A deep male VOICE begins a Cherokee song*"; and, finally, "*a fire begins, first to glow, then to a blaze, from the exact spot of the picnic in Scene One*" (ibid., 198). The lights come up on Gray-Wolf and his eight-year-old grandson, Sonny, who listens to his grandfather's song. It is the first time that we have seen a source for the play's drum score.

The scene, with its ceremonial aspects of scenic repetition, song, and storytelling, is deceptively complicated. When we see Gray-Wolf and his grandson, we might assume that this scene will capture an unsullied time, when questions of culture and belonging were not so difficult; instead, Riggs breaks the peace with violent speech and actions that portray the social upheaval that occurred as non-Native settlers moved into Indian Territory. Sonny and Gray-Wolf talk of death and the dangers facing their community. Gray-Wolf tells his grandson that, "When Death wants you, it's better to sit and wait," and that Sonny's father was shot when he "took a side of beef from the smokehouse on Rucker's Ranch" to feed his starving family (ibid., 200, 201). The homelands are not safe; "Indian Territory is plumb full of men with six-shooters now – cattle rustlers, desperados" (ibid., 201).

As an illustration of these dangers, Edgar "Spench" Breeden, the father of Gar and Bee, breaks into the cabin and holds Gray-Wolf and Sonny hostage. Spench trains his gun on Gray-Wolf, cursing the elder and demanding that he nurse his bleeding gunshot wound. Spench was shot running from a posse of white men looking to capture him for a reward. Gray-Wolf convinces Spench, who admits to killing an innocent shop-keeper, to let Sonny go, while he remains to care for Spench. Alone, the two men begin to talk. Although Spench has repeatedly cursed Gray-Wolf, the older man gently nurses him. Gray-Wolf tells Spench how much Gar, his son, resembles Spench, and how Marthy, Spench's wife, "Still talks about you. Thinks you're sump'n fine, 'stid of a killer" (ibid., 206). Gray-Wolf also says that Florey Newcomb, who is pregnant with Bee, is "Proud to have a kid by a desperado, a man that don't like no one's life but his own, a man that ain't got a heart in him no place" (ibid.). Through their discussion, we see Gray-Wolf's connection to the Cherokee communal values, as he unconditionally treats a cold-blooded murderer with dignity.

Spench asks Gray-Wolf why he is so good to him, why he is not interested in turning Spench in for money; Gray-Wolf claims to be inter-ested in something else – trying to understand why Spench has become so rotten. The answer shifts to issues of blood and the land, as Spench explains, "I tried everything. Tried to farm. Too restless. Cattle herdin,' ridin' fence. Sump'n always drove me on. The bosses! Burned down their barns, rustled their cattle, slept with their wives. Shot the bastards down – ! Sump'n inside – no rest, I don't know – Bad blood. Too much Indian, they tell me" (ibid., 208). Spench has spent his life wandering, placeless, without a community. He has either been a servant to "the bosses" or an outlaw. Gray-Wolf counters Spench's stereotype of savage Indians and responds, "Not enough Indian [...] I'm full-blood – Cherokee. I live peaceful. I ain't troubled. I remember the way my people lived in quiet times. Think of my ancestors. It keeps me safe. You though – like my boy. He's dead. He was half white, like you. They killed him, *had* to kill him! Not *enough* Indian. The mixture" (ibid.). At this moment, Riggs begins to twist the audience's expectations, again. Although Spench's stereotype is self-destructive, Gray-Wolf's proclamation about genetics, which supposes a wretched future for Sonny, is no better. Strangely, Spench is the one who brings balance to their views: "Lost so much blood. Feel my life runnin' out of me, slow. White blood, Indian – it don't matter. It spills out, runs out of me like water. Don't try to stop it any more" (ibid.).

Going against the lessons about death that he taught Sonny, Gray-Wolf begs Spench to fight for his life, but Tinsley and the posse break into the cabin and shoot Spench. The characters' final dialogue resonates with a level of despair that some critics have judged to be Riggs' surrender to the myth of the vanishing Indian. Tinsley, with his white invaders, declare supreme power over the land and people: "It's time someone killed him. A bad half-breed, that un. One of your tribe, Gray-Wolf. Let this be a lesson and a warnin'. Teach your grandson. Tell everybody what it means to oppose the law. You Indians must think you own things out here. This is God's country out here – and God's a white man" (ibid., 209). Marthy Breeden enters with one-year-old Gar, a pregnant Florey Newcomb, and other women from the Cherokee community. Her monologue, like Gray-Wolf's theory of mixed heritage, sounds like defeat. She delivers it as a kind of ceremony, while others draw near:

Edgar. Husband. They got you. We always knowed they would, didn't we? [...] (*Her voice is unemotional, but full of a rich warm, earthy and compassionate power* [...]) What you done was what they call wrong. You couldn't help it, I know that. You tried to do right. It was too much. You was hounded day and night, inside and out. By day, men. At night, your thoughts. Now it's over. Sleep. Rest now. (*She shifts the child in her arms* [...]) But here's your son. In him your trouble. It goes on. In him. It ain't finished [...] Florey. Here's Florey Newcomb, bearin' your child. You're at rest. Sleep. Your disgrace, your wickedness, your pain and trouble live on a while longer. In her child, in my child. In all people born now, about to be born. (*Her face becomes luminous, as her mind gropes toward an impersonal truth.*) Someday, the agony will end. Yours has. Ours will. Maybe not in the night of death, the cold dark night, without stars. Maybe in the sun. It's got to! It's what we live for. (ibid., 210)

Certainly, Marthy's words are problematic. But did Riggs really push against the expectations and suggestions of New York theatre companies only to create a play that ends, as most mainstream Native-themed dramas did in the 1930s, with a grand Native statement of defeat? Could Marthy's words be read any other way? Might her discussion of "all people born now, about to be born" refer literally to *all people* sharing the troubled land of Indian Territory, the place where Native Americans were first sent away from whites, only to be reinvaded later through federal policies and broken treaties? Could "ending in the sun" foreshadow not death but the epiphany their son, Gar, has on Eagle Bluff, when he shouts under the hot summer sun, "You can't kill me! I'm going to live. Live!" (ibid., 186)?

In a letter to his advisor, Riggs said of *The Cherokee Night*'s ending:

What astonishes me and delights me now is that finally, by projection, the play has meaning beyond the story, even beyond the theme. The last scene of all concentrates a statement about and covers the entire field of Indian–White relationships in one dramatic incident such as I could never have foreseen. And it's not a protest – but a triumphant comprehension by an old Indian, a real nobleman, which makes the play dignified and austere beyond my first feeble calculations. I hope it will be my best play. It can be. (qtd. in Braunlich, *Haunted*, 95)

The final moment is Gray-Wolf's sacred declaration, words that powerfully heal the rupture between Spench, the most unloved of all people – white or Native – and his Cherokee community. Gray-Wolf tells the posse, "Leave us. It's *our* dead," sacred words that claim Spench and welcome his spirit in a homecoming, a literal burial-ceremony in his homeland. Riggs writes that when Tinsley's crowd leaves, the Cherokee community members gathered in Gray-Wolf's home transform their actions: "*It is like a curious and solemn ritual. A drum has begun to beat, low and throbbing and final* [...] *A faraway look is in GRAY-WOLF's eyes* [...] *as if he mourned for his own life, for the life of his son, for his grandson, for SPENCH, for the WOMEN, for a whole race gone down into darkness*" (Riggs, *Cherokee*, 211). The characters' feelings about the moment exist on one level, but "by projection" into the future, the audience knows a different story. We know that the path will not be easy for the Cherokee Nation of Oklahoma, but that their survival and remembrance of communal values will continue.

Riggs communicates this hope through two major dramaturgical elements relating to place. The first is an overt use of parallelism in the final moments of staging. Riggs allows Claremore Mound to have the final word in *The Cherokee Night*. The last stage directions read: "*The lights fade slowly. The fire flickers. Claremore Mound glitters in the night. A few stars are in the sky*" (ibid.). The fire, which represents the Cherokee community, both worldly and spiritual, endures; Claremore Mound, which roots the characters' identities, remains their homeland, a sacred place where new generations might connect to ancestral knowledge. We understand this timeless connection to place when we watch Scene Seven and can clearly realize that the spiritual connection Gar makes to Claremore Mound in Scene One is a most profound link to place: he encounters the exact place where both his literal father and spiritual fathers eternally reside.

The second dramaturgical convention relating to Native concepts of place is one that Riggs completes in Scene Seven. The structure of *The Cherokee Night* itself functions as a linguistic, platial ceremony. Each of Riggs' scenes relates to a Cherokee clan; for example, "The Cherokee Night" relates to the one remaining clan, the Long Hair Clan, *Anigilohi*, which was "known to be a very peaceful clan. In the times of the Peace Chief and War Chief government, the Peace Chief would come from this clan. Prisoners of war, orphans of other tribes, and others with no Cherokee tribe were often adopted into this clan" (Cherokee Nation website, "Cherokee Clans"). Gray-Wolf, whose actions exemplify the "Beloved Path" in the face of extreme conflict and in his acceptance of the homeless Spench, aligns Scene Seven with the Long Hair Clan. This association between clans and scenes accomplishes more than representing the Cherokee Nation's entire community: it transforms the plot into a platial ceremony that allows Riggs to communicate an overarching theme of Cherokee cultural continuance.

When Cherokee communities gather for traditional ceremonial events, there is often a particular seating arrangement that places everyone around the sacred fire of the ceremonial grounds (Cherokee Nation website, "Cherokee Stomp Dance"). This emplacement begins in the east with the Long Hair Clan. Then it moves to the left, clockwise: Blue Clan, Wolf Clan, Wild Potato Clan, Deer Clan, Bird Clan, and Paint Clan. Riggs' plot structure and staging devices follow this ceremonial pattern, beginning with the Blue Clan and Talbert's message, moving around Claremore Mound's sacred, ancestral fire, and ending at the chronological and physical place of origin – the Long Hair arbor in the east. Read through its structure, the play ends in hope, at the literal place of new ceremonial beginnings. With this structure, Riggs marks the stage itself as a place of Cherokee communal action – a profound statement for a Cherokee playwright in the 1930s, and an historic moment for Native American theatre. As Riggs moves traditional Cherokee culture into his contemporary, New York world of playwriting, he undoes the defeatist language of the characters and truly stages "the entire field of Indian-White relationships," past and present, seen and unseen (Riggs qtd. in Braunlich, *Haunted*, 95). No wonder he so ardently protected the integrity of the play's dramaturgical style against the wishes of theatre critics.

In *The Fire and the Rose*, Joannie's journey toward a geocentric identity uses language in a poetic way. When Joannie recalls the beginnings of her journey, Native concepts of language weave artistically into those of place and spirituality. Not only does Bernie's task of editing Joannie's poems structure the play's plot, but also each fragment of Joannie's poetry represents a marker along trails of meaning. Bernie acknowledges the power of her friend's poems when, in their third conversation, she confesses to Joannie, "With every poem, I go on a journey too, through you, and each time it takes me a while to recover [...] I feel so close...so near the edge of understanding but then my intellect intrudes" (Oliva, *Fire*, 66). Bernie's statement acknowledges the strength and failing of Joannie's poetry: it has the potential to transport readers to new places of meaning but, due to the book's unfinished state, the work cannot help Joannie reach such final destinations.

At the campfire, Joannie confides in Bernie the direct relationship between her writing of poetry and her quest to develop a sense of rooted-ness. As an adolescent, Joannie's first attempt to reconnect with her deceased, Chickasaw grandmother was driven by language. Joannie remembers, "I wanted so badly for my Grandmother to know how sorry I was that I didn't listen. As a little girl, I laughed at my Grandmother and rolled my eyes. I remember how embarrassed I was that she would speak such a foreign and odd language" (ibid., 40). Not speaking Chickasaw distanced Joannie from her grandmother and, owing to the traditional Native American emphasis upon the oral transmission of culture, from her own feelings of belonging to the Chickasaw Nation. However, by adolescence, Joannie had intuited that language created a passageway to connect, first, to her Grandmother and, ultimately, to her own place in the Chickasaw community. She states:

JOANNIE: One night, when everyone else was asleep, I sat by the fire and pretended to conjure up all my unknown history. The Choctaw and Chickasaw women whose blood seemed to purge through me like the fire in the night. I recited the very few words that I remember my grandmother saying in Chickasaw.
GRANDMOTHER remains in shadows, whispers words.
GRANDMOTHER: Minko.
JOANNIE: Minko.
GRANDMOTHER: Ishki.
JOANNIE: Ishki.
GRANDMOTHER: Inki.
JOANNIE: Inki.
GRANDMOTHER: Loshoma.
JOANNIE: Loshoma.
    [...]
GRANDMOTHER: Kilimpi
JOANNIE: Kilimpi. Loshoma means to be dead and kilimpi means to be strong.
(ibid., 39–40)[13]

The combination of her grandmother, language, and history provides direction for Joannie to resolve her problem with place. By approaching her grandmother through language, Joannie has the ability to overcome her figurative level of displacement, which, in turn, may lead to the healing of her literal-historical displacement.

In *The Sacred Hoop*, Allen explains the vital connection to place through ancestry. She states, "Failure to know your mother, that is, your position and its attendant traditions, history, and place in the scheme of things, is failure to remember your significance, your reality, your right relationship to earth and society. It is the same as being lost – isolated, abandoned, self-estranged, and alienated from your own life" (Allen, *Sacred*, 210). Here, Allen articulates Joannie's obstacle to creating a geocentric identity. Without her grandmother's traditional knowledge, Joannie suffers from a rupture with both place and meaning, breaks she must continue to mend in the afterlife. Although the grandmother's death prohibited Joannie's ability to fully learn of her place in the Chickasaw community, language offers the return path. Oliva theatrically demonstrates the power of language to connect generations by having Grandmother and Joannie engage in the call and response of Chickasaw kinship words. Significantly, the shared-language scene is the play's only scene in which Grandmother speaks.

The topography of language – how language symbolizes the land – is specific and literal in Native American cultures. In "Land Speaking," poet and novelist Jeannette C. Armstrong explains the distinctive relationship between Native American land and languages. She begins by providing an example of her own traditional language called N'silxchn. Armstrong states:

As I understand it from my Okanagan ancestors, language was given to us by the land we live within…I have heard elders explain that the language changed as we moved and spread over the land through time. My own father told me that it was the land that changed the language because there is special knowledge in each different place. All my elders say that it is land that holds all knowledge of life and death and is a constant teacher. ("Land Speaking," 175–176)

Armstrong's statement provides important keys to understanding the significance of Native languages. A traditional Native language is a connection to a specific land; through that language, the land actively teaches people about existence in both life and death. These lessons reinforce Deloria's argument regarding the sacredness of places and the ability for spiritual meaning to change with the needs arising from relationships between people and their homelands. Armstrong asserts that this connection between land, language, and knowledge is not limited to her own

Okanagan Nation but rather "all indigenous peoples' languages are generated by a precise geography and arise from it" (ibid., 178).

The initial barrier to Joannie's ability to use Chickasaw language in order to reclaim her people's knowledge rooted in a direct relationship to place was her recollection of only a few words; consequently, she had to discover a new word path. Eventually, she learned to mold the English language into poetry that not only evoked the sacredness of place, but also began to transform into a map that could guide her return, through her grandmother, to a Chickasaw geocentric identity. Joannie confesses, "I vowed to myself to not ignore that feeling of the fire purging in my veins [...] I started to write and find the words back to my past. 'Dancing on My Grandmother's Grave' was the first time I publicly admitted to being Indian" (Oliva, *Fire*, 40). As a declaration of Joannie's cultural identity, the sonnet aesthetically presents the interweaving concepts of rootedness, the sacredness of place, and language as landscape in a direct relationship to Joannie's figurative and historical-literal levels of displacement. Joannie recites the poem, which reads:

> I dance for my grandmother, on red dirt
> The drums and flute are singing just for you
> I wear the fringe that once was on your skirt
> My words are hands that reach for what you knew.
> [...]
> Brown eyes taught me lessons no longer sung
> For my people have lost their way and I
> With white blood, my beige skin – stranger among
> Those who never knew the Trail of Tears, the lie.
> [...]
> If I could dance backwards into the past
> Beneath the soil I'd look for hands that glove
> My hands, I'd step into your bones at last
> I would accept the you in me, the love.
> Poet daughter journeys forward with rhymes
> For songs whispered from graves the spirit climbs.   (ibid., 35)

In the sonnet, Joannie uses images of land to frame her search for a geocentric, Chickasaw identity. She begins the poem by dancing "on red dirt" and ends it by reaching "beneath the soil" into the eternal home of her grandmother (ibid.). Evoking many Native American ideas regarding the sacredness of burial sites, Joannie locates cultural knowledge in a specific sacred location, her grandmother's grave. It is here that communication between two worlds of existence, Joannie's and her deceased grandmother's, can take place. The exchange of wisdom occurs through a language directly tied to the earth. In writing "My words are hands that reach for what you knew" Joannie creates an image of her words entering into the sacred burial-space to "look for hands that glove/My hands" (ibid.). In this place where language circulates through land, Joannie can ask her grandmother for guidance, and her grandmother can provide the "lessons no longer sung" by Joannie's family (ibid.). The grandmother's "songs whispered from graves" provide Joannie with an understanding of how to live in contemporary society while embracing her geocentric identity. To journey "forward with rhymes" is Joannie's ability to progress through her lifespan while honoring knowledge from the Chickasaw Nation, which she comes to understand and incorporate into her daily life through the creation of poems (ibid.).

In addition to presenting interweaving concepts of Native American platiality, the sonnet provides information about *The Fire and the Rose*'s major plot complication, Joannie's current existence in the boundless place between life and the afterlife. Although Joannie first states that she is using her death in order to reclaim her past, throughout subsequent visits it becomes apparent that she is trapped between two worlds. In their third visit, characterized by the element of wind, Joannie and Bernie meet beneath an expanse of Oklahoma sky, where Joannie makes a kite tail from a line of clothing that Grandmother has stretched across the stage. Although Grandmother "*delivers a kite* [to Joannie] *as if it were a bird flying overhead*," Joannie is unaware of Grandmother's presence and believes that Miles has left the kite for her (ibid., 64). Despite the scene's lighthearted opening, tension between Bernie and Joannie mounts, until Joannie desperately confesses, "I don't have all of the answers, why do you think I'm still…I'm on the worst kind of journey a person could have, looking at my life with dead eyes" (ibid., 65). She admits to Bernie that she has yet to find God, and states:

I never felt wise enough to have a religion. It took me a long time to believe, much less celebrate my spirit, the way I saw the world and how all of me added up […] When I was little I used to sit in church and stare at the perspective painting behind the baptismal. A road leading to infinity, to God, I thought. And I believed with all my heart and soul that I could step into that painting, onto that road and meet God. All my poems are about that. (ibid., 70)

Bernie senses a distance growing between herself and Joannie. She tries to comfort her friend and to keep her from leaving, but Joannie is pulled in a different direction. Oliva's stage directions state that when Grandmother exits the stage chanting and trailing the clothesline behind her, Joannie follows while chanting "*in stops and starts*" (ibid., 70). Joannie's involuntary choice to walk behind Grandmother portrays that, unbeknownst to her, she has already stepped on the road to her spiritual home. The obstacle to Joannie's complete homecoming is that the map that will guide her back to place is the book of poetry left unfinished by her untimely death. The fragments of poetry, the scraps of this map, cause Joannie to remain suspended between life and afterlife, unable to effectively complete her journey until Bernie has finished the book. This conflict compels Joannie to remain attached to the living world through Bernie until the book's completion.

Bernie and Joannie's fourth visit serves as the play's final scene. In it, Oliva's dramatic action and stage directions present the connection between the completion of Joannie's book and the healing of her rupture with place. When the scene opens, the play's living characters have just attended a reading in celebration of the book's publication. With the exception of Bernie, the living characters read their favorite poems before exiting the stage. Bernie is left alone sitting by a fountain and contemplating the changes in her life: the book's completion and her recent choice to divorce Tony.

Grandmother watches from a distance as Joannie comes to visit Bernie a final time. Oliva's stage directions call for the lighting to shift to blues and greens, suggestive of Chihuly's seaforms, and for the sound of waves and seagulls; however, despite these staging shifts, the actors playing Joannie and Bernie do not depict a transition from space to a shared place between the two friends. Unlike for their prior visitations, Oliva's stage directions state that Joannie and Bernie "*are separated in their realities*" – Bernie in the space of living characters and Joannie someplace different (ibid., 81). Although the audience can see Joannie, her character now functions according to the theatrical conventions affecting Grandmother. Joannie and Bernie can feel one another's presence, but their interaction is limited, as Bernie can neither hear nor see Joannie. Bernie acknowledges the difference between her and Joannie's ways of discovering meaning. She states, "I'm moving…somewhere, tomorrow. You were right about ringing the bell backwards. That was your journey, not mine. Good ole T. S. Eliot. If he can find his faith after exploring the metaphysical maze, there must be hope for me" (ibid., 83). When Joannie does not answer, Bernie holds out her arms in the hope of feeling Joannie take them. Instead, Oliva's stage directions state, "*JOANNIE extends her arms to GRANDMOTHER who walks toward JOANNIE*" (ibid.). A Native flute underscores the action as Joannie is reunited with her Grandmother, who begins to enact a Native American custom of honoring the four directions that also mark the reunion's physical location.

The ceremony heals Joannie's rupture with a geocentric identity while transforming undifferentiated space into a sacred place. Explaining the cosmology of place-based societies, Tuan states that such ceremonies honoring the four directions extending from sacred places "make sense of the universe by classifying its components and suggesting that mutual influences exist among them. It imputes personality to space, thus transforming space in effect to place" (*Space and Place*, 91). As Joannie repeats Grandmother's motions, she states, "The four directions. And the four colors of man, red, yellow, black and white" (Oliva, *Fire*, 83). They continue the ceremony by relating the cardinal directions to the four elements, fire, earth, air, and water, which were also the four distinct places shared during Joannie and Bernie's four visits.

Although Bernie is not fully cognizant of the homecoming ritual occurring in her midst, her farewell to Joannie articulates an understanding of how geocentric identity, spirituality, and language all interrelate. She states:

I understand your chapter of revelations, Joannie. Eliot's *Four Quartets*.
Rises, slowly walking away.
You found your way through your words and all is well. "All shall be well and All manner of things shall be well/When the tongues of flame are in-folded/Into the crowned knot of fire/And the fire and the rose are one."
She lays rose on book.
I'm leaving the book here for you. I hope you're dancing with your Grandmother somewhere. Goodbye Joannie. (ibid., 83–84)

With the book complete, Joannie is free to depart limbo and enter her Grandmother's world. The power of her words, even those spoken after death, has allowed her to reach back through time to find a spiritual and ancestral home. Joannie opens the book and begins to read "Dancing on my Grandmother's Grave" to her Grandmother. Together, she and her Grandmother begin to dance the reverent Traditional Women's Buckskin Dance, as Joannie's recorded voice overtakes the live reading of the poem. Dancing, Joannie follows her Grandmother off the stage. Oliva's final stage direction reads, "*Flute music fades as rainbow appears barely visible on the landscape*" (ibid., 84). The appearance of the rainbow, a covenant between God and humanity that is expressed upon the landscape, concludes the play.

The Fire and the Rose portrays the power of language to align people with place. According to Native American platiality, such actions are possible because language not only comes from the land, but also offers a primary means by which humans can interact with place. Language offers Joannie the ability to claim her Chickasaw identity, to access her Grandmother's spirit, and, eventually, to mend her rupture with place. While the powers of language and place share a common historical site of rupture for Native communities, Native American dramaturgy depicts how the power of specific places can be reaccessed through language, even when the language spoken is English. Oliva shows that more important than the tongue spoken is the purpose of speech and the speakers' understanding of how language can draw humans into larger systems of meaning. Through acknowledging the purpose and power of language, Joannie can reclaim a Chickasaw linguistic practice, if not the particular Chickasaw words, of relating to place and its inherent networks of meaning, such as culture, spirituality, and community.

Like *The Cherokee Night* and *The Fire and the Rose*, *The Story of Susanna* also demonstrates the power of language within Native American platial theories. In the case of Susanna, her search to cultivate a geocentric identity and heal her rupture with place occurs through the reclamation of place and the stories that stem from it. Throughout the play, Kneubuhl focuses upon the essential link between place and language by posing questions of ownership. Through Act One's depiction of how Susanna reconstructs herself to conform to Lee's fantasy and Act Two's investigation into the truth behind individual and national narratives, the entire play interrogates religion and society to reclaim knowledge for women in contemporary culture. This knowledge enables the women in Kneubuhl's play to cross the threshold from a place of powerlessness into a place of wholeness.

The Story of Susanna enacts a mythology of place in order to heal the geocentric identities for all of the women in Threshold. In speaking about the link between stories, place, and healing, Pommersheim discusses the importance of platial mythologies. Like Kneubuhl's dramaturgy, Pommersheim sets his theories of place and story in opposition to the American myth of the continent's conquest; he also advocates geocentric identities for people of all cultures. Ultimately, Pommersheim argues that a new national mythology based on place has the capability to heal the rifts between Native and non-Native America:

What both sides already have is space and aridity, but what is more important is a sense of place to meet the deep human need of belonging, particularly in our complex and riven society – a sense of place that provides silence, space, and solitude for the healing of our raw spirits. Yet it is unlikely that we can achieve such a sense without painful introspection, particularly in the non-Indian community.

The mythology of the non-Indian West is grounded in conquest and possession, and it no longer works...This outworn mythology has also been fueled by the excesses of individualism which have hindered the development of communities and traditions. It has robbed much of the non-Indian community of the gods who make places holy. American individualism, much celebrated and cherished, has developed without its essential corrective, which is *belonging*...Yet the key, it seems to me, to generating a long-term coming together is the development of a *story* or *ethic*. There are complex issues aplenty...to bring Indians and non-Indians together, but the development of a greater ethic or story, beyond the particulars of any issues, is needed to hold us together. (Pommersheim, *Braid of Freathers*, 29–30)

Pommersheim proposes "an ethic of place," which respects the reciprocal relationship between humans and the natural world. In this proposal, Pommersheim emphasizes the fundamentals of Native American platial theory: "belonging," "healing," "communities," "traditions," "gods who make places holy," and the final ingredient, "story."

Kneubuhl's *The Story of Susanna* theatrically demonstrates how such an ethic of place can bring healing to people, both Native and non-Native. In order to do this, she first tackles the national myth of America's conquest. The character, Molly Lightfoot, represents the challenge to the mainstream American origin myth. Interestingly, her story is the one contemporary story that most closely parallels the biblical story of Susanna: in both stories, society treats the victimized women as criminals for speaking their versions of the truth. Molly's truth is one that challenges the national myth of America's founding. In direct address to the audience, Molly and Adele share the account while standing in the lower, public circle. Significantly, the story takes the form of a ceremony when it begins to invoke the power of place:

ADELE: This is the tale of Molly Lightfoot and how she stood true with her story. She was working at a place, a place that was once the home of her mother's mother's mothers, a place that was once called home by her father's father's fathers, and in that place she spoke.
MOLLY: In this place, in this very place there once was a night like blue glass, the luminous moon tumbling down on the tanned skins of our dwellings, and the men going down to the river. Once on a night like stars and dark-blue glass, the luminous moon gleamed down on the tanned skins of our dwellings and we the women and children sat to sing. Let us sing.
ADELE: Let us sing.
MOLLY AND ADELE: Let us sing [...]
MOLLY: But once there was a night like stars and dark-blue glass with the luminous moon grinning down across the tanned skins as we sat to sing,

we heard another kind of song. A song like horses' hooves and a deep
pushing breath, a clattering song that killed the luminous moon with flags
and swords and glistening guns, brass buttons shining and boots. And the
moon turned upside down, pouring out our blood and our bleeding –
and our blood you have killed, the tanned skins, you have killed the
singers, the elders curled in their blankets and nothing to stop your blood.
Let us sing [...]

ADELE: But that wasn't the story Molly Lightfoot was supposed to tell, no. (*To
Molly*) You will tell a brave story, a story of the noble courage of the black
boots and shiny buttons. Against all odds and savages you will tell how they,
great protectors, preserving the blessed way of life, the only way of life, how
they forged a nation. One nation under God.

MOLLY: No, I won't tell that story [...] That isn't my story.

ADELE: So Molly told the other story instead, and the people came and listened,
and some liked it and some didn't, but Molly didn't care because everyone
began to wonder which story was really true. And Molly liked that.

MOLLY: One day the man came. He wore a black suit, and he too had shiny
buttons, and he listened very carefully to Molly's story, and when it was
finished, he stood up very straight and hard and said:

ADELE: "You lie! You lie about the blue glass night. You lie about the singing
luminous moon. You lie about women and children and blood in the night.
You lie about men who come on horses. Lies, lies! He was brave and coura-
geous. You tell lies about my father's fathers, great men building this great
nation. One nation under God."

MOLLY: "No," said Molly. "That is not a true story."

ADELE: Then out came the gun so quick and easy.

　(*Adele pulls out the gun and shoots Molly*).　　(Kneubuhl, *Susanna*, 341–342)

In Brechtian style, each actor steps out of her character's usual context to
consciously re-enact the story of how Molly Lightfoot was shot three
times for standing "true with her story." Kneubuhl uses the theatrical
retelling of Molly's story to stage Native American philosophies of place
in a complex manner. Through techniques of alienation, the actors break
the audience's passive relationship with the play and present directly to
the audience a troubling representation of the settling of America.
However, this Native American account of the conquest is not only a
political story, it also incorporates spiritual elements. The story speaks of a
sacred place, a homeland where ancestral knowledge lives. The telling of
the story is conveyed in a ceremonial manner, with repetition and the
joining of voices. The story is also a reclaiming of place. Not only does
Molly tell of the land before the invasion of Europeans, but she reclaims
her history while freely standing in the lower public circle. By placing this

ceremonial story in the most public circle of the stage, the play's staging symbolically recovers the spiritual power of place.

Molly has been placed in Threshold because she is considered a threat to the man who shot her. Her attacker, an ambiguously described wealthy and powerful man, claimed that he shot Molly in self-defense because she was stalking him and his family. As the director of Threshold, Adele believes the legal documentation used to justify Molly's incarceration, yet as the play progresses it becomes clear that the evidence was concocted to frame Molly and silence her activism. Molly's struggle during the play is not for personal justice or freedom, but only to gain Adele's trust and convince her to listen to the story. When Adele, a woman who represents white society and the institutional system, finally hears Molly's story and accepts it as truth, Kneubuhl's plot shifts its focus from challenging national myth to contesting biblical myth.

In the play's final scene, Adele gathers the women together for Threshold's tenth anniversary. Kneubuhl's stage directions call for the party to take place on the stage's lower circle, which now represents the transitional home's outside lawn. As the women celebrate Threshold's continued survival and the obstacles each woman has overcome, the evening stars begin to appear. Under the stars that remind us of Molly's recent story, Adele comments, "Look at the sky. Do we need any more right now?" The women comment:

MOLLY: Yeah, a story, we need a story.
ADELE: Yes, let's tell us a story.
SUSANNA: What story should we tell?
MOLLY: A true story.
HAZEL: Let's tell the story.
ADELE: The story of Susanna.
(*Enter Daniel*)
SUSANNA: Here is the story of Susanna as it comes to us from our own memory.
(ibid., 369)

Outside, in public space and under the stars, the mythical Daniel enters into the contemporary world. Together, the women and Daniel tell the story of Susanna not from the Bible, but from collective memory. This act of storytelling moves the story of Susanna from the biblical book of law into the realm of oral, communal, myth. Significantly, this dramaturgical choice not only reclaims the story for Susanna, but it also returns the biblical story to its oral origins, for the Book of Daniel, like the myths of Native American cultures, first existed through oral transmission.[14] (See figure 2.)

2. Susanna takes back her story in *The Story of Susanna*, 2003, UC Berkeley.

While the worlds of myth and empirical reality coexist, Susanna, now both ancient and contemporary, pulls her hidden story away from the Bible's text. She not only speaks the private story of Susanna in the public circle, she also reconnects the myth to an ethic of place. This mythology of place brings healing to the characters, revives the sacred power of the land, renews communal relationships amongst the women, and restores the reciprocal relationship between the characters and the earth. In this version of the myth, Susanna "remembered what was forsaken" and "took back the things which were always hers" (ibid., 370). The voices of the women and Daniel join together as they each speak a section of the new Susanna myth, while they also enact a healing ritual that re-establishes their connections to the earth:

DANIEL: And the end of the story has its beginning in the first new day.
SUSANNA: And in honor of the day, Susanna called the women, and together they
    came into the garden.
DANIEL: And the first dawn rose.
SUSANNA: And this became known as the Time of Planting.
HAZEL: I give this to the earth, that it may grow you a jewel – clear, deep and rich,
    and of its own nature.
MOLLY: I give this to the earth, that it may grow you a night like stars and dark-blue
    glass, on which there is only peace.

MARINA: I give this to the earth, that it may grow you a place, in which I will always hear your voice.

ADELE: I give this to the earth, that it may grow you a light, by which you will always find your way.

DANIEL: I give this to the earth, that it may grow as a constant prayer, that you suffer no more.

SUSANNA: I give this to the earth, that it may grow you a miraculous garden, where, with each sunrise, arms branch out, unfolding into life.   (ibid.)

In this final action of the play, Kneubuhl's characters, both Native and non-Native, join together to embrace a new mythology of place. In sacred language, they give respect back to the earth which holds them; in doing so, they literally mend the rupture between self and place. Kneubuhl's staging also reclaims space by marking all of earth, public and private, as sacred by the very nature of the powers, myths, spirits, and ancestors who inhabit it. No longer can the divine be separated from the human through written laws or defined spaces: the binaries of myth/social, private/public, sacred/social have collapsed.

Dramatically presenting the interweaving theories of rootedness, worlds of existence, and language as landscape, Riggs' *The Cherokee Night*, Oliva's *The Fire and the Rose*, and Kneubuhl's *The Story of Susanna* work as aesthetic manifestations of Native American platial discourse. Although the playwrights use the same concepts of platial discourse, they do so in very different manners that display the effective way theories of place function across a wide range of artistic and cultural expression. Riggs structures his entire plot upon a platial arrangement of Cherokee communities during ceremonial events, such as the Cherokee Stomp Dance. His *The Cherokee Night* pairs this arrangement with theatrical imagery that allows audiences to see the characters' spiritual experiences from Native perspectives of place. Oliva's dramaturgy demonstrates the differences between Native and non-Native theories of place by portraying the separate journeys of Joannie and Bernie. Her *The Fire and the Rose* also complicates such theories of place by using metaphysical poetry to structure the play and Joannie's own poetic expressions to construct a pathway home. Kneubuhl incorporates both Greek staging conventions and biblical mythology into *The Story of Susanna*, but by infusing these elements with Native concepts of land she re-establishes place as the center of both national and spiritual mythologies. Through their differences, each play provides important information about the interactions between people and places. As these and other Native plays introduce theatre audiences to the complex network of concepts within

Native platial discourse, Native dramaturgy provides a forum for theorizing about the many possibilities of platial theory across the field of Native drama and throughout general theatre studies.

As we have seen in the plays discussed throughout this chapter, the elements of Native American platial discourse offer numerous combinations and manifestations of platial concepts. These combinations are further multiplied by the dynamic, localized relationships created between individual people and specific places, such as the relationship between the Cherokee Nation and Claremore Mound. Thus, how an individual playwright chooses to present each character's relationship with place – and its particular concepts of rootedness, spirituality, and language – is unique. Such diversity is extended even further when one accounts for the many intersections between Native concepts of platial discourse and other Native intellectual traditions. For example, language as landscape presents an area in which two powerful Native discourses, platiality and storying, share theoretical space. At this intersection, the philosophies within Native American dramaturgy become more diverse, for storytelling has its own set of interweaving theories, examined in the following two chapters.

CHAPTER 5

Native storytelling

[T]he reworking of the past in post-colonial theatre is also entwined
with the re-establishment of pre-contact forms of history-making and
history-keeping.

> Gilbert and Tompkins, *Post-Colonial Drama*, III

I am the word carrier, and I shape-change the world.

> Jeannette Armstrong (Okanagan), "Land Speaking," 183

Post-colonial theatre scholars often question how the plays by people who
have endured, or are enduring, colonization work to de-center and revise
the versions of history recorded by colonizers. In many cases, this inquiry
leads theorists to "pre-contact" methods of documenting history. In the
field of Native American theatre, that means focusing on Native storytelling
and oral histories that transmit knowledge through the generations. Native
American concepts of storytelling provide one way to approach Native plays
that seek to revise history, plays that foreground the forgotten and omitted
stories of Native Americans who shaped our present world.

Examples of this revisionist use of storytelling range from JudyLee
Oliva's biographical play, *Te Ata*, which incorporates Te Ata's own
Native stories and performance notes into the construction of its plot, to
Daniel David Moses' history plays, including *Almighty Voice and His Wife*, a
play that amends popular Canadian history by depicting "the last armed
resistance by Native people in Canada" from the perspective of the Cree
man whom non-Natives murdered for killing a cow (Mojica and Knowles,
"Introduction to *Almighty*," 173). *Changes* and *In Search of a Friend*, dramas
from the Inuit theatre company Tunooniq, develop out of elders' stories
and songs, expressions so rooted in their Native community that distinguishing a single playwright is inappropriate (D'Aeth, "Introduction to
Changes," 104). LeAnne Howe and Roxy Gordon's *Indian Radio Days*
incorporates the stories of several characters that provide little-known
segments of American history. For example, the Choctaw character,

Anolitubby, tells of his heroic military service in World War I, service that was denied a medal because Native Americans were not officially considered American citizens until 1924 (Howe and Gordon, *Indian*, 124–125). In *U Da Naa*, Gina Kalloch (Athabaskan) uses Raven trickster stories to present an Athabaskan version of the world's creation, including the story of how Raven protected the earth's beings from the great prehistoric flood (Kalloch, *U Da Naa, 4–7*).

While many Native American plays incorporate storytelling in order to revise and reclaim history, Native American playwrights also use Native storytelling for purposes that extend beyond historical revision. Ubiquitously, Native American playwrights and performers claim storytelling as a central element of their work as theatre artists. Tomson Highway muses, "Why the stage? For me, the reason is that this oral tradition translates most easily and most effectively into a three-dimensional medium. In a sense, it's like taking the 'stage' that lives in the mind, the imagination, and transposing it...onto the stage in a theatre" ("On Native," 1). As we read through Native American drama's diverse field of plays, we see elements of the oral culture everywhere. Marcie Rendon's *SongCatcher*, for example, focuses on the traditional practice of orally transmitting Native cultural property. Rendon then creates a contemporary play with a haunted feeling, as she contrasts those Native values with Frances Densmore's method of capturing on wax cylinders disembodied voices singing Native songs. Bruce King presents yet another example of storytelling in *Dustoff*, as a multi-ethnic cast of military characters exchange battle stories about the missions they have served in Vietnam. For these and other Native American theatre artists, storytelling is not bound by "pre-contact forms of history-making and history keeping." Storytelling is a living, liberated, integral element of *all* creation, artistic and mundane. Native storytelling not only shapes notions of the past, it also affects events to come. Post-colonial theories that focus solely on revisionist history can miss the more profound ways storytelling functions in Native theatre because such theories can overlook the relationship between storytelling and the future.

Native American literary theorists espouse a number of related concepts regarding the nature and function of storytelling in contemporary Native art and cultures. Native dramatists agree with these theorists; accordingly, when Native playwrights talk about their work, one often hears a distinctive way of speaking about the relationships between playwriting, theatrical productions, and storytelling. Because Native American scripts and performances are infused with theories of storytelling, they also work to demonstrate these theories to readers and viewers.

Through two discourses, storying and tribalography, we will investigate how Native theories of language function within Native American plays to create meaning within dramatic texts and theatrical productions. This investigation borrows the term *storying* from Native playwrights, who often use the word interchangeably with the words "playwriting" and "performing." The discourse of storying can also refer to writing novels and poems, delivering formal addresses, or casually exchanging stories with friends or family. The broad use of the term *storying* occurs because it is an intertribal term that contains a nexus of concepts about the power of words, usually spoken. The interrelated concepts of the power of language derive from numerous Native origin stories that link the winds with human breath, and the acts of speech and thought with that of creation. The causal relationship between speech and creation connects to the idea of "language as landscape," in which humans engage in a reciprocal relationship with place through speech. Like platial discourse, storying also involves particular notions of time; storytime, for example, is when a story allows the past, present, and future to unite. Finally, in the same way as "language as landscape" posits that language changes according to place, the discourse of storying embraces the changing nature of stories; it provides an all-encompassing view of stories, in which the boundaries between fact and fiction are unfixed and permeable.

Another discourse closely related to storying is *tribalography*, a term coined by LeAnne Howe, a Choctaw playwright and educator. In her article "Tribalography: The Power of Native Stories," Howe traces the way in which Native stories are believed to create material effects. Howe credits the power of language as the driving force behind such effects. Early in the article, Howe asserts that "Native stories are power. They create people. They author tribes" ("Tribalography," 118). She then goes on to posit:

Native people created narratives that were histories and stories with the power to transform. I call this rhetorical space "tribalography"...[The] power of Native storytelling is revealed as a living character who continues to influence our culture. The study of tribalography is advanced by first looking at how Indian people made story from events and non-events. Secondly, by examining how the oral tradition and written texts are a symbiosis of Old World and New World, it becomes evident that Native authors are important to expanding our understanding of story at the beginning of the new millennium. (ibid.)

Howe never overtly defines tribalography beyond stating that it is a "rhetorical space" within which stories generate transformation; instead, her article centers upon how storying creates material effects. One example

Howe provides is an account of how "a native story helped author America, an act of creation" (ibid., 123). Howe explains that the Six Nations Confederacy's Condolence Ceremony was a performance of a story that inspired the European immigrants in North America to form a United Nation.[1] As another example of tribalography, Howe discusses a theatrical performance of Vera Manuel's biographical, revisionist-history play, *The Strength of Indian Women*, a production that generated partnerships between feuding scholars. Thus, Howe's investigation of tribalography is largely an exploration of a creation process. By telling stories about transformations, Howe challenges non-Native people to re-evaluate "the power of Native stories."

In this study, I use Howe's term *tribalography* to describe a collection of Native American concepts regarding reciprocal relationships between storying, in both oral and written forms, and creation. Tribalography, as a discourse, offers an effective method to understand the ways in which Native American playwrights use concepts of language within their dramaturgy. Because Howe does not set a fixed definition for tribalography, the term takes on various meanings: tribalography is a creative physical force, and it is "a rhetorical space" for theory, or argument. Extending from storying, tribalography is both a subject – an "author of tribes" – and an object – a theory that can be studied. Tribalography encompasses both past and future, tradition and transformation, orality and writing; it symbolizes "a symbiosis of Old World and New World." Moreover, tribalography, a term which literally reads "to write a tribe," also derives its meaning from oral art. Possessing this quality of in-betweenness, the discourse of tribalography is able to investigate how Native concepts of language both inspire and perform within Native American plays.

In the following chapter, I will build upon the foundation provided by Howe's article and then add to it the perspectives of other Native American literary theorists, such as Paula Gunn Allen, Diane Glancy, and Leslie Marmon Silko (Laguna Pueblo), who frequently speak about the power of language in Native philosophies. From the discourses of storying and tribalography, I will examine four interrelated concepts: "Story Cosmos," "Multi-vocal Authenticity," "Constructing Communal Truth," and "Collective Creation." "Story Cosmos" moves beyond the discussion of "language as landscape" to examine several Native American theories that pertain to how language functions. These theories do more than propose a connection between language and land: they suggest that the acts of speech and writing are powerful forces that can generate connections amongst beings and across time and space. After a basic examination of how

Native theories of speech function, I will shift the focus to discuss how Native stories work theatrically. "Multi-vocal Authenticity: Constructing Communal Truth" combines two concepts to examine three Native American plays that focus strongly on the theme of storytelling: Spiderwoman Theater's *Rever-ber-berations*, Vera Manuel's *The Strength of Indian Women*, and Tomson Highway's *Ernestine Shuswap Gets Her Trout*. This section will investigate how these plays model discourses of storying and tribalography. It also concentrates on the in-between nature of tribalography, investigating reciprocal relationships between both compatible and incompatible, and private and public forms of narratives. Through the communal nature of storying, "Collective Creation" adds the character/audience relationship into the analysis of Native theories of language. Investigating what occurs on the stage and how that can affect what happens in the audience's space, this section explores how Native American plays often model the transformative capabilities of storying. As a theoretical point of contact between Native concepts and those from the general theatre, I include Elin Diamond's readings of Brechtian and critical audience-response theories to demonstrate how concepts of tribalography extend critical concepts in theatre studies.

As with my earlier investigation of platial discourse within three Native plays, I will again limit my analysis to specific examples of Native American plays that use the discourses of storying and tribalography. Certainly, the three plays *Rever-ber-berations*, *The Strength of Indian Women*, and *Ernestine Shuswap* are not the only Native plays that incorporate these discourses into their dramaturgy; rather, I select them because they offer clear examples of storying and tribalography through very different performance styles and purposes. Spiderwoman's *Rever-ber-berations* is an autobiographical play, written and performed by three sisters. Manual wrote *The Strength of Indian Women* for productions set within Native American communities seeking to heal from the wounds inflicted by their boarding-school experiences. Highway's *Ernestine Shuswap* was commissioned by Western Canada Theatre and the Secwepemc Cultural Education Society to commemorate an historic event, the 1910 creation of the Laurier Memorial (see p. 115). Although *Ernestine Shuswap* addresses the history of a specific region, Highway writes the play to address a wide range of potential audiences, Native and non-Native, Canadian and beyond.

The one aspect that the three plays have in common is that their performances are linked to specific productions that will allow me to better reference how their concepts of language reach into the audience during the process of collective creation. References to the script, staging practices, and audiences' responses can provide a more thorough examination of how the discourses of storying and tribalography function as both theory and process. The specific performance of Manuel's *The Strength of Indian Women* to which I will refer was the play Howe featured in her tribalography article. It was presented as a staged reading at NAWPA at Miami University in Oxford, Ohio on March 20, 1999 during the conference, A Celebration of Native American Women Playwrights. The audience for this play was a mixed audience of theatre artists and scholars from both Native and non-Native heritages. The women who performed the play were, like Manuel, playwrights honored at the conference. At the time of its reading, *The Strength of Indian Women* had already toured through Canada after its 1992 premiere by Storyteller Theatre at the Firehall Theatre in Vancouver. The play had recently been published by Living Traditions Press.

The Strength of Indian Women concerns a group of women elders who endured a traumatic childhood together in an abusive boarding school. The play is set on an unnamed reservation in the home of Sousette, an elder who is the mother of Eva and grandmother of Suzie. Together, Sousette, Eva, and an extended community of elders from the boarding school, Lucy, Mariah, and Agnes, sponsor thirteen-year-old Suzie's coming-of-age ceremony. The structure of the play chronologically follows the preparation for Suzie's ceremony, her two days of ritual fasting, and her return into the community of women. The two days in which Suzie is away from home for her fasting coincide with two days of storytelling amongst the women. During this time, the elder women break their silence about the years of abuse in the Catholic boarding school. The personal stories told by each woman adhere to a form of witnessing, in which the play's conventions of realism break while each woman stands alone center stage to deliver her story directly to the audience. Through these stories, the elder women heal animosities that were created toward one another by the boarding-school experiences. The stories also help Eva understand the reason for her own mother's distance from her and why traditional practices, such as the coming-of-age ceremony, dissolved during her own childhood. Thus, as Suzie undergoes a ceremonial transformation into womanhood, the audience observes a dramatic portrayal of how storytelling creates a transformation within the women's community. In the preface to *The Strength of Indian Women*, Manuel states:

I didn't make up the stories told in *Strength of Indian Women*. They came from pictures my mother painted for me with her words, words that helped me see her as a little girl for the first time. Each time we staged a performance of the play, I mourned that little girl who never had a childhood. I mourned the mother missing from my childhood, and I gave thanks for the mother who became my loving teacher in adulthood. ("Author's Note," 76)

While Manuel uses stories of the individual elders to structure her play, Spiderwoman Theater creates its plays through a trademark technique called storyweaving. For over twenty-five years the company has shared with the world their concept of creating theatre from storytelling. "The stories created by Spiderwoman [Theater] are not linear," explains Muriel Miguel to participants of Spiderwoman's storyweaving workshops. "They exist like this –": Muriel extends both of her hands away from her stomach, her fingers spreading wider as her arms reach out. It is a gesture of reaching, growing, extending, from one's core outward into a complex network of relationships (Spiderwoman, Storyweaving Workshop). Muriel Miguel and her two sisters, Gloria Miguel and Lisa Mayo, use the term story-weaving to refer metaphorically to their artistic process and to their namesake, Spiderwoman, a Hopi creation deity. In Hopi philosophy, Spiderwoman helped create the world through weaving. Everything she wove became real on earth. She then taught the Hopi people how to weave and instructed them to leave a flaw in every woven work of art so that its spirit could escape.

Spiderwoman Theater's storyweaving theatrically manifests the weaving lesson taught by the Hopi creation deity. The company members state that they are interested in "creating a tapestry" in which there is more than a single layer of meaning. Storyweaving blends various levels of understanding, elements of emotion, and portions of stories. It is a practice that views stories as more than words written on a page. Stories are words spoken in time, through the body. Stories are gesture, vocal sounds, breath, movement, dance, and chant. Individual people's stories connect one to the other, not at "logical" seams, but by overlapping, circling, juxtaposing, synchronizing, and intertwining. Muriel Miguel's story might connect to an element of someone else's story; yet, the connection may be something that cannot adequately be explained. As Spiderwoman Theater teaches, storyweaving connects people by creating a tapestry of narratives which sometimes has no articulated meaning but must be felt instead.

Through this process, Spiderwoman's plays move fluidly from present, to future, to past, to times indistinguishable. At one moment, Gloria Miguel may be a political activist in Panama City, and in the next she may be a girl with her sisters playing a childhood game. An intimate story addressed directly to the audience may be followed by a mock re-creation of a wild-west show performed on (broomstick) horseback. In many instances, Spiderwoman follows the practices of Native American clowning by disarming the audience's defenses with laughter before launching into serious investigations of ethnicity, gender, sexuality, class, politics, prejudices, and abuse.[2] Always intricately structured and well rehearsed, Spiderwoman's plays contain surprising improvisatory moments. The technique of improvising allows the actors freedom to interact directly with the audience and to tailor the dynamics within scenes to each audience's levels of understanding. This reciprocal relationship between performers and audience members creates an illusion of a flawed, or rough, performance that refers back to the legend of the Hopi creation deity's instructions to weavers. The roughness around the edges of Spiderwoman Theater's productions references the artistic flaw from which the spirit of their play can escape into the world of the audience.

The production of *Rever-ber-berations* that I discuss was performed by Lisa Mayo, Gloria Miguel, and Muriel Miguel at the Ohio State University's Roy Bowen Theater in October 2000, to an audience that included Ohio State students and faculty, members of the Columbus Native American community, and other general theatregoers. At the time of the performance, Spiderwoman Theater had been touring *Rever-ber-berations* as part of the company's repertory for ten years.[3] *Rever-ber-berations* is one of Spiderwoman Theater's most serious works. It presents a story of the sisters' spirituality, namely, how each sister developed an understanding of the spiritual gifts possessed by her mother and then how she accepts those gifts within herself. Focused on exploring this lineage of spirituality, the artists celebrate the connections amongst their family members: sisters, mothers and fathers, daughters and sons, grandparents and grandchildren. In the company's signature storyweaving style, the play blends the personal stories of the three sisters with comedic interludes (a repetitious tea party and reoccurring "noise-band" segment, in which the sisters play "music" on trashcan lids and toy violins), elements of pop culture (Cole Porter's "Night and Day," Irving Berlin's "Blue Skies," and Don McLean's "Vincent"), and Native cultural elements (drumming, giving respect to the four guardian directions, Gloria's singing of the Kuna creation story, and the sisters' performance of the Bowl Dance Zuniga). As its title suggests, the play moves like *déjà vu*, repeating scenes and subjects over and over, tracing how repeated experiences mold a person's understanding of self, the world, and the universe.

Highway situates his writing within the long legacy of Native American storytelling that reaches back to Native languages' origins in the earth.

He explains, "the Indian people of this country have a literary tradition that goes back thousands of years. As a people, we are very much aware of the fact that there were mythologies that applied – and applied in a very powerful manner – to this specific landscape since long before the landmark year of A.D. 1492" (Highway, "On Native," 1). His 2004 production of *Ernestine Shuswap Gets Her Trout* brilliantly illustrates Native American theatre's ability to unite Native mythology, historical documents, and the voice of Native lands within the theatre's powerful, embodied medium.

Ernestine Shuswap began in 2000, when Western Canada Theatre of Kamloops, British Columbia (BC) and the Secwepemc First Nation's Cultural Education Society (SCES) commissioned Highway to write a play that dramatized the creation of an historical document called the Laurier Memorial.[4] The 1910 Laurier Memorial is actually a document, a letter composed by the chiefs of three Thompson River Valley Nations, the Secwepemc (also known as Shuswap), the Nlaka'pamux (known as Couteau or Thompson), and the Okanagan. James Teit, a Scottish man who had married into a Nlaka'pamux family and who became the three nations' secretary, translated and recorded the letter, which reads as a narrative that covers the first hundred years of relationships between the Native peoples and the non-Native colonists. Particularly, the letter tells a story about the Native people's relationship to the land, how their traditions of hospitality led them to share their resources with their first non-Native neighbors, and how that hospitality was abused when British Columbia was established in 1858. By August 25, 1910, the day the Thompson River Valley chiefs presented their letter to Sir Wilfrid Laurier, Prime Minister of Canada, the Native people of the region had been reduced to a state of homelessness in their own homelands. The BC government had confined them to small, infertile portions of land that could not sustain the Native communities, who were burdened further by strict limitations on Native hunting, fishing, irrigation, ranching, and gathering. Laurier agreed to help the Native nations, but then lost his re-election.[5] The land grievances and sovereignty debate recorded in the Laurier Memorial are still in play today.

Mitigating the somber tone of the play's subject matter, Highway uses humor to bring the Laurier Memorial's creation to life through the lives of four Native women: Ernestine Shuswap, a fifty-three-year-old woman who faces adversity with humor and wisdom; Isabel Thompson, a forty-three-year-old woman who lords her Catholic piety over the other women; Annabelle Okanagan, a thirty-two-year-old, irascible widow; and Delilah Rose Johnson, Isabel's twenty-one-year-old, nervous little sister who carries the child of Billy Boy Johnson, her white husband. Highway subtitles the play

"A 'String-Quartet' for Four Female Actors," which hints at the way these four characters function. Like a quartet, their distinct voices enrich one another's while they each recount the history of the Laurier Memorial. These accounts come from three distinct nations; thus, the women are archetypal characters, represented by their last names: Shuswap, Thompson, and Okanagan. Delilah Rose represents a new kind of identity in the women's world: Shuswap/English. As the characters' individual stories blend into the actual language of the Laurier Memorial, the play provides its audiences with a vast scope: the effects of British colonization upon the Shuswap, Thompson, and Okanagan Nations, effects that remain a source of conflict.

Because Highway focuses on four characters, the play never feels unwieldy; rather, it flows seamlessly, like its river setting, from one scene to the next. Highway calls for a minimalist set to ease the play's transitions. He writes, "*Four styrofoam cubes – to be used as chairs, rocks, other objects as the need will arise – sit scattered at random. An ancient gramophone (ca. 1900) sits open on the floor by one of these 'chairs.' Last, a plain white backdrop hangs slashed by a line, curved, horizontal: the land in silhouette. The rest is lights, sound, music*" (Highway, *Ernestine*, 10). Throughout the play, the four women prepare for the banquet in honor of the Prime Minister, whom they call "The Great Big Kahoona of Canada." Each woman performs a task. Ernestine readies the recipe for the trout which her husband has promised to catch. Isabel gathers berries for the 624 saskatoon pies she has promised to bake. Delilah Rose sews and sews the long tablecloth for the banquet, and Annabelle prepares her recipe for stuffed beaver, a subject that provides one of many opportunities for Highway to incorporate his trademark, Native humor:

DELILAH ROSE: The English. *They* don't like beaver, Billy Boy was telling me. But the Great Big Kahoona of Canada is French, Annabelle Okanagan, French, not English, so Billy Boy was telling me. And the French *love* beaver – did you know that, Annabelle Okanagan of Kamloops, B. C.? – *especially* young beaver, so Billy has read? This Frenchman, for example, the Great Big Kahoona of Canada? What's his name again? Sir Willpaletch Lolly-some-thing-or-other?

ANNABELLE: Lolly-yay. Sir Wilfrid Lolly-Yay. Prime Minister of Canada, is what they call him, in English as if…

DELILAH ROSE: Anyway, he finds old beaver tough and rubbery, impossible to chew on, and not much juice […] the Great Big Kahoona of Canada, at age sixty-five, can partake only of the juice-filled, soft-fleshed, sweet and tender succulence of very young beaver. I hope that doesn't mean too much extra work for you.

ANNABELLE: Oh, I'll just boil the shit right out of it. Until it's all puckered up. (ibid., 35)

The beaver jokes, the attempts to define the differences between "real whites" (the French) and "plain whites" (the English), and the women's attempts to sound out foreign words (such as Laurier) all contribute to the linguistic humor that drives *Ernestine Shuswap*'s action. Highway's production notes state that productions of the play must never forget that, although the actors present the play through the medium of English, the historic Native participants spoke their own nations' languages. For the sake of dramatic clarity, Highway's characters are all supposed to be speaking Shuswap, a language which *"works according to principles, and impulses, different entirely from those that underlie, that 'motor,' the English language"* (ibid., 11). Highway explains, *"the principle that 'motors' the Shuswap language is, in essence, a 'laughing deity' (i.e. the Trickster), it is hysterical, comic to the point where its 'spill-over' into horrifying tragedy is a thing quite normal, utterly organic. That is to say…the 'laughing god' becomes a 'crying god' becomes a 'laughing god,' all in one swift impulse"* (ibid.).

It is the boundless form of Native humor, that moves from joy to pain and back again, that gives *Ernestine Shuswap* its characteristic movement and tone. Within these rhythms, Highway adds language from the actual Laurier Memorial and then lets the interplay of these two storytelling qualities create his dramaturgy. Manuel, who uses the remembered stories of the elders, also uses storytelling practices to structure *The Strength of Indian Women*, but her play works with a different rhythm. As one story unfolds into the next, the play's structure enacts the same branching and spreading technique that Muriel Miguel has described. Spiderwoman Theater, of course, also uses branching movements to create their plays, but *Rever-ber-berations* places such interconnections into an overriding, cyclical structure that allows us to return to specific moments with an ever-new perspective. Although the plots function in entirely different ways, they all derive from the Native American discourse of storying, which we will explore next.

CHAPTER 6

Storying and tribalography in Native American drama

> It is no accident that the greatest writer in English was a playwright. Shakespeare's language is the language of speech, the soul's breath. In our time and place, and in his, the play is the supreme vehicle of oral tradition.
>
> N. Scott Momaday (Kiowa), "Preface," viii

> Native artistry is not pure aesthetics...Indian writers are trying to *invoke* as much as *evoke*. The idea...is that language, spoken in the appropriate ritual contexts, will actually cause change in the physical universe.
>
> Craig Womack (Creek/Cherokee), *Red*, 16–17

Spiderwoman Theater's use of Native American storytelling through story-weaving, Vera Manuel's use of it in witnessing, and Tomson Highway's use of it through the Laurier Memorial all represent various ways of theatricalizing Native philosophies of storying. Despite the differences in their writing styles and purposes, these playwrights all use storying to both structure their plots and inform their staging conventions. In all three cases, the discourse of storying extends into the discourse of tribalography, which allows the plays to model concepts of Native American storytelling and audiences to experience how Native stories are intended to affect those who hear them. To better recognize this transformative nature of Native American stories in the theatre, it is helpful to understand the basic concepts that reside within Native American views of language.

STORY COSMOS

Storying is the action of telling Native American stories, and it is also a discourse that encompasses concepts about language from Native American intellectual traditions. In a profound sense, storying always involves a sense of its own world, a story cosmos. As realized in Native American theatre, this story cosmos exhibits four aspects: a holistic view of language; an understanding that stories can synchronize diverse moments; the belief that stories connect humans to the natural world; and a faith that language creates material effects. I will refer to these four concepts as holistic communication, storytime, human–world bonds, and acts of creation through speech.

Storying supports a holistic view of communication, in that the term *story* refers equally to history, fiction, and performance. LeAnne Howe explains that there is little need to differentiate amongst types of story, because Native American cultures often view "these things as an integrated whole rather than individual parts. For instance in Choctaw an Anoli is a teller, someone who does all of the above [tells history, fiction, and drama], relating all living things" (Howe, "Tribalography," 118). Holistic views of what constitutes a story derive not from a focus on subject matter, but from an emphasis on the actions of exchanging knowledge. Howe writes, "All histories are stories written down; all stories are the performance of those beliefs, a living theater" (ibid., 123).

Holistic communication becomes significant when we address Native American plays, which often develop out of diverse narrative styles. To understand such plays, one must not focus too much upon defining the styles, but rather investigate how narrative styles actively function to inform one another, the dramatic characters, and theatrical audiences. For example, Spiderwoman Theater's *Rever-ber-berations* uses narratives from personal memories, the Kuna creation song, and accounts of historical events; these various stories construct a sense of the women's spirituality. Manuel's *The Strength of Indian Women* recounts historical events through the personal narratives of the elders. Highway intersperses readings of an historical document with surreal monologues from fictitious characters and playful, comedic scenes. In all three cases, the holistic approach to communication emphasizes how various forms of narrative come together to construct, through multiplying stories, a communal worldview.

Storytime, or the way Native stories envision time, is perhaps the most important aspect of storying in contemporary Native American dramaturgy. Although theatre scholars commonly allude to the use of time in Native American plays, something significant about storytime is often overlooked. In *Post-colonial Drama*, Gilbert and Tompkins speak of indigenous theatre as avoiding chronological renderings of time through the use of mythical figures, Native American tricksters, and Australian Aboriginal dreamers. The authors argue that these figures "collapse present, past, and mythic time and foreground points of overlap and contact between the spiritual world and the more mundane time/space of the 'ordinary' action" (Gilbert and Tomkins,

Post-colonial Drama, 140–142). In an investigation of Native American literature, I would push this idea of time further. Synchronicity *is* the nature of
Native storytime, with or without a trickster figure. Storying represents a view
of time in which the past, present, and future coexist and possess the vital
ability to affect one another. Within the synchronicity of storytime, the
"mythic," including spiritually charged tricksters and creation stories, intermingles with the "facts" of daily experience.

Paula Gunn Allen describes the synchronic aspect of storytime as "ceremonial." In "The Ceremonial Motion of Indian Time: Long Ago, So Far,"
she states, "The traditional tribal concept of time is of timelessness, as the
concept of space is multidimensionality" (Allen, "Ceremonial Motion,"
69). According to Allen, it is chronological time that appears unnatural
when viewed from Native perspectives. Chronological time upholds non-
Native ideologies that attempt to create a human hierarchy by separating
humans from the rest of creation. In contrast, Native American philosophies of time, place, and spirit abide by a holistic view of the world. Allen
explains:

The achronological time sense of tribal people results from tribal beliefs about the
nature of reality, beliefs based on ceremonial understandings rather than on
industrial, theological, or agricultural orderings. Chronological time structuring
is useful in promoting and supporting an industrial time sense. The idea that
everything has a starting point and an ending point reflects accurately the process
by which industry produces goods…Chronological organization also supports
allied western beliefs that the individual is separate from the environment, that
man is separate from God, that life is an isolated business, and that the person who
controls the events around him is a hero…That understanding, which includes a
strong belief in individualism as well as the belief that time operates external to the
internal workings of human and other beings, contrasts sharply with a ceremonial
time sense that assumes the individual as a moving event shaped by and shaping
human and non-human surroundings. (ibid., 70–71)

Allen's assertion that the function of time coincides with a culture's notion
of reality provides theatre scholars with an important frame of reference. It is
not enough to merely observe how a Native American playwright structures
time and then to profess that the play is either linear or non-linear.
Similarly, artistic sovereignty is jeopardized when Native American theatrical criticism posits that the non-linear nature of time used in many Native
American plays is a reaction against the climactic structure of the "well-
made play." Non-linear time in Native American plays is, first, an overt
manifestation of cultural philosophies that weave through Native
dramaturgy.

Spiderwoman Theater's *Rever-ber-berations* is a play that physically demonstrates ceremonial time as it is discussed by Allen.[1] In the play, the interconnection of stories shapes the movement of time. Portraying the sisters' personal, spiritual lives, *Rever-ber-berations* emphasizes a spiraling motion of time. This spiraling creates a sense of *déjà vu* as the play's action repeats two key scenes three different times during the performance. "Noise Band," the first of the repeated scenes, opens the play. In this scene, the performers play themselves as children. In the dark, Gloria and Lisa are startled by a sound under the bed, while little sister Muriel complains that she needs to pee. When the lights come up, the sisters play a "noise-band" song, in which Lisa bangs a garbage-can lid, Gloria plays on a toy violin, and Muriel rhythmically throws a plank of wood on the floor. In the second repetitive scene, entitled "Tea Time," the sisters portray caricatured versions of themselves – ridiculous, stuffy artists arguing over which show to take on the road.

These two repeated scenes function in various ways. On one level, they work to prevent audiences from stereotyping the sisters' spirituality as romanticized history or as cultural mysticism. For example, the first noise-band segment juxtaposes the pre-show's recording of traditional Native American drumming and singing. As the actors add lyrics to the noise-band song, they sing, "Like the beat beat beat/ of the tom tom,/ when the jungle shadows fall" (Spiderwoman Theater, *Rever-ber-berations*, 187). The stereotypes invoked by Cole Porter's lyrics, in which a jungle-man beats a tom-tom, are undermined by the sisters' parody of the song, featuring trash-cans and wood. The arrangement of this parody's following a recording of traditional Native drumming sets up a series of distortions. The imagined tom-tom is as much a distortion of the traditional drumming as the noise-band rendition is of the popular song.

On a second level, the repeated moments work loosely to bookend collections of serious scenes, contrasting their intensity with humor. For example, "Noise Band #1" and "Tea Time #1" frame scenes in which each sister addresses the audience, relates a story of her mother's ability to communicate with the spirit world, and expresses her childhood reactions against her mother's uniqueness. The repeated "Noise Band" and "Tea Time" pairing also encases three other groupings of scenes. One grouping portrays pivotal moments in which each sister experienced and accepted the spiritual gift inherited from her mother. Another grouping presents scenes that portray how the mother's gift has enriched each sister's daily life through humor and meaningful connections with loved ones. The last grouping displays the ways in which each sister's spirituality extends her knowledge of the world and her place within it.

While time in *Rever-ber-berations* continually spirals, Manuel uses a less overt, but similarly ceremonial representation of time in *The Strength of Indian Women*. A story from Sousette's grandfather circles through the life of her granddaughter, Suzie; this circling allows the family to receive messages across the generations. In Act One, Scene One, Sousette tells the story of the coming-of-age dress she gives to Suzie:

I was a girl like Suzie when this dress first came to me. I can still see my grandmother. "I made this special for you," she said, and she slipped it over my head. It was so soft. She took me outside to show grandpa. He told me a story about the hunt, that the deer just stood and waited for him, like they knew they were offering up their lives for something special. They made me feel special. (Manuel, *Strength*, 82)

In the play's last scene, Suzie returns home from fasting with a story about the dress and the deer her grandfather had hunted:

SUZIE: I saw the two little deer that came to great-grandpa, when he was hunting for the hides for this dress. They came right inside the lodge, and they talked to me.
SOUSETTE: What did they say?
SUZIE: That I was going to have a long life, and that my daughter will someday wear this dress.   (ibid., 115)

Suzie's story not only appears to complete a cycle of storying from grandfather to Sousette to Suzie and back again, it also moves in a forward manner. Suzie is to be blessed with a long life and learns that one day her own daughter will wear the same dress. As these two scenes about the deer and dress mirror each other, storytime allows past events to foreshadow the future of those living in the present.

Highway's *Ernestine Shuswap* also dramatizes the concept of timelessness, yet it does so in several ways, through plot structure, subject matter, and staging devices. Although the play is set on Thursday, August 25, 1910, the day the four women prepare for that evening's banquet, the play dramatizes one hundred years' worth of legal changes imposed upon the Native people of their region. Highway accomplishes this condensed notion of time through the tasks he assigns each character. The story of Joe Shuswap's pledge to catch Ernestine a trout opens the play, but quickly we learn that Native people are no longer allowed to fish the Thompson River. New property laws that confine ranchlands and others that limit where Native people can travel to gather food hinder Isabel's attempts to make saskatoon pies with cream. When Annabelle's sons return with just one beaver for 2,000 people, we learn that their failure is a result of new trapping laws affecting Native people. With each successive law, the Native characters are less able to provide for the Prime Minister's banquet. Beneath the characters' preoccupations with creating a banquet, viewers are keenly aware that each law severely limits the Native communities' abilities to feed themselves.

In addition to *Ernestine Shuswap*'s compressed plot structure, Highway dramatizes the concept of timelessness by contrasting the continuous relationship between Native communities and their homelands with the arbitrary, imposed nature of federal laws. Annabelle's first monologue initiates the contrast:

It's true what my dear friend and neighbor, Ernestine Shuswap, is saying when she explains to the people that her husband has been fishing in that river since the morning his mama Minny first let him breathe. We been fishing there, too, my folks and me – and by folks, I mean family, of course, *my* family, *my* kin, my own flesh and blood – we been fishing in that river for a very long time. Me, Annabelle Okanagan of Kamloops, B.C., my dear, late husband Johnny Okanagan of Kamloops, B.C., my father Jeremiah Jerome of Kamloops, B.C., my dear grandfather Benjamin Jerome of Kamloops, B.C., my great-grandfather, my great-great-grandfather, my great-great-great-grandfather, my great-great-great-great-grandfather, my great-great-great-great-great-grandfather, my great-great-great-great-great-great (*pause*) grandfather, and on and on and on, and on and on and on, *and* on and on and on, ever since the cave days, ever since the age of the dinosaurs, ever since the day God said, "Let there be light," yes, ever since that day, we been fishing in that river, my folks and me, the river you can see there in the distance away over yonder? That winding, greenish-blue river that's so busy just a-weaving its way through the mountains [...] right through our hunting grounds, right through our pastures, right through our fields and fields and fields *and* fields of wild saskatoons, right through our houses, through our windows, through our doors, through our children, through our lives, through our dreams, our hearts, our flesh, our veins, our blood [...] Fishing's not allowed? Why, that would be like me, Annabelle Okanagan of Kamloops, B.C., that would be like me coming right into your homes, opening my mouth, and telling you, yes, you. And you, and you and you, and you and you and you, and you and you and you, and you there in the tight red sweater – that would be like me telling you, "No more breathing. Stop right now." (Highway, *Ernestine*, 16–17)

Through the transcendent nature of storytime, Annabelle's account of her family's fishing on the Thompson River connects her to the timeless flow of the river itself. Her language weaves eternity into the very relationship between her people and their homeland. Indeed, the water *is* Annabelle's family. Not only metaphorically, but scientifically, the water in her entire family's bodies comes from the Thompson River. This timelessness floods the singular, disconnected utterance of a law that announces – with no embodied connections to the land – that fishing is not allowed.

Annabelle's story goes further, however, than creating timeless connections between her ancestors and the land: as she breaks the fourth wall to point out audience members, Annabelle brings the story into the present world of the audience. During the play's premiere, this connection between past, present, and future was particularly poignant for an audience comprised of Native and non-Native theatregoers from the greater Kamloops community, where some of the homelands of which Annabelle speaks are still contested.[2] Significantly, even though an additional ninety-four years had transpired between *Ernestine Shuswap*'s setting and the Western Canada Theatre's premiere, the monologue's sense of timelessness still positioned non-Native land claims as haphazard.

Such human–world connections are another significant element of storying which we see in both Annabelle's monologue and Manuel's *The Strength of Indian Women*, when Suzie relates her story about sharing a conversation with two deer. In Native American plays, the bond between humans and non-humans, whether they are animals or departed ancestors, is not merely fantastical: it is performative, connecting humans to the earth. With language as landscape, we traced Native American philosophies that explain how language is rooted in the land. The discourse of storying extends language as landscape by emphasizing the reciprocity that speech enables through humans' relationships with the natural world. This idea is exhibited in Native languages, such as Choctaw and Navajo, where breath, wind, thought, speech, and creation are connected by similar root words (Howe, "Tribalography," 123). In these languages, wind and breath are almost synonymous. The wind breathes over all of creation, and a person's breathing is an embodied exchange with the wind. Imagine the simile: one's breath is to one's body as the wind is to the earth. Human breath is the wind in microcosm. The combination of wind (breath) and thought creates speech. Through the act of speaking, our thoughts enter into the physical universe upon the wind. In turn, the winds circulate our words through all of creation.

The wind, breath, speech relationship exemplifies a significant interaction between humans and natural forces. In "Immersed in Words," Roberta Hill, an Oneida writer and scholar, explains:

Oneida traditions remind us to feel gratitude for earth and water, grass and trees, animals and birds, air and clouds, sun and moon and stars. Daily gratitude gives joy and energy to our lives. Gratitude begins with breath and grows into song and story, for by breathing we exchange our life with the lives that help sustain us…By singing and telling stories, we harmonize the inside of ourselves with manifestations of the universe. ("Immersed," 74)

Philosophies concerning this reciprocal relationship between humans and the world rely upon orality. The concept that speech creates a literal human–earth exchange explains why Native American traditional philosophies often posit speech as a more powerful form of communication than writing. Demonstrating the authority of speech, Elizabeth Woody relates an exchange between Delvis Heath, a Warm Springs chief, and the US Army Corps of Engineers during a repatriation meeting. She states:

[Heath said] "In the way we operate, the word given is to be honored. It seems that in this day and age, agreements are put on paper. Once done, the word is forgotten. If you lose this paper next week, it's as if the word never existed." Through the practice of traditional knowledge, we thank the earth, the life force of the sun, and the Creator; and we bring the earth into our lives by knowing its life. The land, the human individual, and the seen and unseen are connected through the "good word" to the bonds of love's teaching, healing, and strength. (Woody, "Voice," 171)

Orality's authority contrasts with contemporary industrial and legal preferences for written documentation. Interestingly, Heath defines the written word as ephemeral in Native perspectives when he explains that if the paper is lost, the agreements between those who shared the document are also easily forgotten. If relationships forged by writing depend, in part, upon the survival of the written documentation, then speech – the "good word" – creates more permanent bonds through an exchange of one's life, breath, and the timeless universe where, once something is spoken, it exists eternally.

When the discourse of storying combines the concept of the human–world bond with that of storytime, we understand how speech can circulate through past, present, and future. Storying, then, can connect people not only to the land but also to the whole of time and creation, "seen and unseen," the material and spiritual universes. Thus, through storying, humans can use language to connect to non-human beings, to affect ancestors no longer living, and to shape generations yet to come. Hence, Lisa Mayo explains to the audiences of *Rever-ber-berations*:

What I have to say is not sad or heavy. But it is serious. I have not seen my mother since she left her body. But I feel her presence all the time. She comes to me as a breeze around my nose and on my hands when I'm working. She is here in this room now. I feel her. I received a message from her recently. She said she likes my work. She likes my husband. And she is happy for my recognition. (*Rever-ber-berations*, 201)

Lisa's depiction of her mother as a breeze around her nose prepares *Rever-ber-berations'* audiences for understanding notions of storying that blend timelessness, breath and speech, and human and non-human bonds. However, it is the seemingly arbitrary "Tea Time" segments that work most aggressively to draw the audience's focus to these key elements. By repeating the word "blew," the act of blowing, and discussions about the wind, Spiderwoman's "Tea Time" scenes emphasize storying discourse. The ideas repeatedly addressed in these segments are supported further by the theatrical conventions Spiderwoman uses in the play. For example, a set of wind chimes hangs on the line of a hammock which is located upstage center. Lisa Mayo explained to the OSU audience that the chimes represent the spirit world. In the performance, they would ring in response to a breeze, which occurred when one of the actors passed by them or when the performers spoke of communication with spirits (Spiderwoman Theater, Post-performance). As well, the audience hears two repeated "Tea Time" conversations about "blue" or "blew" before Lisa directly addresses the audience with her story of how her mother visits as a breeze around her nose. Simultaneously, the ringing of the chimes and the repetition of blue/blew provide performative evidence of the spirit world.

The "Tea Time" scenes' theatricality presents Native concepts of storying in another way. A large tarpaulin, painted blue, serves as *Rever-ber-berations'* backdrop. It stretches from the top of the set to the stage floor, upon which it extends several feet downstage. Beginning at the center of the backdrop, a black spiral unwinds onto the right-center portion of the stage. The back-drop represents a blue sky, which again evokes images of wind and spirits.

With the wind and sky as a backdrop, a key scene, "Vincent," completes the final "Tea Time" segment. Lisa enters the stage singing, "Hey, hey, hey, dooten day, dooten day, dooten day, starry starry night," mixing Don McLean's lyrics from "Vincent" into her own song (Spiderwoman Theater, *Rever-ber-berations*, 208). As the stage lights dim to indigo, Lisa directly addresses the audience:

Starry, starry night. The world of the five senses is the world of illusion. Reality cannot be seen with the naked eye. With eyes that watch the world and can't forget strangers that they've met.

Starry, starry night. The responsibility of people who make things, build, mold, and shape things, is to interpenetrate the layers, to bring messages between the layers.

Starry, starry night! To go back into the before to use for the future. (*She goes to the hammock and sings "Starry, starry night"* [...] *Sound of wind chimes from the hammock*). (ibid., 208–209)

When Lisa sits in the hammock, she does so with her back toward the audience, as if she is sitting on a swing rather than lying in a hammock. She sings the words "starry, starry night" while she lies back. Her face gazes toward the audience when she is almost upside down, her feet pointing up to the center of the spiral. Her swinging creates the optical illusion that she is flying into the spinning spiral, almost as if she is entering the sky or another world. This scene contains *Rever-ber-berations'* most concrete statement of Spiderwoman's spirituality. "*The world of the five senses is the world of illusion. Reality cannot be seen with the naked eye*" (ibid.; emphasis added). Reality exists beyond the physical. The sisters' mother's body is gone, but her spirit remains, so it is "*The responsibility of people who make things…to interpenetrate the layers, to bring messages between the layers*" (ibid., 209; emphasis added). Time is a spiral in which eras exist adjacent to one another in tight coils. The spiritual gift that Lisa, Gloria, and Muriel inherit from their mother is the ability to journey across these layers of time and physical existence. As easily as Lisa appears to swing into the spiral of time, they can "go back into the before to use for the future" (ibid.).

In a similar fashion, Highway's *Ernestine Shuswap* depicts human–world connections through precise staging conventions in addition to the characters' language. With the use of sound effects, the playwright provides a theatrical voice for the landscape. These effects open and close the play, creating the impression that *Ernestine Shuswap* is not just a play about the people who wrote the Laurier Memorial, but a drama of the land itself. Highway's opening stage directions state, "*First, from the darkness, the gurgle of a river – rich, evocative, the voice of the land. It rises, fades. Out of it 'bleeds' a very low note, on a cello, bowed*" (*Ernestine*, 13). Throughout the play, Highway uses the sound effects of flowing water and cello playing to evoke the land's experiences. These sounds provide transitions between dramatic events and also help highlight dramatic moments, such as when the words from the Laurier Memorial are read aloud in English (mirrored by the river) and Shuswap (which "*'circles' the auditorium like a restless breeze*") (ibid., 86).

The idea that speech connects humans to the world through an exchange of breath and wind contains one other attribute significant to the discourse of storying, that of creation through the spoken word. Howe explains the link between speech and creation by stating, "Choctaws have a mysterious word that represents a kind of creation. It is *nuk* or *nok*, a suffix or prefix that has to do with the power of speech, breath, and mind. Things with *nok* or *nuk* are so powerful that they can create. A teacher, for instance, is *nukfokchi*" ("Tribalography," 123). *Rever-ber-berations* models this concept in an overt, theatricalized manner. Manuel is more subtle. She bases the plotline of *The Strength of Indian Women* upon the concept of creating material effects, the healing of a community, through storying. According to the concept of the creative power of language, once they are spoken, stories have the potential to enact change through the connecting of past, present, and future. Armstrong ("Land Speaking," 194) explains:

In particular, stories that are used for teaching must be inclusive of the past, present, and future, as well as the current or contemporary moment and the story reality, without losing context and coherence while maintaining the drama. There must be no doubt that the story is about the present and the future and the past, and that the story was going on for a long time and is going on continuously, and that the words are only mirror-imaging it having happened and while it is happening.

Manuel's dramaturgy represents this communal nature of seemingly disparate stories. For example, the elders' stories, which appear to return each speaker to a living past as she speaks, ultimately work to restore the women's community and to provide a healthy future for their descendants. Likewise, Suzie's account of the deer demonstrates the ability of a story to create balance in the world. Sousette's grandfather's story returns through the deer to Suzie to mark a new kind of future for the play's Native community.

For Native American playwrights like Diane Glancy, the theatre becomes a space in which to enact the philosophies of story cosmos. In an article entitled "Native American Theater and the Theater That Will Come," Glancy begins with a Cherokee saying, "A Stage is suspended in the air. The earth hangs beneath it on cords. As long as the voices last, the cords will not break. But when the voices fail, the earth will fall into chaos below" ("Native American Theater," 359). She then states, "There is still the belief that story holds things together. The lives of the people depend upon a stage where words take place" (ibid.). While some critics claim that the act of writing marks the "loss of the body as the sole carrier of words," others, like Glancy, propose theatre as one of many solutions (Armstrong, "Land Speaking," 189). Theatre provides a space in which writing and orality come together for the performance of storying discourse. The theatre Glancy imagines, and indeed that which many Native American playwrights create, is one that adheres to Native concepts of speech. Glancy states:

If drama only follows the rules of conflict/resolution, one-point-of-view, plot, chronological order, and the usual, there is something essential in storying that is not included in the above, which is hard to define. It's a migratory and interactive process of the moveable parts within the story. *It's also the element of Native American oral tradition told with what it is not – the written word – then returned to what it is by the act of the voice.* ("Native American Theater," 359; emphasis added)

Theatre provides a powerful vehicle for storying because it can physically realize a "cosmos" with alternative notions of time, while it also restores bodies and breath as carriers of words. As stories "migrate" in the theatrical space, they begin to enact narrative bonds that hold worlds together. Significantly, storying's power does not reside in a single story, a single perspective, or a single truth; rather, storying and tribalography are potent only when the voices multiply.

MULTI-VOCAL AUTHENTICITY: CONSTRUCTING COMMUNAL TRUTH

The discourse of tribalography, which I cover in these next two sections, moves from an investigation of how stories function to an examination of how stories interact, multiply, and work to create material effects. Multi-vocal authenticity is the concept of creating a story by bringing together multiple perspectives, simultaneously. Communal truth refers to the ways in which such overlapping stories often create inconsistencies, which open space for creative action. Incongruity is at the core of tribalography because the discourse is concerned with the process of gathering multiple voices, diverse points of view, and competing perspectives. Tribalography also embraces reciprocal relationships between other seemingly oppositional elements such as theory and action, personal and public, and individual and community. In this particular section, we will investigate how the concept of multi-vocal authenticity helps structure Native plays, which often model for audiences the concept of communal truth.

At this point, it is important to recall the concept of holistic communication because, as we move into a discussion of *Rever-ber-berations*, *The Strength of Indian Women*, and *Ernestine Shuswap*, personal stories, history, myth, and drama will continue to overlap. The multiple use of the term "story" connects to a key aspect of Native American storytelling and theatre, as Muriel Miguel explains:

Storytelling is the way you feel and know where you are within your family, your clan, your tribal affiliations, and from there into the history of how you fit into the world. Storytelling starts at the kitchen table, on your parent's lap, on your aunt's and uncle's laps. Storytelling begins there, about who you are...Then it continues from there about who you are in the family; of where you are as a tribal member, as part of that particular nation; then where that nation is in the community; and where that community belongs in the world. There's always circles upon circles upon circles. And that's how Spiderwoman approaches theatre, through circles upon circles upon circles. (qtd. in Haugo, "Circles Upon Circles," 228)

In her statement, Miguel presents an aspect of multi-vocal authenticity: the gathering of many stories creates the larger story about an individual's sense of belonging in the world. Significantly, knowledge is not gathered from a single perspective; rather, Miguel suggests, it is obtained through various stories, each represented as a circle. As these circles overlap, intersect, and juxtapose one another, knowledge appears somewhere in-between. The idea of relating storytelling to self-knowledge is reflected often on Native theatre's stage. As Glancy explains, Native American theatre rarely makes use of a centralized point of view ("Native American Theatre"). In fact, Native American theatre regularly celebrates the multi-vocal aspect of storying. Thus, audience members often do not derive the meanings of a Native American play from following a single story or protagonist, but from witnessing a multitude of stories. Multi-vocal authenticity not only shapes the dramatic structure of Native American plays, but also sets the stage for audiences to understand the concept of communal truth.

In *Post-Colonial Drama*, Gilbert and Tompkins state that cultures which have endured the effects of colonization often use theatre as a tool for challenging imperialist versions of history. The colonizers' version of history comes under scrutiny for at least two main reasons: "because imperialism precipitated a rupture in traditional ways of recording and relaying history" and "also because that epistemic rupture has often been presented as natural and uncontroversial" (Gilbert and Tompkins, *Post-colonial Drama*, 110). Thus, plays by survivors of colonialism engage with history on two levels, by practicing traditional manners of communicating history and by "establishing counter-narratives" "which refute, or at least de-center orthodox views of history" (ibid., 111).

Incorporating Native storytelling, Native American theatre utilizes traditional methods of imparting history. However, the histories of Native plays often present not one, but many alternative versions of history, and so the sheer number of these accounts works to de-center the monolithic versions of history derived from colonization. The diversity of these narratives is magnified further by the diversity existing across and within Native American nations, each with its own history and narrative. *Rever-ber-berations*, *The Strength of Indian Women*, and *Ernestine Shuswap* are three of many Native American plays that work to revise American history concerning Native American people. While *Rever-ber-berations* relates a more private family history concerning Native spirituality, *Ernestine*

Shuswap revises a public, historical event through the private experiences of four characters who break the fourth wall to challenge audience members to investigate how they fit the gathering history. Meanwhile, *The Strength of Indian Women* strikes at the core of several authoritarian institutions: Christianity, education, and the federal government. By telling stories about how, as children, the First Nations women were forced by the Canadian government into schools run by nuns who beat them and priests who raped them, *The Strength of Indian Women* challenges the charity and good intentions with which churches and governments justified the violent education and assimilation of Native children.

In *The Strength of Indian Women*, Manuel demonstrates how the discourse of tribalography positions the stories of individuals in a reciprocal relationship with the stories of a community. Although each elder's story contains similar episodes of abuse, it is significant that Manuel provides a moment for each woman to stand center stage, face the audience, and tell her personal story. This action presents Woody's reciprocal version of Muriel Miguel's statement about locating oneself within circles of stories. If many stories allow a person to locate their place in a community, then it is equally important that all members of a community tell their own stories. Elizabeth Woody states, "we, who are irreplaceable carriers of our own story, know that self-worth does not come from the measurement of ancestry through blood – it comes from ourselves, our work, and our story" ("Voice," 173). Manuel's play models this reciprocal relationship between the stories of a community and the story of an individual. In the opening scene, Sousette sets the course for the play's action when she tells her daughter, Eva, that she and the other elder women have decided to break their silence. Sousette explains, "I've thought about it a long time, and I talked to the others. We decided that you need to know every-thing, about the school, and about us. You need to know because of Suzie. It's her history, too" (Manuel, *Strength*, 81). While Eva and her daughter, Suzie, must hear the stories of the elder women to understand their own place within their family, among the community's women, within the reservation where they live, their Indian nation, Canada, and their contemporary world, it is equally important for the individual women who carry the stories to speak. Agnes, an elder who left the reservation and survived through prosti-tution before becoming a political activist for First Nations people, explains that she believes that her story provides her reason for living:

You know the Creator left me alive for one reason. It could just as easily have been me that got killed. Somebody has to talk about it. Somebody has to tell the truth about what happened to all those little girls. I figure the Creator saved me because he knew my big mouth would come in handy some day. Still, it's hard to talk about the things that people are so afraid to hear. (ibid., 102)

Agnes' statement demonstrates the idea that storying is not only public and political, but also distinctively private to an individual and that person's specific community. Her story functions in several ways. Agnes' own survival depends upon telling the story; the placement of people within her community depends upon hearing her story; and, finally, her story serves as both a personal and public political tool.

In "Breaking the Silence" Gloria Bird, a Spokane author and critic, links the political act of witnessing, discussed by Gilbert and Tompkins, to the personal act of telling one's story. Bird asserts that her personal story not only works in an overtly public manner to bear "witness to colonization," but also upon a more personal level that aids the Native American community as well as herself. She states that her testimony is "aimed at undoing those processes that attempt to keep us in the grips of the colonizer's mental bondage," for "Autobiography is important to undoing the process of colonization of our minds" (Bird, "Breaking," 29).

Highway's *Ernestine Shuswap* begins with a prologue, a series of personal monologues that emerge out of the initial "voice of the land" and provide each woman's account of the fishing law, the first law that affects them. Their stories build upon one another, offering slightly different perspectives of the same event. In this way, the individual voices develop a sense of community, while the staging conventions provide an air of ceremony. Highway's stage directions state that, as the cello continues to play:

three women will appear, each in turn, under icy pools of light, as from a silvery moon […] The pools of light should be limited to their faces, however, so that these faces look like masks in a Greek tragedy. In fact, that is what their voices should sound like as well, like those in a play by Euripides, that is, a mesmerizing weave of chant and prayer. The point here being: though, at first glance, this may appear to be a very funny play, right from the start, there are undercurrents of darkness, a horrifying tragedy. (*Ernestine*, 13)

As each woman gives her testimony, she speaks *"the words – and thoughts – that will resonate inside her mind, her heart, her body through the course of this day we are about to see her live through"* (ibid., 13–14; 15; 15–16).

First, we hear Ernestine's account of how Joe woke her up early that morning, before the sun. The flirtatious tone of her monologue teases the audience into anticipating that her husband has roused her for sex, but soon we learn of his motive: "'Ernestine Shuswap, I'm getting you a trout'" (ibid., 14). When Ernestine freezes in her pool of light, we are left with images of her daily life: her relationship with Joe, his lighting the woodstove to make coffee for his trip. The next light comes up on Isabel. Her monologue recounts the moment she broke the news to Ernestine, "I says to my dear friend and neighbour, Ernestine Shuswap of Kamloops, B.C., 'How's Joe Shuswap supposed to go down to the river and capture you a trout, rainbow or otherwise, when fishing's not allowed?'" (ibid., 15).

The last monologue is Annabelle's statement about the Thompson River's importance to her people. As she speaks, the lights stay up on the other two faces, so that we remain aware of how the separate, personal accounts build into a communal history. The isolated faces that directly address the audience also dramatize the multi-faceted purpose of storytelling, which Drew Hayden Taylor describes as "metaphorical, philosophical, psychological" ("Alive," 61). The psychological weight of story is referenced each time a character refers to herself or other community members as "so-and-so 'of Kamloops, B.C.'" Throughout the play, this ritualized utterance becomes a convention that continually evokes a sense of place connected to two intersecting communities: the world of the women in the play, and the world of the Kamloops audience. When Annabelle overtly implicates the audience members by pointing them out, her personal story takes on other dimensions. It is not only personal and communal: it is psychological and political. The audience sees her as a character, the member of a fictional world, and the representative of a very real history. Before elements of revisionist history cause the play to veer too blatantly into the political, the scene shifts. Annabelle returns to the mythical mask under the silvery light. She freezes, and the cello music stops. The following scenes are predominantly shared scenes that depict the women's attempts to prepare the feast, despite the pressures of ever-new and changing laws. However, as the play progresses, Highway will increasingly incorporate surreal staging conventions.

Although *Rever-ber-berations* does not target a specific element of history in the same manner as *Earnestine Shuswap* and *The Strength of Indian Women* do, it too insists on the importance of autobiographical stories. In a moment of witnessing, Muriel Miguel's monologue that completes *Rever-ber-berations* is directly addressed to the audience and exposes ideas that link one's personal story to those of family, community, and the world. The monologue simultaneously works as a political action, because it marks the undoing of mental colonization. Muriel explains that speaking, bringing life and breath to the stories of important events that shaped her spiritual life, attests to the legitimacy of her family's beliefs:

> I am an Indian woman.
> I am proud of the women that came before me.

I am a woman with two daughters.
I am a woman with a woman lover.
I am a woman whose knowledge is the wisdom
    of the women in my family.
I am here now.
I say this now because to deny these events
about me and my life
would be denying my children.

(Spiderwoman Theater, *Rever-ber-berations*, 212)

Like the stories told about residential schools in Manuel's play and the story that the Thompson River chiefs brought to Canada's Prime Minister, the stories shared by Spiderwoman Theater are ones that often are met with resistance. This occurs when audience members who – owing to different historical, cultural, or spiritual perspectives – cannot accept the presentation of reality conveyed by the storytelling within Native plays.

Because of the political nature of witnessing, the more people there are to tell a story, the more credibility it can attain. However, multiple narrators of stories in Native American plays perform roles other than staging agreement. More pertinent to the discourse and process of tribalography is the bringing together of stories that often appear in opposition. In Native literature, stories work in a highly complex set of relationships, as Glancy explains:

Native American storytelling is also an act of *gathering*. It takes many points-of-view to tell a story. One voice alone is not enough because we are what we are in relationship to others. Native American writing is also a balancing or alignment of voices so the story comes through. A *relational stance* is the construct of Native American writing. ("Native American Theater," 359)

Manuel demonstrates this multiple perspective of storytelling when Lucy and Sousette take turns telling the first story in *The Strength of Indian Women*. The telling takes on a sense of ceremony as each woman's words provide strength for the other's. Flute music, used to represent breath and wind, underscores the telling of this first story and emphasizes the significance of the words. Lucy, who got pregnant when the priest at residential school raped her, begins the story of why she and Agnes tried to run away:

If it wasn't for that priest, I wouldn't have even run away. It was the first time he ever got me alone. The older girls always warned me never to be alone with him but I was on dorm duty, and Sister sent me to get sheets from the storage room, and he was waiting there. He scared me. He rubbed his tongue all over my mouth before he let me go […] Agnes found me throwing up behind the stairs. She cleaned me up, then she told me she was gonna run. She said some others were gonna go with her, and if I wanted to I could go along. It didn't take me long to decide to go along.

We almost made it over the mountains when they caught us [...] Our own people brought us back. (Manuel, *Strength*, 92)

At this point in the story, Lucy is physically drained. She moves away from the center-stage witnessing area and sits on the couch in Sousette's living room. Then Sousette picks up the story of Lucy and Agnes' attempt to flee the school. She takes center stage and continues:

They made us clear away the tables and chairs in the cafeteria [...] We didn't know for sure what was going on, but we heard somebody saying they caught the runaways and they were going to punish them. They sounded the bell *(A handbell rings three times and flute music begins)* and called us girls to stand in a circle in the cafeteria.
    I saw the Sisters bringing you in one at a time, holding you down so you couldn't get away. I heard your screams, and cries, and I heard that whip slicing through the air, cutting through your flesh. We tried to close our eyes, but those Sisters standing among us forced us to open them and look. The whole top of my dress was soaked with tears. (ibid., 93)

Telling this story for the first time soon tires Sousette, but the brief break she created affords Lucy the strength to finish. In the NAWPA staged reading, the actor playing Lucy stood firm at center stage (Manuel, *Strength* [Reading]). This action was justified by Manuel's stage directions, which state, "*Lucy stands to deliver the rest of her story with all the power she needs to conjure up the image and destroy it*" (Manuel, *Strength*, 93). Lucy continues:

They took turns whipping us. When one of them would get tired, another would step in. They were harder on Agnes because they said she was the ringleader, and because she wouldn't cry [...] The priest was yelling at her, "Cry! Cry! Cry!" but she wouldn't. Then I noticed a trickle of blood running down her leg, and when she fell, it smeared on the floor. She had started on her period, started bleeding, and they still wouldn't stop [...] They broke her that day. (ibid.)

With the end of her story, Lucy leaves center stage and the lights fade on the scene. The stillness punctuates not only the story itself, but also the sharp contrast between the violent context of Agnes' first menstruation and the loving context of Suzie's traditional coming-of-age ceremony. Many aspects of the monologues demonstrate storytelling's relational stance: Lucy and Sousette's dual presentation; the backward-and-forward images relating Agnes and Suzie's coming-of-age events; and the participation of non-Native and Native people who "brought us back" to the residential school (ibid., 92). These relationships are highlighted by the play's theatrical conventions. After Lucy and Sousette's witnessing, a slide of the girls from the residential school fills the stage, showing the audience faces of real children, each with a story like Lucy's (ibid., 93).

Although the stories that begin *Ernestine Shuswap* first appear congruent, as we learn more about the characters we see the ways in which Highway also gathers disparate voices into the larger story of the Laurier Memorial. Annabelle and Isabel bicker about the consequences of the new laws, which horrify Annabelle. Isabel, however, seems immune to the changes and even adopts the language of land ownership as she proclaims her assurance: "It's *my* house, *my* yard, *my* pasture, *my* grass, *my* irrigation system. No one can take it away from me" (Highway, *Ernestine*, 20). While Annabelle and Delilah Rose grumble about having to stage such an elaborate banquet for the Great Big Kahoona of Canada, Isabel revels in the ability to show off her culinary skills to people in power:

[…] *our* banquet? It will be so monstrously, disgustingly, mouth-wateringly, taste-bud-titillatingly spectacular, don't you think? Imagine, just imagine, steaming, juice-effulgent sweet potatoes, wild onions, wild asparagus, wild beans, wild this, wild that, the trout, the stuffing, *your* beaver spread across the table like a carpet for the devil, *my* saskatoon pies, your tablecloths, the squeals of delight, the moans of pleasure, the ambience, the feeling, the rhythm, the cat, oh yesssssss, Delilah Rose Johnson of Kamloops, B. C., yesssssss. (ibid., 28)

The opposing perspectives that are held together by the community's story extend beyond humorous details, which we learn when Annabelle tries to talk to Delilah Rose Johnson, whose frantic sewing produces an ever-growing tablecloth. In awkward pauses, punctuated by the "*rush of 'river-sound'* [that] *balloons and fades – rich, evocative, the voice of the land*," Annabelle tries to confront Delilah Rose, asking "How do you think this whole…fishing/river thing is going to affect you and…well, you know" (ibid., 33). Delilah Rose avoids her friend's questions, first by dodging, "You mean other than kill myself with these tablecloths I was fool enough to volunteer to hem?" and later by sheer denial, "No one's gonna do anything to me. Or Billy Boy. Or our child" (ibid., 33, 36).

Near the end of Act One, we finally hear the fourth monologue, Delilah Rose's, which adds a new perspective on the Laurier Memorial story and affirms why the young woman hems the tablecloths with life-or-death urgency. Billy Boy's gramophone, which plays an unaccompanied cello suite, sits on the floor next to her, and a suspended cowboy hat hangs 6 foot above center-stage, as if on a coat tree. In a spot of silvery light, mirroring the previous monologues, Delilah Rose finally claims her version of the story. Instead of the removed, mask-like appearance, mad moments of laugher occasionally peal through her witnessing, which begins as a love story:

Delilah Rose Johnson of Kamloops, B.C., twenty-one years old, though you can't really tell. Cuz up close, I look thirty-five, bet you a dollar. Why? Because today, I'm in trouble. You see, two years ago [...] I made the mistake, so they tell me, of falling in love with...well, a white boy, a cowboy, in fact [...] Billy Boy Johnson. Why? Because he was different, because he was special, because he liked...classical music, yes, that's what he called this curious music I still don't understand. And wouldn't you know it but he brings along this gramophone just to prove it, to me [...] Said he had a cousin away over in England who played this thing called a cello. Somehow, says Billy Boy to me, that music – that's the only thing that could assuage the pain, the unbearable pain of feeling...out of place, of not belonging. Isn't that bizarre?
    Laughs, beautifully. (ibid., 47–48)

Delilah Rose, the youngest of twelve children, loves Billy Boy's difference, his melancholy homesickness, his appreciation of classical music. Ironically, as her people begin to suffer from their own displacement, Delilah Rose also turns to the cello in order to comfort her own pain "of not belonging."

Delilah Rose's displacement is more complicated than her husband's or her community's, because her allegiance to both marriage and family relations leaves her homeless in the current political atmosphere. Like her Native community, the new laws directly affect her rights and threaten to change her child's future in ways unimaginable. At the same time, some people in her Native community have rejected Delilah Rose for having broken two taboos. She explains, "But you see, around here, in *my* family? An Indian girl does *not* fall in love with, much less marry, a white boy. And neither does an Indian boy dare marry or love or even think of a girl who is white. And, forbidden above all else? A Roman Catholic does *not* marry, or love, a Protestant" (ibid., 48). As Delilah Rose's monologue unfolds, we begin to see the absurd nature of both the federal laws, that can remove an entire river from a community, and those cultural taboos that seek to divide the human heart in the same ways the BC government has divided the Thompson River Valley. Ultimately, Delilah Rose's choice to marry a white man, whom her community rejects, and to live in her homeland, which the white government is stealing, places her in a frighteningly isolated place:

There's a new law on land, Indian land, land used for grazing. And the man in charge of making this new law a reality? In these parts, meaning Kamloops, B. C. and environs? The father of the man I love [...] the father of the father of the child right here. (*pats her little round belly*) My father-in-law? His name? Charles Peter

Johnson formerly of Manchester, England but now from here. His son? [...] The father of my child ... The white man – the *Protestant!* – named – ta-da! – William August Johnson, yes, the very white-skinned cowboy named Billy Boy Johnson, only son and heir to the white man who's just said to my people, "no more fishing," "no more grazing for your cattle," "no more this, no more that." And I'm Delilah Rose Johnson, of Kamloops, B.C. *Laughs. Freeze.* (ibid., 49)

Delilah Rose carries the story's contradictions in her body, and her language predicts the changing relationship between the Thompson River Valley and its inhabitants. While she is still "Delilah Rose Johnson of Kamloops, B.C.," she leaves room to imagine a Charles Peter Johnson and William August Johnson, "formerly of Manchester, England but now from here." Again, we see the timelessness of Native connections in contrast with the newness of the settlers' connections to place, but Delilah Rose hopes for a land that might contain both, peacefully. It is within this imaginative space, this hope, that Delilah Rose hems the tablecloths as if her life depended upon it. In order for her to ever imagine living with her child and husband within her Native homelands, the Prime Minister must be moved to uphold the Native land claims.

Multi-vocal authenticity posits that stories weave relationships not only between people and their sense of belonging within a community, but also between human beings and the world. This human–world relationship through stories is evidenced through prayers, songs, and ceremonial speeches that enter the world on the breath to reaffirm relationships with creation stories, the land, and non-human beings. *Rever-ber-berations* demonstrates the reciprocal relationships formed through storytelling between people and the non-human world. In a scene entitled "Sun Dance Corn Dance," each member of Spiderwoman Theater tells the story of when she came to understand and accept her mother's spiritual gift. Significantly, the sisters' stories intermingle with one another, as if each individual testimony were a part of a greater story about joining a family's spiritual tradition; however, in addition to incorporating a relational stance to one another, these stories also work to relate the sisters to the earth, spirits, and animals. Setting a serious tone for "Sun Dance Corn Dance," Spiderwoman underscores the scene with live drumming,[3] while the sisters take shifts between playing the drum and speaking their stories.

Each sister's account begins with a relationship to place. Muriel's story takes place on the dancing grounds of the Sun Dance; Gloria's, first, outside of the Sun Dance ceremony and, then, in the sacred Black Hills; and Lisa's as she watches the Corn Dance in Taos, New Mexico. Gloria begins the scene by crossing downstage center, while Muriel stays upstage right playing the drum. As Gloria dances, she states:

> I'm not dancing in the Sun Dance.
> I'm dancing in another world.
> I'm not dancing in the Sun Dance.
> I'm dancing in another world.
> I'm not part of the ceremony.
> I'm outside watching my sister and my daughter dance.
> Feeling the power of the dancers.
> The eagles, three of them, swoop down and fly off.
> The dancers honor them.
>
> (Spiderwoman Theater, *Rever-ber-berations*, 196)

From the beginning, Gloria's and Muriel's stories are linked, by place, by ceremonial dance, and by Muriel's playing the drum that Gloria now dances to (even as she recalls that it was her sister, Muriel, who danced). Gloria also mentions the power being exchanged between the dancers, people attending the ceremony, and the spiritual world of non-human beings. As Muriel takes over the dramatic action, her story confirms the relationship between human and non-human beings. The exchange occurs after four honor beats on the drum; Gloria takes over drumming as Muriel comes downstage to tell the story of when spirit messengers spoke to her during her fourth day of dancing. Muriel states:

> I looked down and I saw ants,
> crawling around my feet.
> They crawled up my feet,
> ran up my skirt.
> And on my mola[4]
> were these two ants.
> They talked to me.
> The said they would take care of me.
> They would give me strength.   (ibid.)

While Muriel's story quickly moves to the topic of her place within the spiritual network of humans and non-humans, the seen and unseen worlds, Gloria's and Lisa's stories move more slowly. In the next exchange of drumming and speaking, Gloria continues her story and explains that she came to the Sun Dance in order to "touch this ancient earth," so she drove out to visit the Black Hills (ibid., 197). In-between Gloria's explanation, Lisa begins her account. Unlike her sisters, Lisa relates her story from upstage center, where she stands behind the hammock, which she uses as a rope. Lisa begins, "I was on vacation in my polyester pantsuit at the Corn Dance in Taos, New Mexico, standing behind the rope with the tourists. Beautiful sunshine day. Cloudless sky. I became aware of my heartbeat. And I could hear my blood surging through my veins" (ibid.). The sisters' stories segue from one teller to another as the drum continues to beat. Together, the stories mount in intensity. Muriel's story relates how her father came to visit her in the shape of a cloud: "I looked up into the cloud, and the formation of the cloud became my father's face. My father said it was right that I was dancing. He would give me strength, watch over me, take care of me" (ibid.). In the Black Hills, Gloria tells how she was visited by ancestral spirits who entered upon the air: "Softly I felt a breeze pass by me. The breeze became stronger. I felt them, bodies passing by me. I heard singing coming from way behind the hill. Voices coming from the hills. Singers passing by me. Dancers passing by me. Bodies passing by me. By me, and around me" (ibid.). Lisa tells how from a cloudless, sunny sky, she witnessed "the surging water of a terrible storm raging. Everything changed," and then, "Vibrations from the drums entered my body from the earth on which I stood" (ibid., 197, 198). For each sister, the experience she relates is not only a story of learning her place within the spirit-filled world's network of relationships, but also a story about her active response to that experience. The scene ends:

MURIEL: And I said to myself, "I'm really Indian."
LISA: The message was clear. As I stood in my purple polyester pantsuit, behind the rope with the tourists at the Corn Dance in Taos, New Mexico [...]
GLORIA: (*at the same time as LISA is finishing*) Now I knew what I had to do. Now I knew what I had to do. Now I knew what I had to do.   (ibid., 199)

The actors do not overtly share the personal instructions they each received; as is customary, the details of their spiritual experiences are private. However, it is significant that their stories of having received guidance cannot be separated fully from what Spiderwoman Theater is doing on stage in the very moment they re-enact those scenes. As Spiderwoman tells these personal stories of spiritual awakening to an audience of *Rever-berations*, the audience members can locate themselves in a relationship within the stories' circles. Part of Spiderwoman's art is their legacy, those threads of story-spirit that escape into the world. The women tell their stories; by listening, the audience members assist this process and, so, become a small part of the continuing story.

In *Ernestine Shuswap*, the ways in which stories escape into the world and the ways in which the natural world responds to those stories is a relationship that Highway demonstrates through imagery and overlapping narratives. By the end of Act One, Ernestine and Isabel have come across a stretch of barbed wire that Billy Boy's father, Charles Peter Johnson, has erected in the middle of the Native communities' herb, berry, and root-gathering fields. Isabel vows to poison Delilah Rose's father-in-law with one of her saskatoon pies, but Ernestine comments, "Charles Peter Johnson is simply [...] a pimple on the face of society [...] If you poison anyone tonight, why not the Great Big Kahoona of Canada, hmmm?" (Highway, *Ernestine*, 55). The images that end the act present four distinct views of how the women and the land are affected by the mounting conflicts facing their community. Playing off biblical allusions that position Kamloops as Eden and the Prime Minister as an unreasonable god, the women "*look at the forbidden fruit, ERNESTINE with yearning, ISABEL with rage*" (ibid.). Behind the women are two more frozen "still lives": Annabelle stirring a large pot as she reads what we will eventually learn is the Laurier Memorial, and Delilah Rose in a separate space. Highway describes Delilah Rose:

looking like a goddess emerging from a river (the length of white muslin); again, she is just snipping at her thread with her bright, glinting scissors. From her gramophone [...] *cello music starts: unaccompanied Bach slow, mournful, almost painful* [...] *A billow of "river-sound" and wind, making the shadows of the saskatoon bushes shimmer across* [Ernestine and Isabel's] *faces and bodies, which in turn, makes them look like spirits – the land is talking, through them.* (ibid. 56)

The saskatoon shadows morph into barbed-wire shadows that slash across the women's faces. As the river rushes and the cello music rises, the women let out a "'war cry,' which ends up sounding like the wailing of a widow at a funeral" (ibid.).

In Highway's images, we see both the individual's reaction and the community's collective response to the violence perpetrated on the Native nations' ways of life. Like a fifth person, or an ancestor, the Thompson River Valley adds its voice with the rushing sounds of water and wind. Interestingly, Highway calls for the women's presence to appear ghostly, a reminder to the audience that these "spirits" and their stories still reside in the landscape of Kamloops. Playwright Floyd Favel writes about how Native theatre works to stage this interplay of language, landscape, and ancestors: "Present in the immediate worlds are the ancestors, which go back generation by generation, right back to the day our language bubbled up from the springs and whispers of the trees and grass. [Language] is a doorway, and a window" ("Theatre of Orphans," 33–34).

The linguistic presence of land mounts in *Ernestine Shuswap*'s second act, during which the women begin to "proofread" aloud passages of the historic Laurier Memorial, and Highway's sceneography presents more powerful examples of how the landscape mirrors the stories of its peoples. Delilah Rose, whose tablecloth has grown to surreal proportions, summons Ernestine for advice. Isabel and the Native community have urged Delilah Rose to leave Billy Boy, while the priest has told her to leave her family. She explains that leaving the Johnson family, whose child she carries, or leaving her own family, the land, and "everything I know, everything I love [...] would be like me asking you to neigh, Ernestine Shuswap, that would be like me asking you to act like a horse. It just wouldn't happen, would it now?" (Highway, *Ernestine*, 65). Caught between her Catholic faith, which condemns divorce, and her Native sense of community, Ernestine has no words for Delilah Rose. Instead, she predicts that her husband, Joe, would advise that "they'll lynch him, they'll hang him by the neck from the tallest, most beautiful Douglas fir" (ibid., 66).

Uncertainty increases as Delilah Rose asks who will be lynched, her husband or father-in-law. Her uneasiness travels to her gestures: she "*once again 'billows' out the tablecloth* [...] *so that again* [...] *it looks like a river. It is a river...a river with a 'trout' 'inside' it. As well, a billow of 'river-sound' surfaces, blooms, and fades*" (ibid.). The symbolic Thompson River that Delilah Rose holds and the contested land the women call home enact their own story, as Ernestine tells Delilah Rose about the Jenkins family, the first white people to steal Native land in Kamloops. The feuding between the Jenkins and the Native community climaxed when Don Jenkins, Sr. shot Franklin Coyote in the back for taking a chicken to feed his starving family. The Coyote brothers retaliated. On the banks of the Thompson River, where the North and South branches meet, they chopped off Don Jenkins' head with an axe. Ernestine warns:

And the blood of Don Jenkins Sr. and the blood of Franklin Coyote still hang in the air, like a mist, over the waters of the Thompson River. And they say that inside that mist, late at night, when the moon is out? You can see eyes in them, like lamps, two pairs of them, hanging there waiting and waiting and waiting...I was six years old, Delilah Rose Johnson. I heard the screams of Don Jenkins Sr. I still hear them.

She pauses. And in that pause, we hear the death screams of Don Jenkins Sr., somewhere far, far away, as though filtered through fifty years of memory [...] *Ever so gradually, we see the "eyes" just described, two pairs of them, like lamps, hovering in the air.* (ibid., 67–68)

Highway's staging conventions increasingly present a world in which the land weaves its own story into the language of the characters. Collectively, the land and characters revise history, dramatizing the Native nations' construction of the Laurier Memorial in a complex manner that remains receptive to both Native and non-Native cultures. Ernestine mirrors this acceptance as she remains haunted by the screams of Don Jenkins, and the land itself marks the tragedy with two pairs of eyes that linger above the juncture of the North and South Thompson Rivers. This visual element speaks to the present lives of the audience members, Native and non-Native, who live in Kamloops, the city whose name bears the Shuswap word for "meeting-place," a metaphor for the region's history and future.

Like *Ernestine Shuswap*, Manuel's *The Strength of Indian Women* demonstrates how tribalography's power comes from staging multiple perspectives with narrative incongruities that open the space for collective creation. Glancy explains:

America was once called the Melting Pot, but we are taking out of the pot what didn't melt: our voices, culture, styles, and ways of storytelling. America, as well as Native America, is a fractured, changing, pluralistic society, which our theatre should reflect...It seems to me that art is the best medium for understanding our different cultures, and not only the difference between cultures, but the differences within cultures also. Indian tribes and languages and ways of life are vastly different. ("Native American Theatre," 361)

Manuel demonstrates this difference in *The Strength of Indian Women*. Although they are all from the same reservation and have suffered arising abuse from the same boarding-school experience, the elders are not a congenial group. Mariah is an elder who lives according to her Christian faith. While she remains close to Sousette, Mariah has few friends on the reservation. Agnes is surprised that Mariah has returned there. She states, "I thought she'd stay her whole life in the city. If she doesn't get along with Indians, it sure must get pretty lonely for her here" (Manuel, *Strength*, 97). Lucy is more outspoken. She claims that Mariah "don't really belong here," and questions, "if her [Mariah's] grandmother was a medicine woman, how come she had a half-white granddaughter?" (ibid., 97, 98). Later, when Sousette says that "not a single one of us in the picture [of the residential school students] has had an easy life," Lucy is quick to counter, "Except maybe Mariah, and Sophie, and Joannie, all those teacher's pets with their light skin" (ibid., 102).

Most of the elder women believe that their perspectives tell the whole story of what happened at the residential school. When Sousette mentions that she thinks Mariah has an important story to tell, Lucy rejects Mariah's point of view by claiming, "I know everything that went on in that school" (ibid., 98). Yet, when Mariah finally does break her silence in Act Two, the women learn that, despite her having been favored by the teachers, Mariah's testimony contributes a surprising vantage point to their stories of abuse. Mariah states:

What I seen in that school shocked me into silence, and disbelief in everything that was good. But it was not the Lord that did that. I know that now. It was people just like you and me.
Gregorian chant begins.
I saw that girl, Theresa, refuse to stop speakin' Indian, refuse to quit prayin' to Napika [...] I saw her challenge them repeatedly, daring them to do what they finally did to silence her [...] I saw murder done in that school, and when they wrapped that broken body and sent it home to the mother tellin' her it was pneumonia that killed her little girl [...] I said nothin'.
The hand-held bell rings three times.
I saw little girls taken in the night from their beds [...] returned in a frightened, huddled mass beneath their sheets, and I said nothin'.
The hand-held bell rings three times.
[...] I saw a baby born one night to a mother who was little more than a child herself. I saw her frightened, dark eyes pleading with me to save her child, and later on, when the grave was dug, and the baby lowered into the ground, I said nothin'.
The hand-held bell rings three times. Gregorian chant ends.
When my grandma died, I was only nine, and I had no one. At Christmas and summer holidays, no one came to claim me, so they became my family. They stroked my light skin, and brushed my brown curls, and told me that I was almost white [...] and because I was so good at saying nothin' I became one of them. I was very loyal. When I left that school, Father put this cross around my neck, and he cried and wished me well, made me promise to come back and visit [...]
I walked away. Never looked back. Not once. For a long time after that, I couldn't pray, and for years I believed in nothin'. (ibid., 105–106)

Through the years of favoritism, Mariah's abuse came in the form of silencing. When she left the school, she was doubly silenced by members of her own community who believed her stories to be unimportant. Yet, Manuel shows that Mariah's story is integral to the elders' understandings of themselves, to their histories, and to telling Eva the whole story about the residential school.

In "Interior and Exterior Landscapes," Leslie Marmon Silko explains how multiple narratives contribute to a fuller sense of storying:

the ancient Pueblo people depended upon collective memory through successive generations to maintain and transmit an entire culture, a worldview complete with proven strategies for survival. The oral narrative, or story, became the medium through which the complex of Pueblo knowledge and belief was maintained. Whatever the event or the subject, the ancient people perceived the world and themselves within that world as part of an ancient, continuous story composed of innumerable bundles of other stories. ("Interior," 8)

The characters of *Ernestine Shuswap, The Strength of Indian Women*, and *Rever-ber-berations* demonstrate that a story is a collection of multiple perspectives gathering together through time. After each sister introduces herself to *Rever-ber-berations'* audience, Spiderwoman Theater performs a key scene called "Mama's Caul." The story provides the audience with information about their mother's spiritual gifts, but it also shows how the story of the mother cannot be told fully without the different perspectives of the three daughters:

GLORIA: (*comes forward*) Grandma said: "Your mother was born with a caul so she has strong psychic powers."
MURIEL: (*comes forward*) She could look into the future. She could see through anybody. She could tell the meaning of symbols left by coffee grounds and tea leaves in the bottom of cups.
LISA: [already standing downstage with her sisters] When Mama went into a trance, she said that everything changed in the world [...] she could hear the sounds that had been in the room...
ALL: ...a long time ago.
GLORIA: And she could see the people who had been there too.
(Spiderwoman Theater, *Rever-ber-berations*, 190–91)

The mother's story belongs to all of the sisters, each of whom, in turn, contributes her own part to the story-bundle about Mama's caul. As they lend their voices to the mother's story, the sisters also place themselves within the story's timeless spiral. The scene ends with the performers' words intermingling, as they tell stories that reach backward to their ancestors and forward to their descendants. Overlapping each other, they all "(*Go back in family history with names of those who carried 'the gift,'* [...] *as they say:*) And my mother's children had that gift. And my daughter has that gift. I have that gift. And my son has that gift. And it goes on for generations and generations and generations – " (ibid., 191).

Likewise, stories of Sousette and her friends are all a part of the daughter, Eva's, story. Near the end of *The Strength of Indian Women*, Manuel breaks the present time with a flashback that depicts the moment when Sousette realized how her daughter and granddaughter were part of the women's continuous bundle of boarding-school stories. In present time, Sousette tells her friends, "It was all so long ago, it hardly seemed worth talking about [...] When they started to talk about residential schools, and even started an investigation, I didn't want to be involved [...] I wouldn't tell them nothing. I said it was a good place for me. Then one day, Eva, she opened my eyes" (Manuel, *Strength*, 107). The play's action shifts back in time as a spotlight appears on stage. Sousette remains on the outer edges of the light, as Eva adds her story to her mother's. Eva tells Sousette:

How can you say, it was a good place for you? How can you lie like that? I'm sick of hearing about how you all suffered from everybody else but you [...] Do you remember how you used to beat me, Mom? Do you even remember the bruises? Do you remember the ugly things you used to call me [...] ? Every time I go to hug you, you stiffen up. Do you know you do that, Mom? Do you know how that makes me feel? And now I'm doing the same thing to Suzie. I push her away, Mom. I call her stupid, and I hit her, and I don't want to. Tell me again that residential school was good for you. Talk to me some more about forgiveness. (ibid., 108)

Upon realizing how her own story continues through the lives of Eva and Suzie, Sousette joins Eva in the light. She tells her daughter, "I'll make it up to you, if only you'll forgive me. I'll start talking about it. I'll tell you everything that happened to me, so you'll understand. We'll help one another to understand" (ibid.). The scene ends with Eva and Sousette pledging to use one another's stories to find placement and healing. The flashback emphasizes why the elders' storytelling is such an integral part of Suzie's coming-of-age ceremony: at the same time as Suzie is crossing a threshold from childhood into womanhood, Eva, her mother, also is undergoing a transformation. The stories told to Eva by the elders allow Eva to discover her place – as both a mother and a daughter within her own family, as a woman in the immediate community, and as a strong Native woman in contemporary society. Manuel builds upon Eva's transformation during the end of her play.

COLLECTIVE CREATION

Collective creation refers to the material effects of tribalography. The concept describes a process by which the gaps and fissures of communal truth create a rhetorical space in which audiences critically engage with the discrepancies, add their own personal stories, and create new relationships. To understand how this process works in Native American theatre, we will first examine how Native plays model the process of collective creation through ceremonial scenes. Then we will draw upon the concepts of language I discussed earlier to investigate how collective creation reaches into the world of the audience to generate material effects, the core objective of tribalography. Because these concepts may seem somewhat foreign to certain readers, I will draw upon general theatrical theories regarding historicization and critical response in order to provide points of contact with Native American theories of language.

When Glancy describes her vision for Native American theatre's future, she speaks of both a fracturing and a revolution. Her revolution incorporates two concepts: that of transformation (the creation of something new) and that of continual movement (storying's timeless spiraling). According to the Native discourse of storying, Native theatre – itself an oral art – is inherently infused with the dual potential to continue traditions and create new forms. Glancy states:

Native American theatre is an example of Native spoken-word art. May more be coming down the road: poetic pieces intermixing ethnographic material with pieces of the old language and contemporary experiences and expressions. The brokenness of the culture, yet moving with the power, renewal, and definiteness of it. I hope Native theatre is in a process of continuance, of extending ethnographic monologues to ethnopoetic dialogues in a new mix of oral tradition. ("Native American Theatre," 360)

Native American plays model the ability of monologues to branch into dialogues. The branching occurs when multi-vocal authenticity extends from the world of the play into the world of the audience. Howe describes these actions of continuance, renewal, and new oral traditions as tribalography's "sacred third act" ("Tribalography," 117). Collective creation, then, is built upon the idea that storying has the power to create a new understanding, to transform perspectives of people and situations.

Collective creation is demonstrated in *Rever-ber-berations*, *The Strength of Indian Women*, and *Ernestine Shuswap*. At the end of *Rever-ber-berations* the gathering of stories gives way to a ceremonial act of purification and healing. After the final noise-band scene, the sisters return to the powwow drum and begin to play. Underscored by the drumbeat, Muriel – who begins the play with a rejection of her mother's powers, "My mother's a witch!!/How embarrassing [...] I don't have any sacred powers" – crosses downstage (Spiderwoman Theater, *Rever-ber-berations*, 190). She now sings to cleanse the negative words spoken earlier in the play:

> This is a song for my mother.
> This is a song for my mother.
> This is a song to release the pain,
> the shame, the secrets. (ibid., 210)

The actors then gather to perform "Bowl Dance Zuniga," a pantomimed dance that physically re-enacts important symbols touched upon in the play's stories: corn-grinding, from Lisa's Corn Dance; eagles, from Gloria's memory of Muriel's participation in the Sun Dance; and childbirth, from the women's focus on ancestry. Additionally, the choreography portrays the sisters' intricate relationships with one another. They sway together, support one another from falling, and physically shelter one another (Spiderwoman Theater, *Rever-ber-berations* [Performance]). Final statements, delivered by each sister, complete the ceremony with declarations of acceptance, healing, and responsibility. Muriel's monologue proclaiming her pride in her women ancestors, her Native identity, her daughters, and her sexuality closes the show.

Likewise, *The Strength of Indian Women* ends with a ceremonial transformation. After Sousette delivers the final residential-school story, she and Eva discuss a new beginning, one occurring within the women's community. Eva reminds her mother, "you taught me how to keep Suzie safe and how to celebrate her becoming a woman," and Sousette responds, "Suzie will turn the whole world right side up again, the way it was meant to be, and we will celebrate" (Manuel, *Strength*, 113). Suzie returns from her fast, and the women prepare her for the feast in her honor. While the elders dress Suzie in the buckskin dress, moccasins, a cape, and a blanket, Sousette explains the upcoming ceremony to her granddaughter:

Everyone is waiting for you. Nothing will begin until you get there. Your mom and your Granny Agnes will cover you with the blanket again. The blanket is a gift from your great-granny Marceline. We will surround you when you come into the hall and the aunties who helped you will lead the way, and some will fall behind. There is an arbor built of spruce and cedar inside the middle of the hall. All the medicine people will sit inside this arbor. We will lead you to the very center and we will remove the blanket and place it in a spot set aside for you to sit. There will be an honor song, and a special prayer, which we will all stand for. When this is done, all the women will make the victory call. (ibid., 116)

The transformation of Suzie from a girl to a woman is a change that is equally relevant to the elder women, because the girl's ceremony marks their transition from silence and shame into healing and pride. Suzie embodies their collective creation. While Suzie purified herself during the two-day fast leading up to the ceremony, the women in Sousette's home also isolated themselves to enact a period of cleansing through storying. The culmination of their story-gathering coincides with the feast in which the community celebrates Suzie's emergence into womanhood. The feast is not only a coming-of-age ceremony for Suzie: it is also a renewal of an old tradition, whose practice had disappeared through the boarding-school years. As the elders renew the ceremony, they also create a new tradition. Cleansed by the telling of their stories, the women use Suzie's feast to claim a position of honor for themselves within the community. Manuel emphasizes this collective transformation in the last moment of the play: when the women leave the house together, they are greeted with an honor song.

Collective creation in *Ernestine Shuswap* generates a ceremonial transformation full of disturbing language and imagery. Favel writes, "The use of words is dangerous, risky. The language evokes all manner of entities and memories, and spirits. The word conjures" ("Theatre of Orphans," 34). Likewise, the final scenes that Highway constructs use the historic language of the Laurier Memorial to conjure moments that dramatize the Native nations' suffering. However, to prevent the play from becoming too gritty, Highway relies upon a surreal style of presentation that allows him to communicate through humor, where he can, and poetic images.

Ernestine Shuswap's scenes begin to overlap. While Ernestine proofreads the Laurier Memorial, Isabel and Annabelle engage in a heated debate about the health of the community's cow. Their bickering bodies begin to look like a tango dance. The scene bleeds into Delilah Rose, who now stands on her chair and wears her 50-meter long tablecloth over her head like a bridal veil. Highway writes, *"In the trance-like state that she's in, she looks like a cross between a bride and the statue of the Blessed Virgin Mary"* (*Ernestine*, 77). A string quartet, with elements of "The Wedding March," *"bleeds in and swells and swells, until, later, it will drown out all four women's voices,"* while Delilah Rose turns to the suspended cowboy hat to re-enact her marriage: "I, Delilah Rose Laughingbird of Kamloops, B.C., do take you, William August Johnson formerly of Manchester, England but now of Kamloops, B.C. [...] in love and in hate, in hate and in love, till death...till death" (ibid.). Delilah Rose's vows repeat and underscore Ernestine's own worries that without any dinner, without a trout, "The Great Big Kahoona of Canada will destroy us" (ibid., 78). Dreamlike, chanting her worries as a mantra, Ernestine goes "down to the river to look for Joe" (ibid.). Her cries for her husband weave into Delilah Rose's repeating wedding vows and the rising and falling string quartet, which now includes the sounds of the river. Visually, Highway pairs the sound collage with overlapping images: Delilah Rose's long veil becomes the river, as projections of an underwater world wash over the women. Ernestine tries to grasp a giant trout *"swimming' around her, just out of reach,"* while this scene is layered over with scenes of the two other women, their voices blending into Highway's metaphorical string quartet. (See figure 3.)

Counterpointing Delilah Rose's wedding vows and Joe's promise to get his wife a trout, Annabelle reads from the Laurier Memorial as she

3. Delilah Rose (Cheri Maracle) and Ernestine (Lisa Ravensbergen) during the surreal marriage scene in Western Canada Theatre's production of *Ernestine Shuswap*.

ritualistically stirs her cauldron. Highway writes that *"her voice, eventually, will emerge through the theatre sound system, unreal, dream-like, otherworldly, the document itself, also eventually, nowhere in sight"* (ibid.). The words she reads record broken promises:

"The whites make a government in Victoria. At this time they did not deny the Indian tribes owned the country. We Indians were hopeful. We waited for their

chiefs to declare their intentions toward us and our lands [...] Presently government officials commenced to visit us, and had talks with our chiefs. They told us to
have no fear, the Queen's laws would prevail, and everything would be well for the
Indians. They said a large reservation would be staked off for us and the tribal lands
outside of this reservation the government would buy from us for white settlement.
They let us think this would be done soon, and meanwhile, we would have the
same liberties as from time immemorial to hunt, fish, graze, and gather our food
supplies where we desired; trials, land, water, timber, all would be as free of access
to us as formerly. Our chiefs were agreeable, so we waited for treaties to be made.
We had never known white chiefs to break their word." (ibid., 79)

Simultaneously, Isabel, also in a trance-like state, pulls a string of 624
saskatoon pies across the downstage area while she reads portions of the
document that record the government's broken promises. Her voice joins
Annabelle's circling through the sound system, so now all four women's
voices weave through the music and the river sounds, as Ernestine swims
and Delilah Rose marries her cowboy. Isabel reads:

"What have we received from our good faith? [...] Their government has taken
advantage of our friendliness. They treat us as subjects without any agreement to
that effect and force their laws on us. They have broken down our old laws and
customs. They laugh at our chiefs [...] They have never consulted us in any of these
matters, nor made any agreement, nor signed any paper with us. They have stolen
our lands and everything on them. They treat us as children. They say the Indians
know nothing, own nothing, yet their power and wealth have come from our
belongings. The Queen's law which we believe guaranteed our rights, the B.C.
government has trampled underfoot. This is how our guests have treated us – the
bothers we received hospitably in our house." (ibid., 80)

The Laurier Memorial's reading ends with Annabelle, who repeats the
chiefs' earlier hope, "They will do the square thing by us in the end" (ibid.).
    In this moment, when the real-world document becomes part of the play,
Highway's storying collapses the boundaries between fact and fiction, past,
present, and future, characters and audience. The literal document delivers
a Native account of the nineteenth century, but the women's voices bring
that story into the world of the present. The words conjure a political
question for the characters and the audience alike: when will the BC
government do the square thing for the Native communities of the
Thompson River Valley?
    A lightening-bolt emphasizes the question and breaks the trance-like
movement, but the surreal style of *Ernestine Shuswap* continues to increase.
Delilah Rose is overcome by "*a mad peal of gorgeous, to-die-for silvery
laughter*"; she leaps off her chair and begins to gallop, neighing like a

horse (ibid., 81). Her horse-cries eventually blend into human speech. In the Shuswap tongue that we now know her father-in-law banned, Delilah Rose's frantic story lashes out at all the women, who attempt to wrench the scissors from her hands. Delilah Rose attacks Isabel's hypercritical condemnation of Delilah Rose for marrying outside the Native community, although Isabel herself had defied her Shuswap family by marrying a Thompson man. Delilah Rose screams, "What's the difference? [...] Huh? Huh, huh, huh? Tell me!" (ibid., 84). Annabelle then breaks her gruff exterior to cry, "A white man killed my Johnny [...] Okanagan, my dear late husband. Shot him in the forehead [...] for a piece of land, *his* land, Johnny Okanagan's little piece of trap-line, yes. *And* I forgive him, Delilah Rose Johnson [...] I forgive Oliver Clapperton...*and his people* [...] I just want peace. I just want peace, so I can sleep. Please, God, please, let me sleep!" (ibid.).

Wildly, Delilah Rose rushes about with her sense of self fractured. In the third person she keeps asking, "So what was she to do, this Delilah Rose Laughingbird [...] with a white man in her stomach?" (ibid., 85). Delilah Rose considers cutting the child out so that she can return to her life as it was before, but to "What land, what kind of land, what kind of culture, what kind of country, what kind of world? Huh? Great Gig Kahoona of Canada?" (ibid.). Her laughing and neighs swell until the scissors appear "inexplicably" in Delilah Rose's belly (ibid.). Her last words become the story of the banquet, her people's hope for peace:

So she took her wedding veil, stitched it and put it on her head. And thus did Delilah Rose Laughingbird now Delilah Rose Johnson...and thus...To this day, [...] on nights when the moon is out, a third pair of eyes hangs high over the river in the mist, like lamps. And to this day, these eyes, they look out over a village, which became a town, which became a city, they look out at a banquet, this woman's head in the mist does, it looks out at a banquet that sits on her veil of pure white muslin, a banquet that sits on her beautiful veil, a veil they call the Thompson River. (ibid., 86)

Through Highway's use of theatrical metaphor, Delilah Rose embodies not just the conflict between the Native and non-Native communities, but also the giving nature of the land itself. Significantly, the land – though disputed – holds the future of the merging communities. With no answer to Delilah Rose's question of what world she could return to, Delilah Rose/the land sacrifices part of herself/itself. The sacrifice offers a place for the union of two disparate cultural groups, whose combined actions forge a new city, a banquet of sorts upon the Thompson River. Of course, this poetic transformation does not come without cost. As her eyes continue to watch the development of contemporary Kamloops, Delilah Rose's story, the land's story, is as much a haunting as it is a love story.

Collective creation, however, involves more than placing ceremonial actions on the stage. According to Native American discourses of storying and tribalography, the power of storytelling cannot be limited by the dividing line between performers and spectators. The theatre is a community gathered. The stories told there enter the worlds of both actors and spectators, so that collective creation implicates the viewers. I opened "Native storytelling" (chapter 5) with a quotation about storying from Armstrong, who asserts that the act of speech contains the potential to change the world. Armstrong builds her assertion upon an understanding of story cosmos. She explains, "By speaking my Okanagan language, I have come to understand that whenever I speak, I step into a vastness and move within it through a vocabulary of time and of memory" ("Land Speaking," 183). Armstrong continues by touching upon multi-vocal authenticity. Her words place her within the bundle of stories gathering through time: "I move through the vastness into a new linking of time to the moment I speak" (ibid.). However, the bulk of Armstrong's statement is related to tribalography's final concept of collective creation. Armstrong continues:

To speak is to create more than words, more than sounds retelling the world; it is to realize the potential for the transformation of the world. To the Okanagan, speaking is a sacred act in that words contain spirit, a power waiting to become activated and become physical. Words do so upon being spoken and create cause and effect in human interaction. What we speak determines our interactions. Realization of the power of speaking is in the realization that words can change the future and in the realization that we each have that power. I am the word carrier, and I shape-change the world. (ibid.)

Armstrong's assertion lays bare the heart of tribalography. If words – spoken stories – have the power to "become activated" and create "physical effects in human interaction," then the ultimate significance of collective creation resides not in a play's ability to model concepts of tribalography but in the potential for the play's stories to enter the audience and change the world.

Change, of course, is rarely smooth. It is a process by which individuals, first, wrestle with ideas and seek to find meaning. When Native American plays present multiple versions of the same story, audience members receive various tools with which to build their understanding. Silko explains, "The ancient Pueblo people sought a communal truth, not an absolute truth. For them this truth lived somewhere within the web of differing versions, disputes over minor points, and outright contradictions tangling with old feuds and village rivalries" ("Interior," 10). The practice of an audience's constructing communal truth, replete with gaps and discrepancies, shares a point of contact with theatrical theory. Theatre scholars can turn to the work of Bertolt Brecht to investigate how the general theatre has also evoked critical responses from audience members by presenting them with multiple, often contradictory, perspectives of history. In *Unmaking Mimesis*, Elin Diamond adds a feminist perspective to Brecht's theories, and so extends the analysis of audience reactions into an examination of how viewers critically approach the performers' physical bodies that also reveal a multiplicity of signs. In particular, Diamond's reading of Brecht's concept of historicization offers points of contact between theatrical theory and Native concepts of generating collective creation through communal truth's dissonance.

Brecht's historicization mirrors elements of communal truth in the way it seeks to deconstruct notions of a universal truth and privileges instead the particular relationships between individuals and society. Brecht explained, "The idea of man as a function of the environment and the environment as a function of man, i.e. the breaking up of the environment into relationships between men, corresponds to a new way of thinking, the historical way" ("Alienation Effects," 97). He achieved historicization by investigating the everyday actions of people who function in relationship with localized, social environments. These ideas parallel aspects of Vine Deloria, Jr.'s argument that worldwide, time-based religions fail human beings by focusing on eternal truths, while localized, place-based religions that take into account the changes between individuals and their environments are more relevant.

Diamond defines Brecht's historicization as "a way of seeing," because an audience member is "writing her own history even as she absorbs messages from the stage" (*Unmaking Mimesis*, 49). This perspective of how audience members understand history incorporates notions of active constructions, localized perspectives, and "unofficial" historians. Diamond's emphasis on the transference of stories from tellers to hearers mirrors concepts of Native American storying, which places an equal responsibility upon the performer and spectator. In her discussion of Pueblo storytelling, Silko recalls that "everyone, from the youngest child to the oldest person, was expected to listen and be able to tell a portion of, if only a small detail from, a narrative account or story. Thus, the remembering and the retelling were a communal process" ("Interior," 9). As an extension of Native American storytelling, Native theatre continues the practice of invoking the listener's responsibility. Through storying's gathering of multiple voices, Native American dramaturgy also reflects Brecht's concern with the specific relationships between people and society. Consequently, multi-vocal authenticity and Brecht's historicization challenge "the presumed neutrality of any historical reflection" while promoting "both unofficial histories and unofficial historians" (Diamond, *Unmaking Mimesis*, 50).

As Diamond grapples with contemporary implications of Brecht's historicization upon audience members, her theories parallel Native American concepts of communal truth. She states, "In historicized performances gaps are not to be filled in, seams and contradictions show in all their roughness, and therein lies one aspect of spectatorial pleasure – when our differences *from* the past and *within* the present are palpable, graspable, possibly applicable" (ibid.). She then extends Brecht's theory to investigate how the body and desire function within historicization and how these material signs are read by audiences (ibid., 52). Specifically, Diamond is interested in how bodies become sites for reading meaningful information. She states that, "If feminist theory sees the body as culturally mapped and gendered, Brechtian historicization insists that this body is not a fixed essence but a site of struggle and change" (ibid.). Such a perspective works to undo the objectification of certain performers who are often fetishized by mass-media representations.

Although Diamond speaks specifically about the objectification of female performers, her criticism is equally pertinent to male and female Native American performers whose bodies are "read" as "Indian" through endless veils of stereotypes mass-marketed through generations of Indian characters in theatre, film, television, and popular literature. Diamond explains:

If feminist theory is concerned with the multiple and complex signs of a woman's life – her desires and politics, her class, ethnicity, or race – what I want to call her *historicity*, Brechtian theory gives us a way to put that historicity in view – in the theatre. In its conventional iconicity, theatre laminates body to character, but the body in historicization stands visibly and palpably separate from the "being" of the actor as well as the role of the character; it is always insufficient and open. (ibid.)

In Native theatre, the gathering of various, often contradictory, perspectives expressed through Native stories extends into the gathering of physical images presented by the playwright, the characters, the actors' bodies, and the audience members' various expectations. Audience members not only perceive the gaps between versions of stories (especially versions of history), but also confront the spaces between character and actor. In Native American theatre, this confrontation usually extends to revealing incongruities between the actors' bodies and the many stereotypical representations that historically marked theatrical characters as "Indian." Diamond describes this perspective as "a polyvalence to the body's representation, for the performer's body is also *historicized*, loaded with its own history and that of the character, and these histories roughen the smooth edges of the image, of representation" (ibid.). The activity of critically viewing the multiplicity on stage, however, is not an activity that spectators can control. Because multi-vocal authenticity fractures authority, actors engage in the process of constructing meaning. Witnessing in character, Native actors break the fourth wall to directly present to their audiences these layered accounts of personal and theatrical stories. Diamond states, "Looking at the character, the spectator is constantly intercepted by the subject/actor, and the latter, heeding no fourth wall, is theoretically free to look back," and in such a triangle "no one side signifies authority, knowledge, or the law" (ibid., 54). With no localized point of authority, multi-vocal authenticity gives way to a communal truth that must be constructed by actors and viewers beyond the world of the play.

The process by which tribalography generates material effects can be seen in the stage directions and performances of *Rever-ber-berations*, *The Strength of Indian Women*, and *Ernestine Shuswap*. Spiderwoman's stories of spirituality, Manuel's characters' stories of the boarding school, and Highway's characters' stories of the Laurier Memorial put communal truth into action when they relate history within the theatre. Manuel's elders become historians as they stand downstage center delivering testimony to one another and their live audience. In turn, audience members' critical perspectives are stimulated. For some audience members, the elders' stories are added to a continuous bundle of boarding-school stories spiraling through their own histories. For other viewers, as Howe explains, "the events that happened at government boarding schools, both in Canada and the U.S., are often difficult for non-Indians to hear. They've never read about the boarding-school era in their history textbooks, and if it wasn't written down, perhaps it wasn't real" ("Tribalography," 123–124). NAWPA audience members reacted to Manuel's "unofficial historians" in various ways. Some viewers believed the stories of abuse were exaggerated. One non-Native audience member was offended, for she perceived the play to be about her religious institution, rather than the survivors of boarding schools. She questioned Manuel's choice to associate the residential school within the Catholic Church and worked to redeem her religion, imploring audience members to "remember the good things" done by the Catholics (Manuel, Post-performance).

Within Native American theatre, the incongruities between views of personal/public, history/story, historian/witness begin to construct communal truth as theatregoers seek to add their own perspectives to the gaps and ambiguities they perceive. When audience members attempt to locate their own places within the circles of stories, communal truth gives way to collective creation. Similar to Muriel Miguel's description of storytelling, the characters' stories fall as circles that sometimes overlap and at other times land far apart. Viewers, then, begin adding their own stories to the bundle in an attempt to locate knowledge and their own positions within the gathering of voices. Since communal truth stresses that reality resides within the gaps between narrative accounts, Native American plays invite a continual play of stories. Likewise, according to the concept of story cosmos, if spoken words exist eternally, then all stories of all time are continually at play. There is no one history, no one fiction; there is only the communal truth playing within the gaps and contradictions.

Significantly, multi-vocal authenticity in Native American theatrical performances often moves beyond the subject of the play to implicate the present community of actors and spectators gathered for it. Tribalography, then, is truly achieved when the members of the audience are moved to join their stories with the stories of the play in order to collectively create something new. Commissioned specifically for the Kamloops community, Highway wrote *Ernestine Shuswap* for the explicit purpose of creating such change. The play's first director, David Ross, stated in the program's notes, "It is our hope that this play will make some contribution to a resolution of the land claim issues that have plagued British Columbia for more than a century" (Highway, "*Ernestine* Study Guide"). We locate Ross' hope within the play's final ceremonial actions.

After Delilah Rose "dies," the four women unfurl her veil/tablecloth/river and set the banquet upon it. During this action, which Highway calls a "*truly odd, and very disturbing, combination of funeral and banquet,*" two male voices circulate through the theatre. One is an English voice of the Shuswap Chief, "*ancient, quavering, yet sonorous, like the babble of a brook or Gregorian chant,*" continuing to read the Laurier Memorial; the other voice is the translation, in Shuswap, which Highway associates with the sound of wind (Highway, *Ernestine*, 87). The section of the document we hear reflects Delilah Rose's question, which asks what kind of world will take root upon the land. It reads:

"After a time, when they saw that we might cause trouble if we thought all the land was to be occupied by whites, they set aside small reservations here and there. This was their proposal and we never accepted these reservations as settlement for anything, nor did we sign any papers. They thought we would be satisfied, but we never will be until we get our rights." (ibid.)

With the use of the word "never," the historic Native communities' reaction to the reservations reaches into the present world of land claim issues in the Thompson River region.

Highway continues to blend the boundaries between history and current political issues, characters and audience, Native and non-Native, Native myth and Christian myth as the reading of the Laurier Memorial and the sounds of the river and winds swell. The document records the cultural changes:

"For a long time we did not feel the stealing of our lands very heavily [...] we still had considerable liberty in the way of hunting, fishing, grazing. However, owning to increased settlement, this has changed, and we are becoming more restricted to our reservations which in most places are unfit to maintain us [...] We have also learned lately that the B.C. government claims ownership of our reservations, which means we are landless." (ibid., 88)

Like a priestess in a ritual, Ernestine arrives to deliver a giant trout upon a platter. The women pass it one to another until the fish reaches Delilah Rose, who kneels center stage as if to serve the Great Big Kahoona of Canada. Highway calls for the sceneography to parallel images of Da Vinci's *The Last Supper*, "*with Laurier as Christ and the chiefs as the Apostles*" (ibid.). The stage picture repeats the claims that the Native community has made throughout the play about the Prime Minister, a man whose political power is compared to that of a god. It also juxtaposes this god-like power of Laurier with the Christ-like sacrifice of Delilah Rose/ the land, who gives of herself so peace can prevail and the communities of Kamloops, both Native and non-Native, might have eternal life.

Simon Ortiz writes that the purpose of Native American storying is to "engender life"; it "sustains life, continues it, and creates it. It is this very process that Indian people have depended upon in their most critical times [... Because] of the insistence to keep telling and creating stories, Indian life continues, and it is this resistance against loss that has made that life possible" ("Towards," 258). Highway dramatizes this concept of storying when Ernestine, Isabel, and Annabelle leave Delilah Rose and exit the theatre through the aisles of the audience's space. The physical presence of these Native women from 1910 within the contemporary world of the viewers enacts a Native resistance against loss. The last lines of the play underscore this continuance, as Ernestine relates her fish tale: "Waded in, right over my neck, my head, my hairdo, and got it with my own sharp teeth! (*neighs*)," to which Annabelle replies, "And she'll be fishing in that river till the cows come home" (Highway, *Ernestine*, 90). The last words of defiance, claiming that the Native community will continue to fish in the Thompson River, as they have since time immemorial, are spoken as the women exit the auditorium. No one remains to stop their words or actions. Indeed, in the case of the Western Canada Theatre premiere, the physical presence of many theatregoers, who were themselves members of the surrounding Native communities, bear witness to the continued Native presence and cultural way of life upon the Thompson River. Highway allows that ancestor to have the last word: *"And last-last – the gurgle of a river surfaces, balloons, and fades, rich, evocative, the voice of the land, and blackout"* (ibid.).

Craig Womack argues in *Red on Red* that the belief that Native American stories can change the world is "an element in contemporary Native writing [that] must be continuously explored in building up a national body of literature and criticism – language as invocation that will upset the balance of power, even to the point [...] where stories will be preeminent factors in land redress" (*Red*, 17). Highway's *Ernestine Shuswap* exemplifies this philosophy. His play ends with an invitation to collective creation, a call to redress the land disputes in the Kamloops region. As the houselights come up, Beethoven's "Sonata for Cello, Opus 69 in A-major" plays, a song that – with flowing notes of water – captures *Ernestine Shuswap*'s pain and optimism. On leaving, each audience member receives a copy of the remaining passages of the Laurier Memorial. The document, in the hands of each theatregoer, physically connects the worlds of myth, history, and reality. Each viewer must decide what to do with the paper, and with the story it relates. Their material response is a new creation, a tribalography.

In Spiderwoman Theater's performances, it is the intentional "flaw" the artists weave into each play that invites collective creation. The company also incorporates physicalized historicization. Spiderwoman Theater is known for widening the liberated spaces between character, stereotype, being, and body. Their playing style revels in these fissures, as the artists combat objectification by portraying stereotypical "Indian" roles (such as the "Indian Princesses" in *Winnetou's Snake Oil Show from Wigwam City*) and the roles of non-Natives who physically don the "Indian" stereotypes to "be" Native (such as Muriel Miguel's Aryan "Shamaness" in *Winnetou*). These absurd caricatures are then juxtaposed with serious autobiographical scenes that lay forth the vulnerability and individuality of each sister. By presenting characters that are simply themselves, others that are caricatures of themselves (such as within *Rever-ber-berations'* "Tea Time" scenes), and still others that are imagined characters, Spiderwoman Theater complicates and then plays within the ambiguities created by the layers upon layers of physical historicization.

The way that physical historicization triggers the audience to actively reconcile the differences they perceive amongst representations of characters is readily apparent in Spiderwoman's productions because their plays directly consider identity, a person's placement not only within multiple stories, but also within multiple portrayals of self. In a less overt manner, Manuel's *The Strength of Indian Women* also utilizes such levels of historicization. One example of this occurred when Manuel arrived at the first rehearsal for NAWPA's staged reading of the play. She was shocked to see her cast. Miami University had been unable to recruit enough Native American students to act in the performance. Thus, the initial cast was a combination of mostly non-Native and one or two Native American theatre students. Manuel insisted that Native Americans play all the roles. To meet this need, many of the playwrights at NAWPA quickly assumed responsibility for performing the play.[5]

Manuel's request was more meaningful than a personal desire for Native American actors to play Native American roles. *The Strength of Indian Women* is a gathering of histories by "unofficial historians" who serve as both characters in the play and as witnesses – for each other and for the audience. In this particular performance, communal truth was greatly increased by the presence of Native American actors who could add their own embodied historicization to the play. When NAWPA's reading was finally staged, the testimonies of the characters were delivered by Native American women, many of whom could locate their own families' stories within the story-bundle gathered by Manuel. Furthermore, when standing downstage center, the physical historicization of the performers' bodies took on added significance. Audience members could read the performers' bodies as "Indian women," yet also split character from performer. Unlike Manuel's characters, who shared a common community, the actors who read for the staged reading were women from various Native American communities, backgrounds, and histories. These performers delivered the testimonies of the elders, while their bodies bore simultaneous witness to the possibility of boarding-school experiences beyond the scope of Manuel's characters. Indeed, during the post-performance discussion, each woman who had read for the play mentioned how she was connected to additional accounts of boarding-school atrocities. This splintering encouraged a further multiplication of narratives, an even wider circle of communal truth.

Like Muriel Miguel's gesture of stories branching from her chest, there seemed to be no end to the proliferation of boarding-school stories playing within the spiral of time.

The overwhelming multiplication of boarding-school narratives – those created by Manuel's elders' stories and those carried by each actor – could not escape the critical gaze of the spectators. Howe documents some of the reactions that occurred after the NAWPA staged reading:

In my case, Manuel's story forced me to think about my grandparents, two of my uncles and one aunt, two generations of my family had been placed in federal boarding schools. I know firsthand their stories of the beatings that occurred, their hunger to see family and home, and their desire to escape...As we [Native American performers and audience members] began to tell more stories relating to the churches and missionaries, the non-Indians became defensive...Others began to tell their stories: the Jewish Holocaust, of the horrors of slavery and what was done to African Americans, the hardships that the Italians and the Irish had faced at Ellis Island. What I believe was happening to the non-Indians was that they were threading their lives and experiences into ours. A shift in paradigm, it's generally believed to be the other way around: Indians assimilating into the mainstream. ("Tribalography," 124)

Howe notes that the apparently contradictory stories among the NAWPA audience eventually pulled together into a larger story-bundle, a kind of collective creation.

Communal truth's embrace of gaps, contradictions, and points of comparison inspires the gathering of stories to continue beyond the realm of a play, sometimes formally, as in the case of NAWPA's post-performance discussion, and sometimes informally, in small impromptu gatherings of people. It is, of course, impossible to quantify how frequently Native plays inspire this level of tribalography; however, post-performance discussions do provide effective venues for exploring the way that communal truth gives way to collective creation. Howe's article on tribalography records collective creation occurring on a large scale. In writing about the presentation of Manuel's *The Strength of Indian Women* at NAWPA, Howe states:

If indeed our world is what we, Native people, say it is, acknowledging the wrongs committed against our ancestors is how we speak to future generations. It is exactly what Manuel's play is about. Her story became part of the living theatre connecting everything and everyone. Native and non-Natives continued talking. The conversation moved to another location. We gathered in a kind of council circle before dinner, each one speaking in turn and we talked and talked and talked. Full-blood concerns, mixed-blood concerns, non-Indian concerns, we kept on talking through dinner, until I thought my head was unraveling...[I]n my story, all this interaction, and yes resolution to change our perspectives to change ourselves, to develop new projects together, Indian and non-Indian, began as a result of a native woman's play, a tribalography. (ibid.)

Interestingly, those of us who experienced the collective creation brought about through the presentation of Manuel's play underwent a process that paralleled the play's dramatic action. The conversation began in discord. Then, conflict veered into witnessing. The first testimonies appeared to continue the antagonistic relationship between those who did not believe the residential-school stories and those who knew, often intimately, the truth about such schools. In fact, the early non-Native testimonies of ancestral oppression appeared to be challenges to prove that non-Native people had suffered equal mistreatments. But, as the stories mounted, what began as contrast gave way to points of intersection. Then, when the conversation moved to a dining-room, where the scent of lasagna wafted, our hunger waited for a healing ceremony of sorts to first take place. Artists and audience members arranged chairs in a talking-circle so that all of us could voice our concerns regarding the conference, Native American theatre, the role of NAWPA, scholarship in the field of Native theatre, and our cultural differences. Through the overlapping stories, we searched for our appropriate places within the growing field of Native American theatre. And from this discussion, a community emerged out of what had been anger, pain, and misunderstanding (Manuel, Post-performance).

Glancy writes that she wants "the redundancies and intimacies of language on the page to escape the mouth, enter the ears of other actors and audiences, and to escape again with new words, further words, and on and on, in circular migrations, moving here and there to define our humanity" ("Native American Theater," 361). In effect, tribalography demands that all people present during a play take on the roles of "unofficial historians," who become official through adding their own experiences and perspectives to the communal truth. This continual branching motion of stories is an essential element of Native American theatre, but Native American philosophies of speech involve motions that go beyond the direct transmission of story from speaker to listener. Collective creation also involves unforeseen movements, untraceable movements, movements of chance. Glancy states that, "An important aspect of Native theatre also is the reciprocity of it. *Yourstory* jars loose *theirstory* and *someoneelse's story* jars loose another part of *yourstory*" (ibid., 359). Which stories get jarred loose and how they connect to others can be neither predicted nor adequately traced. How the stories change and what new creations result from their transference cannot be imagined. The perpetual traffic of uncontainable narratives exemplifies the concept of story cosmos and provides an insight into Native American theatre's potential: Native theatre is not merely entertainment – it is creations and transformations. In the following chapters, we will investigate a discourse called "survivance," which allows us to build upon the study of how motion functions in storying in order to explore how theories of radical motion help shape the very characters and actions of Native plays.

CHAPTER 7

Representing uncontainable identities

[Native theatre artists] must work to help untangle the mass of confusions that stereotyping, assimilation, and acculturation have created in the minds of Indians themselves.

Hanay Geiogamah (Kiowa/Delaware), "New American Indian," 163

Most of us, given the opportunity to learn the words, would probably choose "Don't Fence Me In" as our pan-Indian anthem...perhaps crossing boundaries is the first and foremost basis of our tradition and the key to human freedom.

Paula Gunn Allen (Laguna Pueblo), *Off the Reservation*, 12

Most theatrical criticism approaches Native American theatre through critical lenses that investigate how Native American plays challenge stereotypical representations of Indian otherness. These concerns about Native identity, representation, and subject matter do underlie much of the work created by Native American theatre artists; indeed, the playwrights we have explored thus far openly confront such issues. Spiderwoman Theater is famous for lampooning portrayals of Native people in popular culture. In their *Sun, Moon, and Feather*, Lisa and Gloria re-create childhood arguments over who gets to play the leading, red-haired, green-eyed Jeanette McDonald in the girls' re-enactments of the movie *Indian Love Call*. Their conflict exemplifies Hollywood's relegation of Native American characters to the sidelines of Indian-themed movies. Likewise, Spiderwoman's ironic portrayal of "Indian princesses" in *Winnetou's Snake Oil Show from Wigwam City* makes transparent the ridiculous nature of Native women's stereotypes. In Lynn Riggs' *The Cherokee Night* and Tomson Highway's *Ernestine Shuswap*, the playwrights provide detailed stage directions about their characters' clothing. Clearly stating that "*this being 1910, the women are wearing long-sleeved, high-collared white cotton blouses, floor-length black skirts, and moccasins*" allows Highway to prevent any misinterpretations of what Native women living on reservations at the turn of the century looked like (*Ernestine*, 13). JudyLee Oliva addresses the representation of Indianness in *The Fire and the Rose*, when we learn that Joannie faced discrimination from Native and non-Native people who rejected her Native dance and poetry performance as an inauthentic portrayal of Chickasaw identity.

Bruce King explains that even the very subject matter of his plays is often criticized for not adhering to "Indian" topics. He writes, "Those of us practicing theater constantly confront preconceived notions of what Native American people should perform on stage. Most of the time these notions reinforce what others believe Indians should be – sharing, demonstrating, creating, understanding, quaint, colorful and…safe" ("Emergence," 166). In effect, King often feels that his non-Native audience members desire to see their own images of Indianness reflected through his plays. He states, "they ask about pageantry, the sacred dances, the eloquence of historical figures, environmental messages that will save everybody, universal themes and connections reinforcing the brotherhood of man, and cultural bridges to non-Native American people. That, I am told, is what Native Americans should be doing on stage" (ibid., 167). King's accounts demonstrate the need for a critical methodology that can address issues of representation in Native American plays, a methodology that is flexible enough to accommodate the differences across and within Native America. Any theory that seeks to do this must encompass the multi-dimensional nature of Native American cultures, as well as the varied lived experiences of Native theatre artists.

Cultural multi-dimensionality is complicated further in Native American theatre by the unique dramaturgical elements within the plays themselves, where the deconstruction and reclamation of cultural images rarely occurs in a linear, cause-and-effect manner. Similar to other Native dramaturgical concepts, the processes by which Native artists resist stereotypical representations remain unfixed. Likewise, their constructions of individual Native American identities reflect dynamism. Native plays express this fluidity in many ways. For example, the discourse of storying posits that once a story is told, it can splinter outward from speaker to listeners, jarring loose *their* stories, which – in turn – multiply in new directions to other listeners. Such a network of endless connections and further directions incorporates elements of unpredictability, uncontainability, and chance. The quality of chance relates to the natural world through the endless splintering of genetic combinations, mutations, and re-creations. In some Native American plays, the natural element of chance even extends from the physical to the spiritual realm, allowing for humans and non-humans to communicate (such as when Muriel Miguel's father visited her during the Sun Dance within a vision of a cloud). In Native American dramaturgy, these representations of uncontainable boundaries, which reflect concepts expressed in language and time, can extend to physical bodies and make transformations possible. These metamorphoses in Native plays highlight the significance of motion.

The propensity of motion in Native American dramaturgy challenges scholars in this field to implement critical approaches capable of recognizing the destabilization of stereotypes, providing space for the emergence of dynamic self-images, and engaging with the liminal moments of transformations and metamorphoses that often underlie politicized actions within Native American plays. Paula Gunn Allen argues that any critical perspective geared toward a Native aesthetic of changeability should possess the ability to flow with the transformations, rather than simply become spellbound by the fact that such transformations occur. Allen states:

Some of the more bowdlerized accounts of American Indian mystical experiences treat them from a Western point of view, giving the impression that these states are uncommon, eerie, superlatively extraordinary, and characterized by abnormal states of unconsciousness. But tribal testaments indicate otherwise: paranormal events are accepted as part of normal experience – even expected under ritual circumstances. It is just that few of these events are recorded by white observers, largely because Western sophisticates are unprepared to accept the events, or the person who recounts them, with equanimity. (*Off*, 44)

Thus, any critical perspective fashioned to address Allen's concern would ideally not fixate on the transformative events themselves, but rather accept such motions as part of the aesthetic. Such a perspective would allow readers and viewers of Native plays to examine not what, but how transformative events work to create meaning.

Scholars of Native American theatre have used different approaches to critically address Native representations and transformations, but predominantly these inquiries derive from post-colonial theories that can overlook certain essential elements of Native American theatrical self-representation. Such theories often concentrate on Native aesthetic challenges to stereotypical representations of Indianness, for these images of Native American peoples – from the staged photographs of Edward Curtis to Chief Wahoo[1] and today's other "Indian" mascots – come under heavy fire from Native playwrights and performers, as illustrated by DeLanna Studi's tour of *Kick*, Peter Howard's educational play about the Indian mascot debate. While post-colonial theories offer a way to begin an investigation of how Native American artists deconstruct stereotypes, relying solely upon post-colonial perspectives for understanding Native American literature and performance presents a danger, because such theories threaten to erase the significance of Native American intellectual traditions within artistic works. To situate Native American plays within a post-colonial paradigm continually positions their critical significance in a dependent relationship with the European invasion and its aftermath, while also diminishing the unique attributes of Native dramaturgy. This is because post-colonial theories work in a binary manner that investigates how "marginalized" peoples work to regain control of self-images. The discourse cannot exist without the binary oppositions of colonized/colonizer; thus, its meaning becomes dependent upon the very history it seeks to destabilize. Furthermore, due to the way in which post-colonial theories dissect communal histories into a three-phase system (pre-colonial, colonial, and post-colonial) that hinges upon the colonial invasion, there exists an implicit argument that the pre-colonial traditions of a culture are somehow ineffective in the contemporary, or post-colonial, reality. The set of categories leaves little room for the various Native American traditions that artists continue to practice "in spite of colonization" (Thomas King, "Godzilla," 12).

Jace Weaver contends that the theoretical analysis of Native American literature has become a new "critical area for struggle" against colonialism, which one witnesses – especially in the field of Native theatre – when Native intellectual traditions, such as storying, are not *first* viewed as an indigenous enterprise, with or without the effects of conquest. While it would be naive to claim that acts of colonialism have not affected the choices of Native American theatre artists, an over-dependence upon post-colonial theories to read Native plays is equally simplistic. The pre/post-colonial binary is too fixed and unambiguous to adequately address the inherent complexities and uncontainable creations of identities that emerge from the ancient traditions of Native storying to take their physical presence upon the Native American stage.

To imagine pre-contact mythology and epistemologies within the literature of contemporary Native American authors from the United States, Canada, and Latin America,[2] some scholars of Native literature have turned to the genre of magical realism to theoretically speak about works that address issues of representation, embrace multiplicity, and also foreground the transformations often included in Native works. Alan Velie, a leading scholar in the field of Native American literature, is one of the first theorists who suggested the use of magical realism to critically approach Native American novels. He argues that magical realism presents a "coexistence of Indian and European viewpoints" that allows Native American novelists to introduce "apparently supernatural events into a realistic setting in order to demonstrate the value of reality as perceived by Indians" (Velie, "Magical Realism," 60, 61). The significance of Velie's reading is the way in which he uses theory to acknowledge a "reality as perceived by Indians," one that considers the relationships between individuals and their communities, people and their environments, and humans and non-humans (spirits or animals). This perspective reflects the roots of *lo real maravilloso*, as developed by Alejo Carpentier, a Cuban novelist and theorist whose conception of "marvelous reality" drew heavily on South American indigenous concepts of land and mythology.[3] Such perspectives provide contexts for recognizing transformations as indicators of cultural elements in dramatic texts, but they encounter difficulties when we apply them to theatrical performance. Most obviously, the concept of magical realism confronts a conceptual redundancy in an art-form that depends on the audience's suspension of disbelief in order for viewers to buy into whatever construction of "reality" that is before them. This basic theatrical convention occurs as strongly in other styles of theatrical performance as it does in the presentation of theatrical realism, a genre in which few Native American dramatists write.

While post-colonial theories encounter limitations when addressing the independence of Native American philosophies, and the mode of magical realism meets with frustration when applied to theatrical performance, there does exist a gathering of theories, rooted in Native intellectual traditions, that provides an important and effective critical point of entry into contemporary Native theatre's portrayals of self-images and transformations. As articulated by Gerald Vizenor, an Anishinaabe novelist, poet, and philosopher, the word *survivance* becomes an umbrella term to speak about the doubled action of honoring Native intellectual traditions while moving in critically deconstructive manners. Vizenor uses survivance to address the unique attributes of Native American aesthetics, which are often – at once – activist, experimental, fluctuating, diverse, and traditional. He defines survivance as the combination of Native resistance (to stereotypical representations and reductive studies) and survival (continuance of traditions splintering into the ever-changing, multi-dimensional lived experiences of contemporary Native peoples). He states:

Survivance, in my use of the word, means a native sense of presence, the *motion of sovereignty* and the will to resist dominance. Survivance is not just survival but also resistance, not heroic or tragic, but the tease of traditions, and my sense of survivance outwits dominance and victimry. *Survival* is a response; *survivance* is a standpoint, a worldview, and a presence. (Vizenor and Lee, *Postindian*, 93; emphasis added)

Vizenor's theory of survivance offers to Native American theatre scholars a crucial methodology with which to approach those unique attributes of Native dramaturgy that deconstruct stereotypical images through Native concepts of motion.

Vizenor draws a direct correlation between motion and Native American sovereignty, or independence, when he proclaims that "Native sovereignty is the right of motion" (*Fugitive*, 182). Part of this correlation derives from the troubled history of Native American and federal government relations.[4] One of the most obvious ways the federal government dealt with Native American peoples' resistance to invasion and colonization was through physical containment. The freedom of Native peoples' movement was restricted, first by borders between "civilized" and "frontier" lands and then by the more specifically defined boundaries of reservations. Next, the movement of Native peoples was limited further to land allotments within those reservations and, finally, to urban ghettos by means of "relocation" programs that promised city jobs to youths from destitute reservations. In addition to these literal restrictions on mobility, the government imposed limits on the metaphorical movement of Native Americans.[5] An overt example of this form of metaphorical containment can be seen in the relationship between tribal and federal law. Although Native American nations are called "sovereign," or self-governing, the federal government restricts their independence by also classifying them as "domestic dependant nations." This dependant status is highlighted in cases when Native American people have gained rights but must continue to fight in order to realize them. For example, the 1995 Native American Graves Protection and Repatriation Law (which requires museums to return to their original Native nations Native American human remains, sacred objects, cultural patrimony, and funerary objects) places the entire responsibility for locating, identifying, and proving rights to these objects on individual Native American nations (Peter Jemison, "Repatriation Law"). Due to the doubled physical and metaphorical restriction upon Native American sovereignty, Vizenor locates motion – the ability to cross physical and figurative borders – as the crux of Native resistance and continued survival. More importantly, Vizenor defines the many journeys, transformations, trickster actions, and metamorphoses that reoccur throughout Native American stories as an intellectual tradition of Native sovereign motion, a tradition celebrated in Native cultures since time immemorial.

Vizenor's discourse of survivance incorporates three conceptual strands of motion: mythic, material, and visionary. Together, these strands work to achieve what Vizenor calls *personal sovereignty*. Personal sovereignty extends the concept of national sovereignty to address the individual's realization and will to self-governance, opportunity to establish self-representation, and choice to select or reflect elements of Native traditions within the ever-changing context of one's personal life.

"Mythic Motions" connects loosely to theories of deconstruction. In Vizenor's critical methodology, Native trickster figures are characters who open critical perspectives. By relying upon the mythic trickster tradition, Vizenor shows how Native American actions of deconstruction were born from pre-existing Native practices, not out of a reaction to colonialism. "Material Motion" relates to how Native Americans enact resistance against future classifications, which can lead to stereotypes, by creating art and identities that defy easy categorizations. For example, Native humor, stories, and journeys often utilize unpredictable motions – twists and turns – that work to evade fixity. Lastly, "Visionary Motion/Transmotion" blends the previous two conceptual strands of motion with the discourse of storying and concept of worlds of existence in order to envision personal sovereignty. Vizenor's term *transmotion* signifies an extreme idea of in-betweenness that allows for the criss-crossing and intermingling of individuals, events, places, worlds of existence, species, and stories. He uses the term *visionary motion* to refer to a person's ability to apply the concept of transmotion to him- or herself in order to achieve a critical positioning that defies limitations. Visionary motion allows people to first imagine and then realize their personal sovereignty. Significantly, these three conceptual strands of motion correlate directly to Native American dramaturgy.

Vizenor does not use survivance to analyze Native American theatre, yet his emphasis on motion offers an ideal perspective for not only addressing the depictions of transformations within Native American dramaturgy, but also for imagining the transference of these metamorphosis-rich scripts onto the stage. Indeed, tricksters and mythic figurers populate the dramatic landscape of Native American theatre. They receive top billing in Native play titles such as Sharon Shorty's (Tlingit) *Trickster Visits the Old Folks Home*, Darrell Dennis' *The Trickster of Third Avenue East*, and Native American Theatre Ensemble/Geiogamah's *Coon Cons Coyote*. Their humor shapes entire play series, such as Drew Hayden Taylor's collection of *Blues* plays. Mythological figures teach children about their heritage in Joseph Bruchac's plays; and in Armand Ruffo's *A Windigo Tale*, they provide metaphors for adults attempting to understand tragedy. In Spiderwoman Theater, which passes its style of humor through the generations to Monique Mojica and Murielle Borst, sacred clowns loosen the audience's inhibitions through laughter that opens viewers to receive the serious messages presented in the plays. In Bruce King's *Evening at the Warbonnet*, the realization of trickster characters presents plot twists. Tomson Highway and Daniel David Moses, two playwrights who imagined the trickster to be an ideal figure for Native American literary expression, in half-jest created "the Committee to Re-establish the Trickster" in order to draw audiences to Native peoples' literary works.[6] Of course, Highway's fame as a playwright comes from two plays, *The Rez Sisters* and *Dry Lips*, that feature shape-shifting tricksters who balance the respective female and male perspectives presented in each play. Vizenor's survivance offers an effective critical entry into all of these dramatic works, but to demonstrate the discourse I have selected three one-act plays: Hanay Geiogamah's *Foghorn*, Diane Glancy's *The Woman Who Was a Red Deer Dressed for the Deer Dance*, and Marie Clements' *Urban Tattoo*. All three dramatize politicized resistance to representations while also employing elements of motion that critically unfix identities.

Geiogamah's *Foghorn* is the most overtly political of the three plays. Written in 1973 for the American Indian Theater Ensemble (AITE),[7] *Foghorn* articulates the concerns of Native American activists during the AIM's rise to notability. In 1973, many AIM members were on trial for events stemming from their having occupied Wounded Knee as a gesture of support for Pine Ridge Oglala Lakota traditionals seeking protection against the violence taking place at Pine Ridge. Trouble on the reservation had started when land rights guaranteed by the 1868 Fort Laramie Treaty were rejected.

In addition to addressing the political events of its time, *Foghorn* functions as a compact version of American history from a Native American perspective. The play's episodic plot works to present a Native journey spiraling through time. Some episodes depict the history of colonization, such as Columbus' "discovery" of the new world's "Indians," the Christian crusades to save the "savages," and boarding-school atrocities. Other episodes satirically portray legendary figures – Pocahontas, Tonto, and wild-west warriors – but the majority of the episodes depict the political actions that AIM engaged in to foreground injustices against Native Americans. These include: the 1969–1970 occupation of Alcatraz Island; the 1972 Trail of Broken Treaties; the 1972 occupation of Washington's Bureau of Indian Affairs Office; the 71-day siege on Wounded Knee; and the Wounded Knee II court cases. Significantly, these trials occurred simultaneously with the first performances of *Foghorn*.[8]

Between 1973 and 1974, *Foghorn* had a number of significant productions. AITE premiered the play in West Berlin at Germany's Theater im

Reichskabarett. The US premiere was in 1974 at La Mama Experimental Theater Club in New York City,[9] after which AITE toured *Foghorn* across the country.[10] In the field of Native American theatre, *Foghorn* has achieved the status of a classic, published first in 1980 and again in 2000. Geiogamah's continued presence and activism in the development of US Native American theatre, in concert with *Foghorn*'s rich history as a theatrical companion piece to the Red Power Movement, gives the play its rightful, classic status. *Foghorn* is one of Native theatre's touchstones, for it is intersected by: the events of the Red Power Movement; the struggles of AIM; the history of early Native American theatre companies; the relationship between Native theatre and American experimental theatre; the emergence of Hanay Geiogamah as a leading Native theatre artist; the early careers of other Native theatre artists; and international recognition of Native American theatre and political issues.

As much as *Foghorn* serves as a touchstone for the nascent Native American theatre movement of the 1970s and 1980s, Marie Clements' *Urban Tattoo* is a touchstone for the diversity of work occurring in the current, professional Native American theatre in both the United States and Canada. Clements collaborated with Native Voices in 1994, the first year that Native Voices co-founders Randy Reinholz and Jean Bruce Scott organized the festival for staged readings of Native American plays. Out of the three plays workshopped by Native Voices that year, Clements' *Now Look What You Made Me Do* was selected for Illinois State University's 1995–1996 main-stage season. The play was subsequently performed for the American College Theater Festival's Evening of Scenes in Ohio's Riffe Center.

In 1996, Clements joined with Native Voices again, this time to workshop *Urban Tattoo*, her one-woman, multi-media play with music and dance/movement. This physically demanding play that Clements performs was first presented off-Broadway at the American Indian Community House. The production was part of the Native Voices in New York festival. As a play-developing organization, Native Voices worked with Clements to conceptualize how multi-media elements – video, slides, and music – might be incorporated into the poetic, movement-based script. The New York workshop utilized minimal staging, relying upon Clements to create the transformations physically and vocally from moment to moment as Reinholz, the production's director, read stage directions that indicated where video and slides would appear. Full production elements were incorporated in the 1999 production, when Native Voices paired with Los Angeles' Autry Museum of Western

Heritage. *Urban Tattoo* "was chosen to complement the Autry's exhibit *Powerful Images: Portraits of Native America*. The Autry wanted a theater piece that would cause people to confront the stereotype of the 'American Indian as a figure frozen in time'" (Reinholz and Scott, "Native Voices," 275). The success of *Urban Tattoo* gained critical recognition by *LA Weekly*, which named Clements' performance "pick of the week" (Hernandez, Review, 82). With such success, a Native American play development partnership, renamed Native Voices at the Autry, officially began in 2000.[11] Beyond her collaboration with Native Voices, Clements works independently as a Native playwright based in British Columbia. She has shared her success with others, founding urban ink productions, a First Nations theatre company dedicated to creating new interdisciplinary, multi-media performances, and also its offshoot, Fathom Labs, that accelerates the creation and promotion of Native works. In 2005, Native Voices commissioned her to write *Tombs of the Vanishing Indian*. Clements' edgy works bring multi-dimensional aesthetics to social issues that the playwright dissects with an unflinching gaze.

Clements' *Urban Tattoo* has a post-modern sensibility that intermingles prose, poetry, and music with a collage of still and moving video images that project behind and upon Clements' body as she transitions from pedestrian to dance-like movements. It is a play deeply entrenched in the trickster tradition. Rosemarie, a young Metis woman, moves from her rural, Native community to the city of Edmonton in order to earn money for her family. The plot traces Rosemarie's journey from innocent child-dreamer to poor, urban, Native woman and to independent survivor. Throughout the play, Raven, the trickster, appears periodically to take over Rosemarie's voice when she is unable to move forward. This convention makes the play rich with metamorphosis, which the audience witnesses when Clements' physical movements and voice transition between Rosemarie and Raven. Due to the performance-specific qualities of *Urban Tattoo*, my discussion and analysis of the play reference the play's typescript and two live productions, the 1996 New York performance and a 1999 performance sponsored by NAWPA.[12]

Similar to Clements' wide-ranging visual-aesthetic scope, Diane Glancy's writing draws from various literary styles. Her artistic and theoretical works are known for enacting literary experimentations in the vein of Gertrude Stein. Theatrically, Glancy pushes boundaries both of representations of Native American identities and structures of dramatic plots. Her play *The Woman Who Was a Red Deer Dressed for the Deer Dance* is no exception. Glancy describes it as "a dialogue/monologue between a grandmother and her granddaughter, each arguing against the other for her way of life" ("Author's Statement," 275). She explains:

I think *The Woman Who Was a Red Deer Dressed for the Deer Dance* is an example of Native spoken-word art. The poetic piece is an intermixing of ethnographic material (the story of *Ahw'uste*), with pieces of the old language (Cherokee), and with contemporary materials (the granddaughter's life in the soup kitchen and dance bars)…I want to work more with experimental poetics in a combination of fiction, poetry, myth/magic/ethnography, and the drama of Indian life in the harsh reality of poverty and commodities in the urban/reservation life. (ibid., 271)

Elements of survivance weave throughout Glancy's *Red Deer* as the two characters – Girl and Grandmother, both separated by a line painted on the stage floor – shift between monologues and dialogue, interaction and direct-audience address, storytelling and conversation. The two characters enter-tain two very different worldviews. Grandmother exists in a world shaped by her faith in the power of Ahw'uste, a small, mythical deer that connects humans to the spirit world. Conversely, Girl functions in the world of observable reality, relying on her daily work – not stories – for survival. Girl invests her spirit in male companionship rather than in visions of Ahw'uste. As a whole, the play investigates how spiritual traditions function within the harsh conditions of poor, urban Native populations. It also points to the importance of creating an individualized belief system out of the communal stories and mythical figures of one's culture.

TRICKY DISCOURSE

Before we examine how Vizenor's theories can serve as a critical approach to Native American theatre, it is important to address some of the aspects central to his work, in particular, how Vizenor's theoretical and artistic writings often resonate with Native American trickster figures, Jean Baudrillard's theories of simulacra, and Vizenor's own concept of the post-indian. *Postindians* are Vizenor's answer to post-colonial theories. Simply stated, postindians are diverse, contemporary Native American people who are enacting survivance within a world that has been inundated with fixed representations of Indianness. Vizenor's fierce literary theories weave together postindians, tricksters, and the analysis of simulacra to create the critical context for his discourse of survivance.

Shaped by both Native American traditional and post-modern philo-sophical influences, Vizenor's novels and essays wrestle with issues of Native

American representation within a rhetorical space that can accommodate the dynamic intricacies of multi-cultural and multi-dimensional Native realities. Two crucial questions often underlie Vizenor's theoretical explorations. The first asks: how does one "reimagine if need be, each tribal culture as situated within its own lived time-space and calendar," its own trickster and creation figures, its own religion and myth, "its own sumptuous, performative oral legacy of ceremony and story?" (Lee, "Introduction," 7). The second question, rooted in the answer of the first, asks: once individual tribal cultures are reimagined as diverse and contemporary, how are "cultural hybrids" – those created not only through genetics, but also through language, geography, and consciousness – to be understood? (ibid.). Vizenor's answers derive from the way he characterizes the history of how Indianness has been represented.

Throughout his writings, Vizenor visually presents the term, Indian, ironically, in lower-case, italicized letters: *indian.*[13] He claims that in order to reimagine Native peoples, one must first address the notion of what *indian* is and what *indian* means. To support his assessment, Vizenor turns to post-modern theories. He starts by looking at the name, Indian, and uses semiotics to explain that the signifier is arbitrarily connected to the signified, that the term *indian* has nothing to do with the people who first populated the Americas. The indigenous inhabitants of this continent did not see themselves as one cohesive people but as distinctly different peoples of many nations. However, upon Columbus' both geographically and culturally misinformed utterance of the word, Indian, hundreds of diverse nations were collapsed into a single category created by outsiders. In accordance with deconstructivist theories, these diverse individuals are "traces" of dynamic Native lives that the transcendental signifier, Indian, ignores. Vizenor turns to Baudrillard's theories of simulacra to argue that the created idea of *indian* not only overshadowed the reality and diversity of individual Native peoples, but that this abstraction – with the help of academics, politicians, activists, the media, and even Native American people themselves – also continued to grow beyond Columbus' first mistaken categorization of Native peoples. Thus, Vizenor borrows Baudrillard's discussion of simulacra to define what *indian* means to him:

The *indian* is the invention, and *indian* cultures are simulations, that is, the ethnographic construction of a model that replaces the real in most academic references. Natives are the real, the ironies of the real, and an unnamable sense of presence, but simulations are the absence, and so the *indian* is an absence, not a presence...[T]he simulations of the other have no real origin, no original reference, and there is no real place on this continent that bears the meaning of that name. The *indian* was simulated to be an absence, to be without a place. (Vizenor and Lee, *Postindian*, 85)

According to this theory, when people buy into the construction of the *indian*, they erase the real presence of Native peoples' identities. This happens because the *indian*, the abstraction, is built upon an ideology of stereotypes which limits the diversity of Native peoples in several ways: by grouping Native nations into a single ethnic category; by viewing Native Americans through defined binaries (noble/savage); by forbidding Native peoples to function in a post-modern world because of their supposed unbending adherence to pre-conquest traditions; or by locking Native peoples into a story of victimization, cultural eradication, and absence. Vizenor calls these fixed stereotypes "simulations of dominance," and he claims that many contemporary studies contribute to the construction of these creations when they work to erase the ambiguities of culture and identity. He argues:

Clearly the seams that need to be loosened were sewn too tightly. The irony here, the cultural irony, is that the seams are simulations of dominance. The seams are sewn over and over by social scientists and other inventors of the American Indian. And the invention is a conservative, national allegory of cultural difference and distinction. The seams get even tighter as more studies are conducted to eliminate all of the loose ends and ambiguities, and to explain away every doubt and nuance. (ibid., 79)

Neither the good intentions of the social theorists nor the positive-versus-negative values of *indian* simulations matter: they all lead to the absence of Native peoples. Vizenor provides an example of the link between simulations and absence in a discussion of Hollywood. Speaking of the legacy of cinema's presentation of Native peoples as savage, then as romantic, and finally as war heroes, he argues, "Reversed civilizations or not, we know what happens to *indians* at the end of movies. They vanish, as the tragic simulations of *indians* must do in the movies, because their absence is better understood than their presence" (ibid., 157).

According to Vizenor, the simulacra of *indian* are also a continuation of the historical process of physical eradication *and confinement* of Native Americans. These ideological boundaries work to trap Native dynamism when physical boundaries have failed. Vizenor argues that "manifest destiny" depended as much (or more) upon the restriction of Native American dynamism and sovereignty as it depended upon the actual "clearing" of lands for non-Native settlers moving west. The need for absence was more philosophical than literal:

Natives were represented in narratives, and in the comparative notions of race, but not in the foundational sense of the nation. The reasons of vindication were aesthetic; natives were named in connection with the vast distances of unexploited nation, and as a potential threat to the government. Natives…had negotiated treaties and formed alliances with other governments; these associations were considered to be dangerous to the new constitutional democracy. Natives, in other words, were removed as vindication of the environment. The *absence* of the *indian* in the histories of this nation is an aesthetic victimry. (Vizenor, *Fugitive*, 12)

Myths of victimry focused on Native American peoples residing in the west, those whom the American government had fewer interactions with and less knowledge of, allowing for easier classifications of savagery. This western focus worked to overshadow (and thus erase) America's knowledge of Native diversity and sovereignty, especially the sovereignty of eastern Native American nations with whom the United States and other countries had previously engaged in "civilized" nation-to-nation negotiations. What followed was a pattern of US policies working to confine Native American peoples both physically and ideologically. These are doubled boundaries that Vizenor works against. A. Robert Lee Explains:

Vizenor, moreover, has steadfastly refused to buy into the "Vanishing American" ethos. This he identifies as a mix of romanticized victimry and belief in "Indians" as fixed (heroically or otherwise) first into a frontier or wilderness past, then in reservations and increasingly in cities he calls "urban exclaves," but always, and throughout, denied anything resembling their own unabating human variousness. (Vizenor and Lee, *Postindian*, 4)

Instead, Vizenor addresses the material ramifications of imagined *indians*. For this rhetorical action he relies upon motion. He argues that since the name, Indian, and the simulacra associated with it contribute to the creation of fixed boundaries, then a different process of naming can allow Native peoples to reclaim dynamic identities beyond static limits. If *indians* are "absence, victim, fixed," Vizenor's reply is that postindians are presence, survivors, continual flux. To resist the simulations Vizenor offers many alternatives, the first of which is to enter resistance through reclaiming the original names of Native nations, which bespeak individuality and sover-eignty. He explains, "the semantic slaves bear that name, the *indian*, and at the same time, the name invites our evasion and resistance. So the post-indian names, in an ironic sense, are the actual names of native creation, such as *anishinaabe*, that transpose the *indian* simulations" (ibid., 156). By reclaiming names that are native creations, Native peoples break the façade created by the single term *indian*.[14]

Vizenor, though, goes beyond naming to resist the simulation of the *indian*. His other methods of defiance build upon upsetting the naming process through concepts of perpetual motion. These methods of resistance – humor, chance, nature, tricksters, stories, visions, liberation – all disregard established limitations. Instead, they embrace the essence of being unbound, incapable of capture, unnamable. Praising the tactics used by the playwright Samuel Beckett, Vizenor states:

Beckett teases the silence, the absence, and he overturns the dead voices as he creates an unnamable sense of presence in his plays. I stand with him on stage...I write out of silence, and the unnamable, and the chance to create characters in the nick of time to hear me. Beckett is my obligation to say something, to go on...We must go on. Silence is the tricky start, not the end of our stories. (ibid., 142)

In Vizenor's critical analysis, the silence – or absence – of Native peoples occurs as a result of categorizing which can only happen when the object – in this case, human beings – is motionless long enough to fit within the boundaries created by a category. Once this happens, the category – the simulation – speaks for the people, rather than the people speaking for themselves. To combat this, postindians must resist being captured by definitions or theories that limit their diversity and individuality. One way to not get captured by semantic traps is to move.

It is not surprising that a key player in this game of escaping categories is the Native American mythical trickster, who Vizenor defines as "a liberator and healer, a comic sign, communal signification and a discourse with imagination...a language game in a comic narrative" ("Trickster Discourse," 187). The trickster is a character, from traditional Native American stories, who opens pathways of critical action through his utter freedom of motion, both physical and visionary.[15] Like the imagination, tricksters wander freely, unbound by place, time, or ideology. They personify Native American concepts of movement, transformations, metamorphoses, and chance.[16] In the south-western United States, Trickster is often a coyote; in the north-west, a raven. However, Trickster is not bound by these physical forms. He can transform from animal to human – demonstrating the equality between humans and animals – and from male to female and back again – demonstrating gender equality. The tricksters of Native American oral mythologies are both creative and destructive: Trickster can re-create the world after the great flood and then create disruption by making the once two-way rivers run in a single direction. Often, Trickster displays an insatiable appetite for food. In the pursuit of such desires, Trickster can be both the hero of some stories and the butt of the joke in others. When Trickster's antics lead to his/her death, she/he lives again in the next story.[17] In short, Trickster demonstrates the vast range of social behavior. While trickster stories do teach lessons about the importance of self-elected limits on otherwise unrestrained actions, the stories neither preach absolute versions of good and evil nor suppress the investigation of actions taken to extremes. Instead, they work to reveal the ultimate possibilities of human existence. Thus, tricksters demonstrate the fluidity across the boundaries of the natural and the visionary/spiritual worlds, and so exhibit the vast potential of individual Native American identities.

Reclaiming these trickster actions, Native American artists create new stories, which are comic in the sense that they do not end in tragic absence but, instead, with survival and active resistance. Vizenor learned trickster stories from his cultural heritage and later discovered how the trickster figure modeled critical methods to enact his own survival and resistance:

Naturally, the tease of Naanabozho, the *anishinaabe* trickster in stories, was my best teacher in motion, for a time, but the trickster comes to naught, evermore a transmutation, and that was never enough for me. So my stories in *Earthdivers* loosen the seams and outwit the weavers of terminal cultures [people who see Native peoples as victims doomed to vanish]. *That, a trickster hermeneutics, and a tease of presence, is my sense of native creation and survivance.* (Vizenor and Lee, *Postindian*, 81; emphasis added)

For Vizenor, it is not just the trickster, but trickster methodology expressed through this tease of presence/absence – now you see me, now you don't – and derived from his capacity for shape-shifting that creates Native identities incapable of becoming bound by definitions or held by stereotypes. This mutable presence bespeaks survival because it is capable of movement, dynamism, vision, and action. Moving traces of presence – as opposed to an unambiguous, stationary absence – resist cultural completion and, subsequently, the fate of vanishing behind endless reproductions of simulations.

One other element that teaches people to avoid stagnation through transformations is the role of chance within nature, which Vizenor also emphasizes as a contributing factor to Native presence. Because of nature's unpredictable qualities, he likens it to a game of chance. Vizenor states, "Nature is tricky, a constant tease, and even the most obvious native traces of the seasons are creative sensations, a chance of stories" (ibid., 65). This raw creative energy, rather than energy that merely re-creates and simulates, is where Vizenor locates "the real." He argues that Native peoples' survivance depends upon presenting this reality, which – like tricksters, nature, chance, and visions – cannot be bound and simulated. Vizenor's creative and theoretical writings are his contribution to presenting the real. He calls these writings "trickster stories" and speaks of their power, stating, "Trickster stories break out of the heavy burdens of tradition with a tease of action and a sense of chance. That, then, is the threshold of native survivance" (ibid., 60).

The plays we will examine in the following chapter represent "trickster stories" for the theatre. Although different in both style and purpose, they all model trickster actions that draw from nature, chance, visions, and humor. Ranging from the 1970s Red Power Movement through the late 1990s, these plays model the trickster's ability to shift with the historical moment in order to arise anew in boundless forms of Native creations.

CHAPTER 8

Acts of survivance in
Native American drama

In trickster narratives the listeners and readers imagine their liberation;
the trickster is a sign and the world is "deconstructed" in a discourse.
Gerald Vizenor (Anishinaabe), "Trickster Discourse," 194

[A] healing…takes place on stage, in the audience, and between the
stage and the audience, a healing that is part of the mutability of
Coyote, part of the humour, and part of the ritual.
Monique Mojica (Kuna/Rappahannock) and Ric Knowles, "Introduction to
Staging," v

MYTHIC MOTION: TRICKSTER GAMES

Probably the most reoccurring battle that Native American artists face is the
deconstruction of stereotypical representations and the reclamation of self-
images. Vizenor represents this fight with the metaphor of an annihilated
city when he states, "The *postindian* must waver over the aesthetic ruins of
indian simulations" (*Fugitive*, 15). The *indian* simulations, so widely recognized around the world, render postindians invisible to anyone who compares Native American people to the small pool of stereotypical images.
How Native American people are represented by Native Americans and
non-Natives alike remains a critical issue at the forefront of Native
American theatrical works. Most often, theatrical scholarship investigates
Native theatre's active deconstruction of *indian* representations from post-
colonial perspectives. Departing somewhat from that strategy, this chapter
focuses on the concepts of survivance discourse, beginning with "mythic
motion: trickster games," where the inconsistencies between absence and
presence are exposed and the tight categories of *indian* behavior unraveled.
This mythic motion makes use of the kind of playful irony often used in
trickster narratives. It exposes what Vizenor calls "terminal creeds," concepts that support *indian* simulations. The word "terminal" recalls the myth
of the vanishing Indian, which assumes the appearance of truth when

simulations work to erase the visibility of contemporary Native Americans. In order to undermine such simulations, Native American playwrights, such as Hanay Geiogamah, Marie Clements, and Diane Glancy, often confront audiences with the clash between terminal creeds and Native presence. Their respective plays, *Foghorn, Urban Tattoo,* and *The Woman Who Was a Red Deer Dressed for the Deer Dance*, depict methods of Native resistance and survival through trickster transformations, deconstructions, and representations of Native American dynamism. In some instances, these playwrights open their plays with a simulation and then undermine its meaning. In other instances, they present terminal creeds within the context of scenes that jar the audience into recognizing discrepancies between *indian* simulacra and individual Native people.

Foghorn begins with a projected image of a *"large, painted Indian face... apparition-like, moving slowly as it is projected about the stage, its eyes gazing toward the audience"* (Geiogamah, *Foghorn*, 107). The face, ghostly and disembodied, works to evoke notions of the vanishing Indian. He is literally an image, an Indian representation, like the heads of Native Americans on placards in schools around the United States that bear Indian names, a presence of imagined history but not an acknowledged living presence.[1] Geiogamah underscores this construction of the vanishing Indian with the first dramatic actions of the play. As the face, unbound by place, floats in the theatre's darkness, the voice of an excited sailor cries out, "¡Señor Captain Columbus! ¡Mire! ¡Mire! ¡Mire! ¡Alla! ¡Mire! ¡Dios mio! ¡Estos hombres, cho-co-la-tes! ¡Los indios! ¡Los indios! ¡Ellos son los indios!"[2] (ibid.) With his identity negated by an invented name, the face vanishes.

Geiogamah transitions from this metaphorical erasure, caused by the mistaken name that the sailor conferred upon the individual Native peoples, to physical acts of erasure. The lights come up on the ensemble, whose moments enact a stylized journey. Geiogamah's stage directions state, *"They carry bundles of belongings, pull travois, and so forth. The costumes and movement should suggest a forced journey, such as the Trail of Tears, spanning the centuries from 1492...*[The first lines] *must convey an evolving attitude toward Indians"* (ibid.). The journey and following dialogue of Scene One traces how stereotypical images helped non-Natives justify the removal of Native Americans from their homelands. As the ensemble performs the forced journey, sounds, music, and dialogue collapse over 300 years of genocidal practices:

MALE SETTLER: You're only an Injun. Don't talk back! (*Now louder.*) You're only an Injun. Don't talk back! (*Sounds of mixed gunfire: rifles, old muskets* [...])

TWO WHITE MEN: (*Voices colliding.*) Vermin! Varmints! Vermin! Varmints! Vermin Varmints! [...]

FEMALE SETTLER: Filthy savages. Murderers! Scalpers! [...]

ANGRY MALE VIGILANTE: I say let's force 'em off the land! Move 'em with force, guns! Now!

(*Electronic journey music, group movement, mixed gunshots, high volume* [...] *More gunshots. Electronic journey music and group movement now become fragmented.*)

UNITED STATES SENATOR: The Indian problem is a matter for the courts and the Congress to deal with. We've been victorious over them on the battlefield, now they must settle on the reservations we have generously set aside for them. They have stood in the way of our great American Manifest Destiny long enough! (*Electronic journey music concludes as performers exit.*)

(ibid., 107–108)

The scene portrays a familiar story of the "settling" of America. With the images and snippets of dialogue concerning "the Indian problem," Geiogamah's portrayal echoes the uncomplicated versions of American history that valorize the European conquest and work to erase Native American diversity. However, as Geiogamah uses the popular version of history, he simultaneously undermines it. The live and diverse Native bodies of AITE's actors testify against erasure; they are a physical contradiction to the story of attempted erasure that they re-enact. The ironic portrayal prepares *Foghorn*'s audience for the play's use of mythic motion and presentation of survivance.

Clements' one-woman play, *Urban Tattoo*, begins with an image that, for a brief moment, might be mistaken as a portrayal of a romantic, spiritual, *indian*; however, the playwright, who also performs the play, makes immediate use of ironic trickster actions to combat erasure and claim individuality. The play's first lines are poetic and supported by video images projected behind Clements' stylized movements. Rosemarie stands beneath a lamp-post, lifting her eyes to the sky. Through physical movements, Clements depicts how Raven "*swoops down into her and breathes an old memory into her body and mind. Lifting her all* [the way] *to the sky, and beyond backwards to her place of being*" (Clements, *Urban*, 1). As Clements' body moves in a dance-like portrayal of raven flight, a large screen behind her shows layers of sky warming from rainy gray to blue while a large, white cross rises into the raven's flight path. In the persona of Raven, Rosemarie states, "A grey mist washes my face with its ghost's hands and the whispering of a thousand ancestors yawn past my ears. I fall in a layer of blue and hit the tip of a white cross that stretches so far up piercing this blue to try and shake its God's hand" (ibid.). Clements immediately complicates the spiritual metamorphosis and the romantic visions of flight. Rosemarie/Raven continues, "I perch here for an eternity and take a deep chalk [...] and let the shit fall proud how it blots the landscape" (ibid.). Simultaneously, the video shows a raven swooping across the screen followed by a white streak and blot of bird excrement. Raven soon spots a young Rosemarie, walking through town. He lands on her head and enters her body stating, "In the walk I become her and she me. I look down. My walk different. I laugh inside because I am mud walking on two legs not so forked but with flat souls. I watch my new feet squish into the mud one after the other and it feels good" (ibid.).

The following scenes build upon Rosemarie's personal trickster qualities. She shares Raven's irreverent attitude toward the limiting boundaries of Christian doctrine's "good and evil" and the stifling simulacra of *indian* women. Oddly, Rosemarie has a very particular relationship with her community's church. For her, the church serves neither as a source of cultural eradication, nor as a typical house of worship, but rather as a location for her to dream her future. The ceiling of the sanctuary is painted with hundreds of yellow stars, lined in white upon a cobalt background. They create the sky where Rosemarie's dreams soar. Explaining her unusual love for the church and presenting the contradictions between her relationship with the building and the building's origins, Rosemarie states:

(Baby Jesus stars painted by an ancient French priest surrounded by Indians. This must have been his haven from us. His place to come when the brown faces engulfed him on the land. Here it was just him and his God and his painting hand and he controlled the stars here and the front door and the Good Indians could come and go as they liked as long as he was holding the door.) I sneak in here when there aren't any good Indians around (or the good priest). I lay between the pews and trace my future from star to star...I-wishes to I-wishes [...] or sometimes I just stand tall and trace the painted stars as if I am the painter, as if those stars come from inside me. As if we have an understanding. (ibid., 3)

Just as Rosemarie finds possibilities within her twist on church-going, she locates personal potential, rather than limitations, in images of idealized feminine beauty: her greatest dream is to travel to Hollywood and become a movie star like Jane Russell. Accompanying her grandfather to the Hudson's Bay store, Rosemarie meets an African American road-construction worker who is looking through a magazine of pin-up girls. He is the first black man Rosemarie has ever seen, and she begins to stare at him and his magazine. When the man sees Rosemarie staring, he invites her to look at the magazine with him. Rosemarie states:

My favorite was a girl sitting on a haystack. He said it was Jane Russell. I said I looked like Jane Russell. He just smiled and after a while of looking at Jane Russell he tore the page out and handed it to me. That's when I thought I could be just like Jane Russell the movie star and maybe I'd even take the man from Africa's road to somewhere. (ibid., 4)

The first bout with erasure that Rosemarie encounters comes not from outside of her community, but from within her own family. While Rosemarie envisions a limitless future for herself, her sister counters her dreams with terminal creeds, statements of victimry for those called Indian. Clements depicts the contrast between the two visions of reality with the use of projected images. A color image of the golden, Hollywood sidewalk stars gleaming down the isle of the star-painted church appears on the screen behind Rosemarie. Rosemarie directly addresses the audience:

My sister says I shouldn't want to be a movie star because no one gets out of here except for Mary who got pregnant and wasn't married [...] But I'm not going to get married or pregnant for a long time not until I'm a movie star. My sister says how can I even be a movie star when I haven't even seen a movie. I just said I hear about it and I can picture it all in my head. My sister just laughed and said no Indian's ever been a movie star. I said well I am part Irish. (ibid., 6)

As Rosemarie shares her sister's rebuttal, the colored slide transforms into a gray photograph of the town. The image is of a fading-away of possibility, a vanishing of individual dreams and identity. Rosemarie finishes her story: "My sister laughed harder and said, 'Yeah with a combination like that all you could hope for is being a good drinker'" (ibid.). As the plot of *Urban Tattoo* unfolds, the audience follows Rosemarie's attempts to claim personal sovereignty by navigating through the simulacra, which work not only to limit her dreams but also to shape the way people see or erase her.

In Glancy's *Red Deer*, absence is also dramatized in the way the characters categorize and limit themselves. Girl struggles with financial issues. She works as a manager of a church soup kitchen, where co-workers steal her belongings and the commodities from the storeroom. Financially strapped and forced to use a large portion of her paycheck to purchase a new lock for the storeroom door, Girl must then choose between paying her rent or the repayment on the loan for her truck. With four payments left on a ten-year-old loan, she chooses the truck over her home. When Girl arrives at her grandmother's home, she no longer has a vision for her future. She confesses, "I already know I don't fit anywhere – I don't need to be reminded – I'm at your house, Grandma, with my sleeping bag and old truck – I don't have any place else to go…" (Glancy, *Red Deer*, 281–82).

Red Deer portrays Girl's living in a world where *indian* simulacra limit her actions and imagination. Although Girl and Grandmother live together, the conversations between them are forced. Grandmother speaks mostly of the mythical deer, Ahw'uste, and occasionally of her disapproval of Girl's way of life. Girl wishes that her grandmother would relate to her more intimately, claiming that conversations with her grandmother feel hollow, as if the two women were not related. In the play's fourth scene fragment, the two women speak to one another in a kind of dialogue that resembles their emotional distance:

GRANDMOTHER: I don't like this world any more. We're reduced to what can be seen and felt. We're brought from the universe of the head into the kitchen full of heat and cold.
GIRL: She fought to live where we aren't tied to table and fork and knife and chair. It was her struggle against what happens to us. Why can't you let me in just once and speak to me as one of your own? You know I have to go into the *seeable* – live away from the world of imagination. You could give me more.
(ibid., 277)

Compartmentalizing life into the *seeable* and mythical worlds, Girl detaches herself from her grandmother's wisdom. (See figure 4.) In contrast, Grandmother recognizes that the binary between spirit and daily life is one that has been constructed, one that has "reduced" Native American people's visions of self-images from a limitless universe into a small room, "a kitchen" of empirical "heat and cold" evidence. Because Girl lives a life that recognizes the categories as separate and incompatible, she feels as if her grandmother's stories of Ahw'uste are empty gestures, useless in her life. Girl's desire for a fulfilling life in the physical, *seeable* world leads her into unfulfilling sexual relationships. In hopes of filling her spirit, she sleeps with numerous men. In one encounter, a man uses her for her truck and her money: the first to tow his broken-down van, the latter to buy him dinner. The two have sex before the man quickly leaves. Abandoned, Girl laments, "I could have thought you were a spirit. You could have been something more than just a dude" (ibid., 282).

In *Postindian Conversations*, Vizenor speaks of the need to resist absence by reveling in the apparent contradictions of categorical limitations. He states, "[We] are mythic by conversation, conversion, and remembrance, and *the pleasure is in the contradiction*. Natives have always been on one road of resistance or another, creating postindian myths and tricky stories in the

4. Girl and Grandmother herself from Sage Theatre Company's production of *Red Deer*.

very ruins of representation and modernity" (Vizenor and Lee, *Postindian*, 21; emphasis added). Although Girl believes that her grandmother's way of life conflicts with her own, she harbors a desire to connect with Ahw'uste and the spirit world. She wishes to pull myth into the mundane world that appears to reject such beliefs. She states, "I want to wear a deer dress. I want to deer dance with *Ahw'uste*," but rationalizes her rejection of tradition by claiming that the deer stories would "get crushed in this *seeable* world"

(Glancy, *Red Deer*, 280). Likewise, Girl believes that her contemporary life would be made impossible by traditional ways. She asks her grandmother:

> Why would I want to be a deer like you?
> Why would I want to eat without my hands?
> Why would I want four feet?
> What would I do with a tail? It would make a lump behind my jeans.
> Do you know what would happen if I walked down the street in a deer dress?
> If I looked for a job?   (ibid., 281)

Throughout the play, Girl's struggle is to eventually name her own identity and to find a way for the traditions of Ahw'uste to exist within her own, contemporary life. Because Girl and Grandmother have had two very different life experiences, Girl's task is not to simulate her grandmother's traditions of Ahw'uste but to discover how to embrace the "pleasure of contradictions" within her own postindian identity.

Like Girl, Rosemarie and the ensemble of *Foghorn* combat absence by presenting audiences with representations of diverse, contemporary, Native American characters. Sometimes this portrayal of radical Native American presence takes place within scenes that incorporate acts of naming. For example, at the end of *Foghorn*, the actors in the ensemble step forward, one by one, and reclaim the names of their tribal nations, stating "I am Creek," "I am Ojibwa," and so forth (Geiogamah, *Foghorn*, 125). More often, the postindian trickster games occur through the ironic inversion of "fixed" categories or of the language once used to define and control both land and people. In *Foghorn*, the inversion of such limiting rhetoric occurs immediately after Scene One's images of absence. Scene Two takes place on Thanksgiving Day 1969, the day when AIM and other activists occupied Alcatraz Island in a political action born out of trickster irony. This significant event focused media attention on contemporary Native Americans and the pressing need for change in political policies toward Native peoples. *Foghorn*'s narrator describes the novelty of having actual Native American individuals in the nation's media spotlight by stating, "We are discovered, again" (ibid., 108). Images of the Alcatraz occupation are projected onto an upstage screen. They reflect not *indians* frozen in the nineteenth century but activists in the late 1960s, people whose presence is mirrored by the intertribal cast onstage.

The images of Alcatraz segue into a map of the United States, which is marked only by outlines of reservations that dot the nation's landscape. The narrator explains, "It was the first time that we had taken back land that already was ours" (ibid.). The map is not only a visual representation of the immense appropriation of Native lands: it also represents limits on Native mobility, as well as the more philosophical restrictions placed upon Native peoples. The ensemble mimes arriving on Alcatraz Island; they stand behind the narrator, whose following lines become a trickster game of naming. The narrator's speech mimics and exposes the ridiculous language of ownership used by European settlers and treaties against Native Americans:

We, the Native Americans, reclaim this land, known as America, in the name of American Indians by right of discovery. We wish to be fair and honorable with the Caucasian inhabitants of this land, who as a majority wrongfully claim it as theirs, and hereby pledge that we shall give to the majority of inhabitants of this country a portion of the land for their own, to be held in trust by the American Indian people – for as long as the sun shall rise and the rivers go down to the sea! We will further guide the majority inhabitants in the proper way of living. We will offer them our religion, our education, our way of life – in order to help them achieve our level of civilization and thus raise them and all their white brothers from their savage and unhappy state. (ibid., 109)

By renaming Native Americans as possessors of the land and Caucasian inhabitants as wards of the American Indian nations, the meaning of the map is transformed from a depiction of Native American reservations to one of Caucasian reservations. The image confronts non-Native people with the prospect of how constraining such tight limitations must be. All the while, through the trickster act of naming and proclaiming, the narrator reveals that even if one were to follow the arbitrary English rules of ownership by right of discovery, Native Americans should still control the American soil.[3]

Clements plays trickster name games in a less overt manner. Rosemarie rejects being limited by the categories her sister attempts to impose upon her. She defends her dreams to leave home and to live a life defined by her own standards. In response to her sister's comment about growing up to be a drunk, Rosemarie states, "I don't care what she says. I'm getting out of here" (Clements, *Urban*, 6). She is right. Her father soon secures a job for her as housekeeper for a wealthy Edmonton family. When he takes Rosemarie to the Hudson Bay store for new city clothes, Clements uses the girl's naivety to loosen the borders created by naming. At the store, Rosemarie runs into her friend. She states:

He was sitting in the exact same place I left him last time I saw him looking at his magazine. He said "How are you doin Miss Jane Russell." I said "Just fine thank you soldier." When I came out some big white trapper was in the big black guy's face. Called the black man a nigger and no nigger should be reading a magazine with white women in it. No nigger should be looking at any white woman [...] So I went over there and told the trapper it was my magazine thank you very much and that the man from Africa was holding it for me while I went in the store. He finally walked away. The black man just sat down all sad sorta. What's a nigger? He said that's what white men call black men where he comes from in the United States and that's how white men treat Indians in Canada. I said, "I guess we're just two niggers then." He laughed and laughed real hard for a real long time. I didn't get it. (ibid., 7)

Not until Rosemarie moves to Edmonton do her daily actions become restricted by categories created by others' names. Only then does she begin to exhibit *indian* behaviors, which are really her practical reactions to loneliness and fear.

In a world of non-Natives, Rosemarie seems to adopt *indian* traits which, as the audience knows, are quite unlike Rosemarie's persona. Warned by her father not to disappoint him, Rosemarie goes to work for "a real nice family cleaning up their real nice…stuff" (ibid., 8). She crams her Jane Russell picture and paint chips from the starry church ceiling in her pockets and works very hard to be an invisible cleaning presence in the house. Rosemarie states:

I stuff my words deep down [in my pockets] with them, I stuff. I clean. I stuff. I clean. I clean I clean I clean…don't disappoint him. I clean I clean I stuff I clean I stuff I stuff I stuff until I thought my head was going to explode. They said with nice smiles that Indians don't talk much but really I had no one to talk to. Jane was a way down deep, there was no stars, there was only this tight house and tight polite words that meant different things. (ibid.)

Already, the stereotype of the silent, stoic Indian stands in sharp contrast to Rosemarie, a young girl who has entertained the audience with endless stories about her life. She has proudly shared how she places the picture of Jane Russell on the church altar, and they sit together under the stars while "[I] press my lips together like this, and cross my legs like this and stick my boobs out" (ibid., 5). It is clear that Rosemarie's persona in Edmonton seems silent and stoic because the family she works for expects such a demeanor from *indians*.

In an insensitive environment where Rosemarie is asked to erase her own identity, other people see her as a reflection of their own preconceived notions. Not only do they see her as a "silent Indian," but when the woman of the house discovers her husband molesting Rosemarie, she accuses Rosemarie of being a whore. Sexually abused and now homeless, Rosemarie is thrown out on the streets of Edmonton, where she fights to reclaim her identity from the simulacra cluttering her head. Raven takes over her story, stating, "She remembers I am a nigger. She remembers someone saying crazy Indians…circles…someone asking her if she had a family anywhere circles…She remembered Indians don't talk much…She remembers don't disappoint me" (ibid., 9).

In the city, on her own, Rosemarie must learn to survive. However, the battle has emotional as well as physical stakes. It is not enough to merely resist the existing categories and labels that have worked to victimize and erase her presence. Rosemarie must also work to resist falling prey to future categories that can limit her vision and potential. Like Girl and the characters in *Foghorn*, Rosemarie must find a way to break through boundaries in order to move independently. While the first strand of survivance's discourse is rejecting absence through exposing the limiting classifications of *indian* simulations, the second strand of discourse incorporates a resistance to all future limitations through the tactic of perpetual movement.

MATERIAL MOTION: RESISTANCE

Once trickster games have worked to deconstruct, invert, and expose *indian* simulacra, the next task toward personal sovereignty involves resistance to new simulations through creations that incorporate endless movements. Material motion – the splintering and reconfiguring of many traditions and ideas – infuses Native American creations and allows them to avoid becoming trapped by simple definitions. Material motion and resistance focus on acts of Native creation. The creations of resistance can be expressed in the form of humor, journeys, and/or liberation stories. All of these are movement-based, in that they share the quality of transcending stagnant categorizations. The motion of resistance is practical; by remaining unclassifiable, the creative expressions of Native American people help defend their personal identities from those who wish to fashion new, but nonetheless stagnant, images of Native American experience.

Native American humor, a common form of resistance, is a shifting ground. It works against tragic victimry by destabilizing the images of *indians*, while moving outward to embrace a vast array of contemporary subject matter. Native humor acknowledges the harsh realities of contemporary Native American lives. It does not ignore the grim statistics for infant mortality, teenage suicide, deaths from tuberculosis, and the prevalence of alcoholism and poverty; rather, it can contextualize contemporary Native peoples within such surroundings while focusing, instead, on Native endurance and survival. Native humor concentrates on living perceptively within a world where simulacra profess disappearance. Vizenor calls it "the touchstone of native presence" (Vizenor and Lee, *Postindian*, 190). It is a radical presence, a radical humor – replete with scenes of violence and lunacy – that demands attention by stealing focus from the repetitive images and statistics attempting to imply Native American victimry.

Foghorn's scenes work to overwhelm the stories of victimry by replicating humorous scenes of radical presence. Much of *Foghorn* provides scene after scene of Euro-American dominance rendered powerless by comical forms of liberation. These funny scenes – depicting an evil nun, an idiotic boarding-school teacher, a sexually powerful Pocahontas, an insecure Lone Ranger, and a paranoid First Lady – often incorporate a violent form of humor. The violence, according to scholars of Native American trickster literature, mirrors traditional trickster stories which "often combine violence with humor" (Velie, "Vizenor," 160). In an "Author's Note" for *Foghorn*, Geiogamah warns against a heavy-handed playing of the action, which could contribute to an angry production. He states, "Almost all the characters in this play are stereotypes pushed to the point of absurdity. The satire proceeds by playful mockery rather than bitter denunciation. A production should aim at a light, almost frivolous effect" (Geiogamah, "Author's Note for *Foghorn*," 106). To emphasize the moments of violence in a brutal manner would work against the play's political objectives by not only reinforcing *indian* acts of savagery, but also by championing the same methods of dominance enacted by settlers against Native peoples. Trickster violence mocks by using metaphors of death that do not recognize death as a "fixed" state. Thus, while the scenes of *Foghorn* may simulate violence, it is used not as redirected colonialism but for providing means for new creations. (See figure 5.)

One of *Foghorn*'s strongest presentations of violent humor that moves toward the creation of liberation occurs in Scene Four, the boarding-school scene. The ensemble actors portray young children on their first day of classes. A teacher, dressed in a stars-and-stripes skirt, "*dances onstage, ringing a bell, carrying a bundle of small American flags singing 'Good Morning to You*" (Geiogamah, *Foghorn*, 110). Immediately, the teacher becomes upset that the students do not give her their full attention, or respond to her greeting of "G – ood morning, savages!" (ibid., 111). She complains, "These stupid children should be left on their reservations and forgotten about. What a bunch of worthless things" (ibid.). Soon her disdain turns to suspicion and violence when she sees a young girl gesturing to a friend:

([The teacher] *pummels the girl, who pulls back wide-eyed with surprise.*) What are you doing there? What was that? Was that an Indian sign-language gesture I saw you making there? Was it? Was it sign language? Well, there won't be any more of

5. *Foghorn*'s angry nun preaches "beautiful faith."

that in this classroom, none of that! I'll rap your knuckles hard if you do that again. Do you hear me? Do you understand me? It'll be the dark room for you. (*Pause.*) That's one step out of savagery for you. (ibid.)

Once she is near the children, the teacher turns her anger toward the children's hygiene. Accusing them of being filthy and lousy, she demands that they cut their hair and undergo sanitation. The students respond by laughing at the teacher, whose ranting and gesturing appear to grow in absurdity. This leads the teacher into a diatribe on American civilization:

Here in this school you are going to learn the English language. You are going to learn how to be Christians, how to worship God and live a clean, wholesome, decent life. You are going to learn how to be civilized people, civilized Indians, Indians who can earn an honest living, Indians that the American people can be proud of, not shamed by, so that we can hold our heads up high and say, "They are just like us, they are civilized. They aren't wild and on the warpath any more. They are living the American way." (ibid.)

The teacher's patriotism inspires her to break out in song, singing *The Star Spangled Banner*. The odd nature of her behavior tickles the children. Afraid to giggle, the little girl gestures again to her friend. The gesture triggers another violent rampage from the teacher that exhibits qualities in direct opposition to her patriotic speech. It is she who becomes the wild savage as she:

(*lunges at* [the girl], *yanks up the child, shouts directly into her face.*) This is not the reservation, child! This is not that awful place you came from where you all run around half naked, filthy, living in sin! This is a white man's schoolhouse […] (*She shakes the child violently.*) You are going to be a lesson for the others. You, child, are going to be punished. (*She pulls out a bottle of castor oil and pours it down the struggling child's mouth.*) It's the dark room for you. (*She pushes the child into a dark closet space.*) You will stay in here all day. No food! No water! And no toilet! (ibid., 111–112)

Although the teacher has created conditions of savagery in the classroom, the scene's humor does not end upon that irony; rather, it begins to fashion resistance out of the children's negative situation.

The teacher decides to instruct the children in English, "The language that has brought hope and civilization to people everywhere" (ibid., 112). She tells the children that their very first English word, "hello," will lead to their civilization, and that once they learn it, they must speak it to all the white people they meet. She begins to coax the students to repeat the word: "Listen closely. The word is hell-o. Hell-o. H-E-L-L-O. Hello. Listen to the way I say it. Hello. Hell-o. It's the first word of the American way. The American way begins with hello. Say it, children, say it. Hell-O. Hell-O" (ibid.). At this moment, trickster humor focuses on resistance. It acknowledges that indoctrination into the English language holds a prophecy: the American way will be hell. The students respond to the prediction, "Oh, hell. Oh, hell" (ibid.). As the students begin to repeat the word, the teacher becomes elated. The more animated she becomes, the more the students mock her actions. She soon becomes the manipulated pawn of the Native children. Geiogamah's stage directions describe the end of the scene:

The TEACHER hands the girl a small American flag, then takes it back to demonstrate how to wave it while repeating hello. The girl clowns crudely with the flag in her hand as the TEACHER turns to coax the class one by one to say hello. The students ape the TEACHER with strong gestures as she continues to instruct the remaining students. The

TEACHER soars on her success. The pupils form into a tight group, fists clenched, close in on her, and attack. (ibid.)

The children's attack can be read as their creation of liberation through resistance. By following the teacher's instructions, they read a more sophisticated message than she intends to communicate. Their continuance depends on this ability to see the multiple meanings and ride the humorous twists out of terminal situations.

Glancy's use of humor in *Red Deer* is subtler than *Foghorn*'s. Her humor serves to create pathways between the mythic and objective worlds by playing upon the differing versions of mythical and realistic worldviews. Girl interrogates the plausibility of her grandmother's claim to be both a human and a deer. She asks, "How can you be a deer? You only have two legs" (Glancy, *Red Deer*, 279). Grandmother responds dryly, "I keep the others under my dress" (ibid.). Grandmother's answer contains a double dose of humor. On a surface level, the droll response derives humor from the grandmother's matter-of-fact manner paired with the incongruent image of an elder hiding a pair of deer legs beneath her skirts. Yet, from the grandmother's mythic perspective, humor derives from others' inability to deal with her very simple explanation. Although Girl challenges her grandmother's spiritual world, she also accepts parts of the traditional story of Ahw'uste. At one point, Girl tells her grandmother, "Sometimes your hooves are impatient inside your shoes. I see them move. You stuff twigs in your shoes to make them fit your hooves. But I know hooves are there" (ibid., 281). Girl's wavering rejections and confirmations of Ahw'uste center upon her current inabilities to integrate the spiritual tradition into her personal, daily life.

The liberating form of humor used by Clements' Rosemarie in *Urban Tattoo* comes from the simultaneity of multiple perspectives. This kind of perception derives, in part, from trickster humor. Since she shares an identity with Raven, Rosemarie looks at situations from various perspectives even as she is in them. Louis Owens, a Choctaw/Cherokee author of novels and literary theory, describes the humor created by Raven's multiple perspectives. He states:

a remarkably accurate description of a raven examining and dissecting an object of interest – we find a precise definition of the humor and method of the Native American trickster, he/she who brings the world close and directs this "comical operation of dismemberment," laying bare the hypocrisies, false fears and pieties, and clearing the ground "for an absolutely free investigation" of worldly fact. (Owens, *Other Destinies*, 226)[4]

When Rosemarie shares her story of molestation, she speaks not from a sense of victimry, but from Raven's perspective of a reality spiked with humor that allows her to gain distance from the destructive event and so ensure her own resistance to domination. With a close-up image of a bald man's sweaty head projected behind her, Rosemarie states:

He undid one of my buttons on my clean white Edmonton blouse…I just knelt there…he said to be quiet…I just knelt there…he put his two hands on my breasts and started milking me just like a cow or something…all the time the beads of sweat waltzing down his shiny bald head. I just stared at those beads of water balancing on his skin head till they tumbled down. I just knelt…It's like I wasn't even breathing. I just knelt there…one of his hands undid the zipper of my skirt and one of his milking hands went down there. I started to cry…he said, "Shut up," it wasn't like I was a virgin or something…I said it wasn't like he was a movie star or something. (Clements, *Urban*, 8)

Rosemarie's multi-leveled description of the molestation exposes the weakness, the hypocrisy, of the rich "man of the house." Although he is a predator, the man's insecurities are revealed in his perspiring head, his unmanageable milking hands, and finally his own lack of desirability, reflected in Rosemarie's statement that he is no movie star. The trickster humor does not diminish the gravity of the terrible situations. Rather, as Vizenor states, "Survivance stories honor the humor and tragic wisdom of the situation, not the market value of victimry" (Vizenor and Lee, *Postindian*, 37). As such, Rosemarie's story provides a tragic kind of wisdom, a knowledge that allows her to move forward by reflecting on the hypocrisies that lie beneath images of power and dominance.

For Rosemarie, tragic wisdom gives way to liberation. Her transition from naive child to adult occurs immediately after the Edmonton family throws her out onto the streets. With this abrupt transition into maturity, she undergoes a metamorphosis. Clements' stylized movements portray the transformation of Rosemarie into Raven. As Rosemarie runs through the rainy night and strips off her Edmonton clothes, Raven takes over the telling of her story. Black-and-white projections of rain wash over Clements' body as Raven/Rosemarie states:

She took her nice clothes off and she just walked all the while the rain soaking into her more and more…little streams becoming big streams and flowing down her taking away that burning where his hands had touched her…taking away. She just walked…it was just raining. She walked until she saw this lamppost with a big beautiful light way up in the sky and water crystals floating down to her…touching her softly…talking to her softly…talking to me. (Clements, *Urban*, 9)

Raven carries Rosemarie through the immediate crisis, as visions of simulacra – quiet Indians, crazy Indians – cloud her mind. Once she survives the
immediate experience, Raven allows Rosemarie to take her story back. She
stands in the same position, under the lamp-post looking up to the sky, as
she had during the play's opening. At this point, the audience views the
images with a perspective that is critically aware. They see this stage picture
through the veil of Rosemarie's unique and complicated intricacies.
The audience also comprehends that, although she is now wise to life on
the streets, Rosemarie has lost her sense of self. She states, "I must have fell
from the sky on a rainy night. Drizzle down and just sat here for what
seemed like an eternity [...] I look for my reflection. I see no relation – just
myself" (ibid., 10) A numb but liberated woman, Rosemarie must move
forward to reintegrate dreams and possibilities into her story of self.

Vizenor classifies the act of storying as liberation, a kind of creative
motion that resists stasis. He states:

I am a storier, and my stories enfold the creation of a voice, a time, and a place that
is always in motion, or visionary transmotion. And the stories create me. I say that
because the circumstances of reading and critical interpretation create stories in the
storier. I tease these ideas in my stories and create a voice and sense of presence.
(Vizenor and Lee, *Postindian*, 61).

As I discussed earlier, the discourse of storying posits that narratives function through continual movements, interactions, intersections, and multi-
plicities which all lead to new perspectives. Vizenor envisions the motion of
stories as a form of liberation. In the case of Native theatre, the motion of
storying often occurs in a doubled manner. It happens not only through the
live performance, but also through the plays themselves, when they incorporate storytelling into their dramatic action. For example, *Urban Tattoo* is
a play about survivance that, simultaneously, depicts Rosemarie's liberation
through storytelling. Literally, the plot is Rosemarie/Raven's story, which
creates her even as she tells it.

In Glancy's *Red Deer*, the Grandmother's tales function to depict the
relationship between storying and liberation. Grandmother often spends
her time telling stories about the mythical deer and the first time she saw
Ahw'uste. As Girl listens, she becomes irritated by the way the stories seem
to change. After one of Grandmother's stories about seeing Ahw'uste with
four other mythical deer, Girl challenges the apparent inconsistencies:

GIRL: I thought you said *Ahw'uste* lived in a house in Deer Creek.
GRANDMOTHER: Well, she did, but these were her tribe. She was with them
    sometimes.

GIRL: She's the only one who lived in a house?
GRANDMOTHER: Yes.
GIRL: In Deer Creek?
GRANDMOTHER: Yes, in Deer Creek.
GIRL: Your deer dress is the way you felt when you saw the deer?
GRANDMOTHER: When I saw *Ahw'uste*, yes. My deer dress is the way I felt, transformed by the power of ceremony. The idea of the forest in my head.

(Glancy, *Red Deer*, 284–285)

Unwilling to entertain the multiple perspectives created by the fluctuating motion of her grandmother's story, Girl criticizes Grandmother:

GIRL: Speak without your stories. Just once. What are you without your deer dress? What are you without your story of *Ahw'uste*?
GRANDMOTHER: We're carriers of our stories and histories. We're nothing without them.
GIRL: We carry ourselves. Who are you besides your stories?
GRANDMOTHER: I don't know – no one ever asked.   (ibid., 285)

Grandmother views her stories as her liberation from the daily hardships that worked to reduce her personal sovereignty. She explains that her belief in the spirits and her ancestors was what inspired her to endure when her husband left her with a house full of children. She recalls, "all those kids and no way to feed them but by the spirit"; yet, simultaneously, she acknowledges that day-to-day living incorporated more than a passive faith. She states, "Sometimes I think the birds brought us food. Or somehow we weren't always hungry. That's not true. Mostly we were on our own. Damned spirits. Didn't always help out. Let us have it rough sometimes" (ibid., 288). The grandmother combines her traditional beliefs, her personal stories of Ahw'uste, and her unique history into her stories of survival. Girl is not inspired. By refusing to learn from her grandmother's experiences of poverty, Girl rejects the power of stories and claims to have none of her own. Without stories, Girl appears to remain fixed, stuck in her grandmother's house with no job and perpetually looking for a man to rescue her from victimry.

Stories provide liberation through a form of creative motion that allows people to speak themselves into different situations through the creative power of language. Material motion also incorporates a literal sense of motion in the form of journeys. In *Red Deer*, storying and journeying come together in a moment that allows Girl to break out of victimry. Frustrated by her life and her grandmother's disappointment in her, Girl complains, "I can't do it your way, Grandma. I have to find my own trail – is that what you won't tell me? Is that why you won't speak? I'm caught? I have no way through? But there'll be a way through – I just can't see it yet. And if I can't find it, it's still there. I speak it through" (ibid., 282). When her grandmother dies, Girl attempts to speak her own stories into a trail toward liberation. By accepting the creative power of storying, Girl quickly embarks on a literal journey of resistance which, in turn, leads toward her survivance.

Vizenor argues that while treaties and government policies worked to restrict the physical movements of Native American people into tightly bordered areas, ultimately an individual's movement is something that governments can never fully control. He states, "motion is never granted by the government. Motion is a natural human right that is not bound by borders…and not the common provisions of treaties with other govern-ments" (Vizenor, *Fugitive*, 188–189). Connecting a human's right to motion to issues of sovereignty, Vizenor's theories posit that an individual's move-ments provide the means toward not only resistance to confining borders but also toward the insurance of an individual's right to self-determination. Like Girl in *Red Deer*, Rosemarie and the characters of *Foghorn* literally perform acts of motion before claiming personal sovereignty.

Generally speaking, *Urban Tattoo* is a story about Rosemarie's journey toward personal sovereignty. As an adult in the city, Rosemarie struggles to gain control of her destiny. She rejects the prophecy of a Jehovah's Witness who claims Rosemarie is bound for "Hell. Hell. Hell. Hell," avoids the advances of a man named "Jackal," and peers into the windows of bars where people trade personal power for alcohol and impersonal sex (Clements, *Urban*, 11, 12, 13). Eventually, Rosemarie realizes that her life, like that of the city people around her, is under the control of outside forces. As people push past her on the crowded streets, a projection of tall buildings dwarfing tiny people and whizzing cars looms on the screen behind her. Sounds of rain underscore the scene and then segue into sounds of hooves on cement. These sounds are then layered by repeated "yes's" which grow louder and louder. Rosemarie soon notices that the people of the city live according to so many guidelines that their humanity no longer exists. She says:

The animals here file past me in a steady blow.
From where I am sitting I watch the shuffle of their shoed feet hit the pavement in
    clacks. Nick nack patty wacks…
I know they are being herded but I see no great herder.
I smell their fear of going the wrong way.

[...]
This animal whispers yes's I hear it under their marching breaths.
Even when they are saying no they are nodding yes.
Even when they are saying no they are pushing yes.
Even when they are saying no they are smiling yes.
[...]
Smiling yes, meaning no
In the welfare line, the food line, the booze line,
follow that line, yes follow the design.
[...]
Smiling yes, scheming no, no no.no, don't you know.
There is no parking, no barking, no shitting, no smoking, no men, no women, no
    children, no minors, no dogs, no Indians, no family, no clothes, no shoes, no
    service.
No entrance – No exit. Enjoy your stay.   (ibid., 15)

This moment is the first time since the childhood argument with her
sister that Rosemarie is fully aware of the limitations defining her personal
freedom. The determination of the younger Rosemarie clashes with the
older version's complicity. The image on the screen changes from
Edmonton to the narrow streets of Barcelona with buffalo, rather than
bulls, running. As the running buffalo freeze, the sound of raven wings fills
the stillness. The wings swoop and flap. Then, sounds of the herds' hooves
fill the theatre. Raven takes over Rosemarie's story one last time:

She had wanted to run with the buffalo – too late. She had wanted to run with the
bulls since she read about it. She had wanted to run through the thin streets of
Barcelona – wild eyed, hair flowing, panting, laughing-mad through the streets
of Barcelona hooves behind gaining ground…She wanted to swill a gulp or two of
tequila, taste the salt, and head out strong through the bodies of macho men clad in
white shirts with the stained brains of real men. She wanted to run. Feel the breath
surge up in fear, paralyzing fear that could motivate one to run, to live. She wanted
to run from the beasts and with the beasts. She did not want to run with the sheep
that file through these wide streets the sheer number of them a fearful rhythm. So
she just stopped. (*Rosemarie closes her eyes.*) (ibid., 16)

The younger Rosemarie's will to self-determination returns. Rosemarie
desires personal liberty, the power to run wild. She longs for her potential
to be recognized as equal to that of "macho" and "real" men. By stopping
abruptly against the steady stream of sheep-like people, Rosemarie defies the
"predefined" path for her life. She reclaims her right *"to run, to live."* It is a
physical act that prepares the way for Rosemarie's personal sovereignty.
    The final scene of *Foghorn* also depicts Native resistance through the
determination to move beyond imposed physical limitations. Scene Eleven

depicts the 1973 siege of Wounded Knee. Geiogamah's stage directions state that the ensemble forms a semicircle around a bare-chested drummer as "*He drums and sings the AIM song, building to a spirited pitch. A single rifle shot rings out and the drummer falls forward, his body taut, glistening in the lights. The helicopters, armored cars, and more gunfire are heard*" (*Foghorn*, 124). On the upstage screen, a series of photographs of the Wounded Knee siege appears. Off stage, a voice of a US marshal informs the AIM members that they have been surrounded and "cannot escape" (ibid.). The marshal then begins to command the physical response of the group:

I must caution all of you not to make any sudden moves[...] All of you who do not surrender without resistance are hereby warned that additional charges will be filed against you for resisting arrest. Your hands must be held high above your heads until the handcuffs are placed on you. Again, I warn you, do not make any sudden moves (ibid.)

The ensemble files off the stage, and quickly returns. Handcuffed with their arms above their heads, the performers form a line across the stage facing the audience. The narrator steps forward and begins to deliver a manifesto of resistance and self-determined movement. The scene combines the conceptual strands of survivance, as actors reclaim their original nations' names, vow to move on, and incorporate visions for future directions. Geiogamah writes:

NARRATOR: We move on. To a courtroom in Rapid City, South Dakota. To a courtroom in Sioux Falls, Iowa.
PERFORMER: (*Moving out from the group, he thrusts his hands toward the audience.*) I am Pawnee.
NARRATOR: We move on.
PERFORMER: (*Repeating the action.*) I am Creek.
NARRATOR: Back to our homes, our people.
PERFORMER: I am Winnebago.
NARRATOR: We move on.
PERFORMER: I am Sioux.
NARRATOR: To the land.
PERFORMER: I am Apache.
NARRATOR: To the sky.
PERFORMER: I am Ojibwa. (ibid., 125)

The characters' reclaiming of their individual nations' names, coupled with the pledge to resist boundaries by "moving on," prepares for the final discourse of survivance, visionary motion/transmotion. Significantly, the first claims of movement in *Foghorn*'s ceremony of repossessed motion begin in a relatively straightforward manner: "we move on to the courts, to our homes, to the land." However, the final statement of movement, "to the sky," speaks of motion that exists through a visionary understanding of a Native world with permeable boundaries. Paula Gunn Allen writes of this world stating, "The hoop dancer dances within what encircles him, demonstrating how people live in motion within the circling spirals of time and space. *They are no more limited than water and sky*. At green corn time, water and sky come together in Indian time to make rain" ("Ceremonial Motion" 72; emphasis added). This is the ultimate, transformative world of survivance.

VISIONARY MOTION/TRANSMOTION

Visionary motion/transmotion combines elements of mythic motion and material motion with aspects of deconstruction theories. Vizenor presents the idea as a critical strategy for Native American people to both unfix and resist the stagnant representations contested within contemporary Native identities. The term *visionary motion* refers to a critical awareness maintained by individuals with regard to the construction of their identities by self and others. It is an avowed state of readiness that allows Native American people, at any given moment, to call upon the resources of trickster action, Native creations, and life experiences to strategically counter simulacra and categorical limitations. *Transmotion* is the literal enactment of the strategy.

Within visionary motion/transmotion are theoretical concepts of trace and play, which Vizenor uses to deconstruct *indian*. The radical Native presence that Vizenor equates with survivance comes from the numerous, distinctly different nations, cultures, languages, and traditions of Native peoples that are erased by the singular, popularized term, Indian. Vizenor equates these overshadowed differences with deconstruction's notion of the trace. The word, Indian, as a transcendental signifier derives its meaning by collapsing and then disregarding the individuality within and across Native American nations. Vizenor summons unique Native lives, or traces, to materialize. Yet, he does not call for the mere presentation of differences, but for their play. He theorizes that the destabilization of *indian* will occur through the abundant combinations of individual elements whose multiplicity resists closure. Such combinations can occur across the history of one Native nation, across multiple Native nations, or across Native and non-Native nations.

Visionary motion also suggests crossing realms of being. Containing elements of mythic motion, visionary motion continues to position Native American peoples in relation to trickster stories. Vizenor classifies these stories as "the threshold of native survivance" stating that they "break out of the heavy burdens of tradition with a tease of action and a sense of chance" (Vizenor and Lee, *Postindian*, 60). The trickster allows for Native peoples to incorporate aspects of traditional cultures without being trapped by them. Trickster's ability to transform at will mirrors both strategies of visionary motion and the changeability inherent within place-based ideologies. Thus, visionary motion/transmotion incorporates aspects of platial theory by referencing the dynamic reciprocal relationships between people and nature. As Vizenor states, "Native transmotion is an original natural union in the stories of emergence and migration that relate humans to an environment and to the spiritual and political significance of animals and other creations. Monotheism is dominance over nature; transmotion is natural reason, and native creation with other creatures" (*Fugitive*, 184–185). The union between humans, natural environment, and the stories that arise from it provide the philosophical foundations for the many transformations that occur within Native plays. In theatre, such transformations are theatrical manifestations of transmotion.

Foghorn ends in a state of transmotion. The naming ceremony begins by bringing critical awareness to the traces of Native identity and finishes with a vow to continually engage in transmotion. The pledge, "We move on. To a courtroom [...] to our homes, our people [...] to the land [...] to the sky," reclaims both physical and mythic motions within a context of vigilant strategic maneuvering (Geiogamah, *Foghorn*, 125). After the ceremony, the stage lights dim and the actors remain on stage. Again, the projected face from the prologue reappears and "*moves slowly around the playing area*" as it overlaps the bodies of the ensemble (ibid.). From an audio-taped recording, the voice of the Spanish Sailor is replayed. The repeated image and words now take on a different meaning. The floating face is no longer a simulation mirroring back exotic difference to the sailor who misnames him; rather, the individuality of the face is a literal trace of Native presence. Spirit-like, his image washes over the performers, who each have already claimed a separate national identity that fragments the sailor's exclamation of "¡Los indios!" (ibid.). The play's final statement, "I am...NOT GUILTY!" also supports the declaration to "move on" by means of transmotion (ibid., 126). *Foghorn*'s narrator makes this claim between the sailor's repeated "discovery" and the play's final blackout. By countering the legal claims against AIM in 1973, the statement acknowledges the contested position of Native sovereignty while it simultaneously adopts qualities of mythic motion. It reflects back through time, appearing at crucial moments of Native history to defy settler discourse used to create the *indian*. It answers not just the AIM trials but also accusations of doomed extinction, Native brutality, savagery, and other simulations of absence. Together, the statement and the floating face link time, space, and communities through a play of traces – one streaking backwards, the other reverberating forwards.

In "Further (Farther)," Glancy's description of Native American theatre expresses attributes of transmotion. She states:

A native play is often orbiculate. To circle back to terms: realized improbabilities probably describes the network of possibilities for the unlikely elements of the topography of the native stage. The improbable happenings that fill the native stage. The acceptable improbabilities. The indirect directions. Blizzard, the cold and heat, thunderstorm, humidity, humor and bleakness, tornado and calm, flood and drought, – all the other upheavals of native theatre. (Glancy, "Further," 130)

Glancy's statement describes the Native creations that arise from the reciprocal relationship between human life and nature as "acceptable improbabilities." She takes away the unfamiliarity of transmotion's mythic qualities by reminding her readers that such improbabilities are as normal as nature's chance presentations of tornadoes and blizzards. The Native theatre Glancy describes exists, in part, to present transmotion. Through a connection to nature and natural metamorphosis, a woman can be a Grandmother who is also a deer who sometimes frees her four deer feet to dance in communion with ancestors. Grandmother in *Red Deer* speaks stories of survivance that represent her ability to attain self-determination through visionary motion and transmotion. To cultivate her granddaughter's understanding of transmotion, Grandmother links the stories of Ahw'uste to the regularly occurring metamorphoses within nature. She links Ahw'uste to her dancing place, a forest floor covered with red maple leaves. Her explanation that the leaves always contain the power to transform is Grandmother's way of teaching Girl to remember the traces of Native identities. Just because the maple tree's leaves appear green most of the year is no reason for the tree to deny the leaves' potential to become red. Grandmother states, "The leaves only get to be red for a moment. Just a moment, and then the tree grieves all winter until the leaves come back. But they're green through the summer. The maple waits for the leaves to turn red. All it takes is a few cold mornings. A few days left out of the warmth. Then the maple tree has red leaves for a short while" (Glancy, *Red Deer*, 282). Through the red-leaf story, Grandmother hopes to inspire Girl to look beyond the world of fixed identities and envision her potential. Grandmother speaks from a perspective of natural reason, one which Vizenor calls the "tease of native season, the myths and metaphors of human and animal connections to the environment – shamanic visions, transmotion, and territorial reciprocity" (*Fugitive*, 183). Although she urges Girl to gain a critical perspective of the many strategies for Native survivance, it is not until Grandmother's death that Girl understands the meaning behind the stories. Girl states:

> She said once, there were wings the deer had when it flew. You couldn't see them, but they were there [...] Like the stories that rode on her silence. You knew they were there. But you had to decide what they meant. Maybe that's what she gave me – the ability to fly when I knew I had no wings. When I was left out to the old world that moved in her head. When I had to go on without her stories. (Glancy, *Red Deer*, 280)

After her grandmother's death, Girl begins to shape the Ahw'uste stories into her own technique of transmotion. She travels from one job interview to another, unable to secure employment. At her fourth interview, Girl begins to tell the stories of her ancestors. Significantly, the story Girl tells is not a repeat of her Grandmother's, but a new combination of the mythical story and her lived experiences. Girl states:

> At the fourth I told 'em – my grandmother was a deer. I could see her change before my eyes. She caused stories to happen. That's how I knew she could be a deer.
> At the fifth I continued – I'm sewing my own red deer dress. It's different than my grandma's. Mine is a dress of words. I see *Ahw'uste* also.
> At the rest of the interviews I started right in – let me talk for you, that's what I can do.
> My grandma covered her trail. Left me without knowing how to make a deer dress. Left me without covering.
> But I make a covering she could have left me if only she knew how.
> I think I hear her sometimes – the crevice you see through into the next world. You look again, it's gone. (ibid., 289)

In this manner, Girl creates a critical positioning for herself that extends beyond the material world of jobs and money into a world where she, too, is part-deer and able to draw upon the knowledge of ancestors. The play ends with Girl in transmotion, pushing against the harsh surroundings of her impoverished environment.

Transmotion also weaves throughout *Urban Tattoo*. Beginning as Rosemarie's unconscious survival skill, the metamorphoses of Rosemarie/Raven soon shape the play's action. Raven not only begins Rosemarie's story, but also takes over her story during the times when Rosemarie feels powerless. This provides Rosemarie with the ability to escape capture, victimry, and absence. Likewise, portrayed through stylized movement, the metamorphoses become transmotion when Rosemarie makes a conscious choice to critically position herself against fixity. Rosemarie claims visionary transmotion during the moment that she refuses to move with the compliant city crowds. She opens her eyes and sees, with trickster vision, a critical strategy emerging from the play of her differences. Owens describes this kind of trickster vision as "Embodying contradictions all possibilities, trickster ceaselessly dismantles those imaginative constructions that limit human possibility and freedom, allowing signifier and signified to participate in a process of 'continually breaking apart and re-attaching in new combinations'" (*Other Destinies*, 235). In her act of transmotion, Rosemarie begins to speak her own multi-faceted destination into existence. The screen behind Rosemarie presents "*a collage of images: A bright lamppost, street scenes, rain, the Jehovah Witness woman, pizza signs, the jackal, the colour blue, sheep perspectives, buffalo, the city street, people standing around looking at her,*" while overlapping sound effects mimic this collage of Rosemarie's experiences (Clements, *Urban*, 14). Rosemarie faces the audience and states:

What do you see? What do you see? Why would I be asking the sheep anything?
What do I see?
I see I am no buffalo.
I see I am no bull.
I see I am no star.
I see I am no Jane Russell.
I see I am no girl.
I see I am no Indian.
I see I am no nigger.
I see I am no white.
I see I am no raven.
I see I am no victim.
I see I am no saint.
I see I am no slut.
I see I'm not rain.
I'm not blue.
I'm not a no-body.
I see I am everything.   (ibid., 17)

Rosemarie's question "What do I see?" and answer "I see I am everything" assert transmotion. Rosemarie adopts a critical positioning that works to resist classifications by decisively playing across the continual fragmenting and reconnecting of her identities and experiences. In the closing monologue of *Urban Tattoo*, Rosemarie ends her story with a decision to remain unfixed. For the first time, she deliberately incorporates Raven into her presence as she states:

It was the other day it became obvious. It was the other day it grew. First just an odd feather and then they multiplied. First it just tickled. Then they caused a black fluff. Then they began to stretch and span out beneath my arms like wings. They attached themselves to me. I wondered about this. I wondered if this is what everyone here had been seeing and that's why they didn't recognize me...

A Native man on the slanted sidewalk was the only one who did. He was a mid-square talking Cree crying Cree to the wind. He looked up and looked me in the eye. We knew each other. We floated away laughing at our wings.

It's easier to live here if you have wings. It's easier to avoid being flattened. It's easier to take a thought or a memory and drift back to it. Drift back to the beginning if you need to. Close your eyes and lift your wings and fly above all the shit and go to the beginning. I thought that was it, that was what it was all about and then Rosemarie showed up, gumboots and all. Leaving mud boot marks clear up to the skin on my calves, then came those church stars, they came at night... they painted themselves right there on my stomach [...] I have a blue paint chip that rests on my hip the same colour. It thinks it's in a pocket. Jane Russell showed up too. I didn't get her boobs but I did get a small picture of her somewhere you don't need to know about right now. The Hollywood stars showed up too they placed themselves accordingly. The tattoos I'm not so crazy about are the bald man's hands, the crosses, a Jehovah Witness pamphlet, the jackal's smile, the pizza slices but I did survive them so they take their own place – the bottom of my feet. The blues they tint my hair, my feathers. The rain falls on me and dries tears [...] The sheep are too scared to show. And that just leaves me to show, all coloured with blood memory and stained cells. Right here. (ibid., 18)[5] (See Figure 6.)

Rosemarie ends with a tease of presence, "that just leaves me to show [...] Right here." What she reveals is that the fracturing and multiplying traces of presence enable her survivance. Rosemarie ends not a victim bruised by abuse, poverty, and rejection, but a survivor who embarks on the critical path of transmotion. Neither a tragic nor heroic simulacrum, Rosemarie, the sovereign individual, vigilantly chooses how others will see her. Rosemarie's visionary motion is her ability to remain in that state of readiness which will allow her to strategically counter future simulacra through mythic and material motions. Her enactment of the critical strategy, her transmotion, closes the play. As soon as Rosemarie claims to be "Right here" the stage lights quickly fade to black.

Like Rosemarie, the characters of *Red Deer* and *Foghorn* present stories of radical, Native presence. As the Native creations of Clements, Glancy, and

6. Marie Clements as Rosemarie/Jane Russell in *Urban Tattoo*.

Geiogamah, the plays themselves are manifestations of survivance discourse. They theatrically demonstrate the deconstruction of simulations and categorical limitations, while they also present strategies for developing a critical positioning of self that works against the constant threat of new simulacra. It is significant that the end of each play resists closure by depicting characters who embark upon paths of critical action. While offering hope, these theatrical presentations of survivance do not present a utopian vision of neat resolutions and tranquil eternities. Instead, the plays acknowledge how Native sovereignty is constantly limited and pairs that reality with a sustained commitment to advance autonomy. The plays also emphasize the reciprocal relationship between individuals and communities by depicting the personal actions as political. Geiogamah's ensemble is a gathering of individuals from different Native nations, while Glancy and Clements focus on the singular experiences of three unique women. As demonstrated through these characters, Native survivance begins with the individual, and it is through the radical presence of each person that the *indian* is contested.

CHAPTER 9

Interconnected theories and the future
of Native American drama

I believe in theatre. I *believe* in Theatre. Theatre is my faith, my church, my spirituality. And all the things I do in the service of theatre, that is my way of witnessing, of proselytizing.

Yvette Nolan (Algonquin), "Selling," 104

The Black Theatre Movement is a good example of how a theatre movement…changed Broadway, and employed lots of Black actors… Why can't that happen in Native theatre? That *has* to happen.

JudyLee Oliva (Chickasaw), qtd. in Stanlake, "Interview," 117

I began this book with an origin story of sorts, a brief overview of the history of Native American theatre in the United States and Canada; and, in the tradition of creation stories, I end by returning our imaginations to that tale. What does that historical account tell us about Native American theatre, but that Native theatre artists have been present and active for a very long time – since before the Red Power Movement – and that their voices are still waiting to be gathered into the communal tale? Somehow, the distinguished presence of Native theatre artists has been erased from theatre history. Perhaps that is because, as Gerald Vizenor might say, these artists rarely presented the *indian*. Although artists such as Lynn Riggs and Will Rogers made no pretense about their Native heritage, audiences – from their generations to ours – have not quite accepted these artists' dynamic, contradictory, and radical presences as *really* being Native.

Luckily, a dichotomy exists between theatre historians and Native American historians, who have continually collected the accomplishments of Native theatre artists in reference books: biographical dictionaries and encyclopedias. These, I imagine, will inspire the beginning research for a full history of Native American theatre. Such a study will not only lead to a fuller understanding of the field of Native American theatre, but will also offer new insights into the national theatres of the United States and Canada. After all, what theatre could be more uniquely American or Canadian than plays by the nations' first peoples?

The other reason I began with an origin story was to feature the sweeping visions of Native American playwrights. From the minimalist, lyrical plays of Diane Glancy to the multi-layered, haunting images of Marie Clements, Native drama stages the landscape of the continent and of the human soul, brought together on stage through ceremony. Tomson Highway writes that Native American theatre inherits this power from Native mythology, which is:

filled with the most extraordinary events, beings and creatures [that] lend themselves so well to visual interpretation, to exciting stage and visual creation: the cannibal spirit Weetigo (Windigo in Ojibway) who devours human flesh...the young man Ayash who encounters a village populated by women with teeth in their vaginas and has to deal with them as part of his vision quest, the woman who makes love to a thousand snakes...Not only are the visuals powerful, the symbolism underlying these extraordinary stories is as basic and as direct as air. And they come from deep, deep within the flesh and blood of a people who have known this particular landscape since time immemorial and who are so close to it they have become an integral part of it, like rock. ("On Native", 2)

Highway's description of the imaginative resources of Native American playwrights flows directly into the aim of this study, which is to provide a critical methodology for approaching the rich diversity and mythic visions of Native American theatre through critical lenses capable of addressing Native theatre's unique dramaturgical attributes, those that directly reflect Native epistemologies of land, language, and motion.

Native American theatre is its own field of drama; it is different. What one encounters in Native plays does not neatly fit into the paradigms of mainstream, western drama (if one can even claim there is such a thing any longer – still, Native plays are different). My overriding concern in this study has been to offer critical strategies for appreciating the intricacies of Native dramaturgy without reducing the multi-dimensionality of these plays, or their larger field. To do so, I have privileged Native American intellectual traditions that relate directly to theatre's performative medium. We can view these Native philosophies through four discourses: platiality, storying and tribalography, and survivance. These discourses coincide with the basic performative elements of space, speech and action, and movement.

So that we might closely examine each discourse and view how its interrelated concepts create meaning in Native American plays, I explored each discourse in an isolated manner. The discourse of platiality concerns characters' relationships with their physical homelands. It comprises the concepts of "rootedness," "worlds of existence," and "language as landscape." Rootedness posits that relationships between people and their homelands create a sense of identity and belonging within a community. Worlds of existence references how human beings can connect to non-human beings through the conduit of sacred places. Language as landscape expresses the concept that language comes from the natural world; thus, through speech, we can enter into a reciprocal relationship with place.

Story and tribalography are interconnected discourses. Storying presents theories that create an alternative paradigm for viewing reality, one that I call "story cosmos." Story cosmos offers different ways of understanding time, the power of words, the material effects of language, and the ability to communicate with the natural and spiritual worlds. Extending from these concepts, tribalography applies storying's views to communities. The discourse of tribalography contains three interrelated concepts: "multi-vocal authenticity," "communal truth," and "collective creation." Multi-vocal authenticity posits that many voices actually create a single story. Communal truth embraces the contradictions found within a single story composed of multiple perspectives, and it theorizes that from these gaps and fissures people build new understandings and relationships. Collective creation goes one step further to argue that the multiplying, contradictory stories can generate material effects.

Survivance is a discourse that addresses the survival and resistance of Native American people against boundaries and stereotypes. It contains three concepts: "mythic motion," "material motion," and "visionary motion/transmotion." Mythic motion refers to the ways Native people undermine stereotypes of Indianness. Material motion concerns strategic moves that Native people can take to avoid stagnation and labeling. Visionary motion is about imagining a radical Native presence, one that teases viewers and evades confinement; transmotion is the act of placing visionary motion in action.

As one reads through the chapters' play analyses, it is easy to envision the symbiotic relationship between the discourses and the plays: the plays model the discourses in action, while the discourses help shape the plays' plot structures and characters. One also probably notices how the concepts within each discourse interconnect with one another. For example, theories of how human beings exist in reciprocal relationships with the natural and spiritual worlds appear in the concepts of language as landscape, story cosmos, and visionary motion. Likewise, theories of identity formation play within the concepts of rootedness, multi-vocal authenticity, material motion, and visionary motion/transmotion. The interplay of theories across and within these three discourses provides the capability for us to address the distinctive qualities of Native plays without losing the multi-dimensional essence, the vast diversity across the field of Native American theatre.

I offer this critical study of Native American theatre not to explain away the intellectual and aesthetic brilliance of these plays – which I doubt is possible – but, rather, to contribute to this field of theatre, which has quickly gained an exceptional level of visibility in grassroots, academic, and professional circles. While programs and communities such as Project HOOP and the Chickasaw Nation are sponsoring the development of community-based theatre companies, mainstream academia, with its commitment to encouraging diversity, is also increasing its interest in the field. The last decade has seen over seven major Native American play anthologies published. Those and the recent launch of the Alexander Street Press *North American Indian Drama* Collection will bring Native American theatre to circles of readers and viewers who may have never before read or seen a Native play.

The world of professional Native American theatre is also expanding through independent theatre companies and development programs, such as urban ink, Fathom Labs, and Native Earth. Strategic partnerships, such as Native Voices at the Autry Museum or those offered by the Smithsonian's National Museum of the American Indian, provide opportunities for showcasing Native American plays. Significant mainstream productions, such as JudyLee Oliva's *Te Ata* World Premiere, William S. Yellow Robe, Jr.'s *Grandchildren of the Buffalo Soldiers*, and Highway's *Dry Lips* are beginning to traverse theatrical boundaries to eradicate the misconception that Native American plays are for niche audiences. Still, there is much work to be done.

Despite the extra attention Native American theatre has recently received, Native plays are still more likely to receive publication than productions. Many playwrights speak about this frustration. In "Selling Myself," Yvette Nolan places the blame on stereotypes that have severely limited non-Native people's imaginations of what a Native American playwright can create. She states, "Here's the thing. The people who make the decisions about what gets onstage, on film or on radio want certain things from First Nations writers. They want certain representations of Indians. They want you to write Indian" (Nolan, "Selling," 98). She goes on relate a story about how her play *Blade*, which addresses Native invisibility, was viewed as not "Indian" enough.

At one point in their careers, Nolan, Highway, and Oliva all have had to work as their own producers just to get their plays seen by the public. Even when companies have been interested in Native American play scripts, they have rejected Native plays on other grounds. Oliva recalls:

I wrote a play, *Call of the River*, which is about the Trail of Tears and the movement of the Indians to Oklahoma. It spans a long period of time; it's epic in nature like *Te Ata*, it's big. I sent it to Syracuse Rep, and they wrote back and said, "We love the play, but we don't think we can do it. We don't think we have an audience for it." I think they're wrong. They said…they didn't think they could do it because…they couldn't cast it. And, yes, casting is difficult, but there are Native actors out there; there are a lot of Native actors out there. Most of them are doing film; they're not doing theatre because it's so hard to make a living in theatre. But I'm determined that I have to make a break-through in that way. (qtd. in Stanlake, "Interview," 116)

In some ways, the skepticism expressed by Syracuse Rep was disproven when the Chickasaw Nation helped produce Oliva's *Te Ata*, an Equity-level production that cast many professional Native American actors, including DeLanna Studi, whose photograph is on the cover of this book. Studi played Young Te Ata, and the pose she strikes is one she copied from the cover of Te Ata's own 1930s publicity brochure. After the production's first week, Studi spoke about the hope of Native American theatre in mainstream venues. She stated, "I don't think Native theatre is risky…the truth is people want to see our stories" (personal interview). She then recalled a non-Native family from Dallas, Texas who had read about *Te Ata* in the newspaper and then drove several hours to get to the Oklahoma production. Studi recalled their telling her that "they didn't want to miss the story," and laughed, "When we do Native pieces, we get a crowd" (personal interview).

In the spirit of such stories from Native theatre artists, I offer this critical approach to Native American dramaturgy in order to demystify this field of theatre that producing organizations often believe is too dangerous to invest in. I offer it to discredit the misconceptions that all Native plays are alike, or that non-Native audiences will be uninterested in Native plays. What is more theatrical than plays based on perspectives that take our art form to the extreme: that return the stage to a place of ceremony, that revel in the power of language, that feature limitless characters, that profess plays can change the world? Such dynamic Native dramaturgies challenge those who mistakenly believe that Native American plays cannot entice the imaginations of contemporary theatregoers.

I imagine the future of Native American theatre branching out the way storying does, the way Muriel Miguel's hands gestured when she spoke of the movement of stories, their moving from one's soul and stretching, reaching, splitting, multiplying outward, and ever more outward. I believe that this theatre movement will eventually transform how we see Native

American people and how we understand the broader discipline of North American theatre studies. It is significant to our understanding of American theatre history that a Cherokee from Oklahoma, Lynn Riggs, wrote *Green Grow the Lilacs*, the play upon which Rodgers and Hammerstein based *Oklahoma!* It is equally important that North America's oldest continually performing women's theatre company is a Native American feminist company, Spiderwoman Theater. In terms of theatrical criticism, Native dramaturgy offers valuable perspectives that can extend current general theories. Platiality, with its emphasis on homelands, politics, and the natural earth, intensifies both theatrical and literary criticisms' notions of spatial theory. Storying and tribalography apply new dimensions to actor/audience relationships by enlarging the idea of "witnessing" to incorporate viewers' narratives into the creative process. Aspects of survivance allow theorists to break through reactive tactics in post-colonial theory to imagine alternative ways of claiming and maintaining agency.

This vision of how Native American theatre can alter general theatrical studies includes only half of the story, however. *Native American Drama: A Critical Perspective* expands the work I began in my 2002 dissertation, and so presents the first in-depth critical approach to Native American dramaturgy from the United States and Canada.[1] A theoretical book about Native theatre from Latin America still waits to be written by scholars who specialize in that field. What might a bilingual study that bridges these two, related fields teach us about indigenous drama from across North and South America? Could it adjust the way we perceive theatre in the Americas? When Craig Womack traces the literary roots of Native American cultures to the Mayan hieroglyphs, he takes a political and academic stance regarding literature arising from these two continents, claiming:

I say that tribal literatures are not some branch waiting to be grafted onto the main trunk. Tribal literatures are the *tree*, the oldest literature in the Americas, the most American of American literatures. We *are* the canon. Native people have been on this continent at least thirty thousand years, and the stories tell us we have been here even longer that that, that we were set down by the Creator on this continent, that we originated here. For much of this time period, we have had literatures. Without Native American literature, *there is no American canon*. (Womack, *Red*, 6–7)

Following upon Womack's sentiment, might future studies in Native theatre from North and South America come to claim the pre-colonial, Mayan *Rabinal Achi* as the tree whence all Canadian, US, Mexican,

Brazilian, Peruvian, Chilean (and so on) dramaturgies branch? Could that revised perspective, with its emphasis on interconnections – human relationships to the planet, to national and global communities – transform the way all people imagine the possibilities of theatre?

And sometime, if he is fortunate, he may hear from the people that he has set in motion…things to astonish him and things to make him wise. (Riggs, "Preface," 5)

Notes

1 A HISTORY OF NATIVE AMERICAN DRAMA

1. In addition to the Chickasaw Nation's major contribution, other sponsoring organizations included the University of Science and Arts and the USAO (University of Science and Arts of Oklahoma) Foundation, the Craig Foundation, James and Pamela Crowe, the Inasmuch Foundation, and the Kirkpatrick Foundation.

2. Incidentally, OCW later became a co-ed institution, which is now the USAO. The *Te Ata* World Premiere occurred at USAO, on the very stage where Te Ata Fisher first began her performance career.

3. For a full history of Te Ata's performance career, please see Oliva, "Te Ata – Chickasaw," 3–26.

4. Curtis was Kansa-Kaw/Osage and has a controversial history as a Native American in federal politics. He sponsored the Curtis Act of 1898, which extended the Dawes Act of 1887 into Indian Territory. (For more, see the following chapter.)

5. Te Ata was born in Indian Territory, which became the state of Oklahoma in 1807.

6. The Cherokee Nation is one of the "Five Civilized Tribes" who were moved to Oklahoma during the Trail of Tears. These five nations – Cherokee, Choctaw, Chickasaw, Creek, and Seminole – were called "civilized" because they had developed governance structures and organized their communities in ways that white settlers approved of and could not criticize as "savage." Despite their high literacy rates, legal negotiations with the federal government, and adoption of Christianity, these five nations were forcibly marched from their southeastern homelands to Indian Territory, along with thirty-seven other Native nations. Because Indian Territory, now Oklahoma, became an intertribal region of Native nations, including those that had adopted governance styles that appeared to be more "white," some people claim that Native people from Oklahoma lack an "authentic" Native heritage. Please see Baird, "'Real' Indians," 4–23.

7. Please see Womack, *Red*, 271–303. Womack's discussion of Riggs' "code talking" goes beyond examining Riggs' Cherokee identity to investigating Riggs as a

homosexual Native American man from Oklahoma living in an era that was not accepting of Native peoples or homosexuals.

8. Spiderwoman Theater's original company included Peggy Shaw and Lois Weaver, who split off from the original group to create the feminist theatre company Split Britches (Haugo, "Native Playwrights," 328).

9. Monique (Kuna/Rappahannock) is a founding member of Turtle Gals Performance Ensemble, a Native women's theatre group, and has co-edited major anthologies of Native drama. Please see Mojica and Knowles (eds.), *Staging Coyote's Dream.*

10. For a discussion regarding Native Hawaiian identity, please see chapter 4, "Platiality in Native American Drama," note 12.

2 DEVELOPING A CRITICAL PERSPECTIVE FOR NATIVE AMERICAN DRAMA

1. All terms – Native American, American Indian, and First Nations – are generalized categories that pertain to hundreds of nations. I've chosen to use the term *Native American*, as opposed to American Indian, in this book because the term relates closely to Gerald Vizenor's (Anishinaabe) theories, which greatly influence this study. Consequently, I will use the terms "American Indian" and "Indian" only when quoting others, providing names of texts or organizations, and referencing cultural mythology, such as "the myth of the vanishing Indian." I'll use the term "First Nations" only with regard to Native playwrights from Canada, where First Nations is the preferred term. Throughout this book, I will attempt to honor the distinctiveness of Native national identities by identifying Native authors' nation(s) when I first introduce the writers.

2. Sources for approaching some of these issues include Warrior, *Tribal Secrets* and Pommersheim, *Braid of Feathers.*

3. I borrow the term "intellectual tradition" from Robert Allen Warrior's work.

4. Here, Weaver uses "secular" in a way different from that in which I do at the beginning of this chapter. While I discuss the secular in terms of Native plays' not staging any specific Native American religion, Weaver's use of secular refers to worldly, or irreligious, perspectives.

5. The work expands ideas originally presented in my doctoral dissertation, "Mapping the Web."

6. Certainly, Spiderwoman Theater's Native heritage, which radically traverses federal boundaries, belies the notion that Native American identity can ever fit neatly into critical studies that attempt to construct a scope with which to view Native works.

7. For a more detailed discussion addressing issues of Native Hawaiian identity, please see note 12 in chapter 4, "Platiality in Native American Drama."

3 NATIVE AMERICAN PLATIAL HISTORY

1. Stiffarm and Lane ("Demography," 24, 47) state that in his 1928 book, *The Aboriginal Population of America North of Mexico*, Mooney provides no justification for his mistrust of the counts.

2. For more on these estimates, see Herbert J. Spinden, "The Population of Ancient America," *Geographical Review* 18 (1928): 640–660.

3. Marshall is also responsible for creating a legal precedent for the federal recognition of sovereign tribal nations. In the 1831 *Cherokee Nation* v. *Georgia* case, Marshall declared that the state of Georgia had no jurisdiction over the Cherokee Nation because Native nations were "domestic, dependent nations." In the 1832 *Worcester* v. *Georgia* case, Marshall upheld Native nations' rights to self-government independent of state government. While these decisions upheld tribal sovereignty, they also created a ward–guardian relationship between tribal nations and the federal government.

4. Stiffarm and Lane cite Locke's *Second Treatise of Government* as a source for his discussions on Norman Yoke. For a history of the development of Norman Yoke into the Doctrine of Discovery and Rights of Conquest, they refer to Williams, Jr., *American Indian*, 233–275.

5. For an analysis of Locke's articulation of Norman Yoke, Stiffarm and Lane refer their readers to Macpherson, *Political Theory*.

6. The beginning date of 1816 marks the end of the War of 1812, a time in which the American government began to focus on "Indian Removal." The (1816–1890) "Indian Wars" period can be deceiving if one takes into account that European warfare against Native Americans began with the European invasion of the continent.

7. The dates for the period of "Indian Removal" are approximate. Certainly, financial negotiations for land occurred earlier and later in history. See Hagan's *American Indians* (75–101) for a further discussion of this period.

8. Out of necessity, the writings of Hagan and Pommersheim speak in a general fashion about Indian removal policies. Each tribal nation affected by removal policies has a unique story regarding these negotiations and this time in history. To cite just one example, the Cherokee Nation attempted to avoid losing its homelands by adopting European standards of "civilization." The success of the Cherokee Nation to use the US judicial system to protect their lands only fueled President Andrew Jackson's anger. In 1831, Jackson willfully went against the Supreme Court's decisions regarding the sovereignty of the Cherokee Nation and demanded its removal, stating, "'John Marshall has made his decision, now let him enforce it'" (qtd. in Hagan, *American Indians*, 85). The brutal, forced removal of the Cherokees, Creeks, Choctaws, Chickasaws, and Seminoles to Oklahoma's Indian Territory came to be known as the Trail of Tears.

9. For more information of the specifics of the General Allotment Act, see Otis, *Dawes Act*.

10. Originally, the Five Civilized Tribes' lands were exempt from the Dawes Act, but the Curtis Act of 1898 amended Dawes and opened up their previously protected lands. The new act was supported by Vice President Charles Curtis, who was Kansa-Kaw/Osage.

11. This quotation is also linked to Francis Leupp's (Commissioner of Indian Affairs) policy on assimilation.

12. Noriega notes that in certain boarding schools, the custom of beating Native American students for speaking their native languages continued into the 1970s in both the United States and Canada ("American Indian," 398).

13. Taken from Francis Leupp's (Commissioner of Indian Affairs) famous quotation: "Kill the Indian, but save the man." See Leupp, *The Indian*.

14. As with many federal decisions regarding Native American issues, the American Indian Religious Freedom Act of 1978 did not succeed in giving Native peoples full freedom of religion. See Deloria, Jr., "Trouble," 267–290.

4 PLATIALITY IN NATIVE AMERICAN DRAMA

1. An example is my article "JudyLee Oliva's *The Fire and the Rose* and the Modeling of Platial Theories in Native American Dramaturgy," 819–841.

2. *The Cherokee Night* was premiered at Hedgerow Repertory Theater in Pennsylvania June 18, 1932. Riggs directed that production and two subsequent ones at the University of Iowa in 1932 and Syracuse University in 1934. In 1936, the Federal Theatre produced a ten-day run of the play in New York (Braunlich, "Chronology," xviii–xix).

3. A staged reading of *The Fire and the Rose* took place at Miami University in Oxford, Ohio in March of 1998. A workshop production of the play occurred the following month at Hofstra University in New York during the Native American Experience Conference. Although the play has yet to receive publication, a public copy of the script is housed in NAWPA at Miami University, www.staff.lib.muohio.edu/nawpa. The *Fire and the Rose* has won several awards, and it was a finalist for the Jane Chambers Playwriting Award.

4. *The Story of Susanna* was first produced in 1998 at the University of Hawaii, Honolulu after having received readings in 1996 at the Women's Community Correctional Center in Kailua, Hawaii; the T. J. Mahoney, Transitional House for Women in Honolulu; and the Kumu Kahua Theatre in Honolulu. The play received a Jane Chambers Playwriting Award honorable mention in 1997 (Kneubuhl, *Susanna*, 294).

5. The Roman Catholic Bible includes Daniel, Chapter 13 within its canon. The Jewish and Protestant canons relegate Daniel, Chapter 13 to the apocrypha, writings omitted from the biblical canon owing to questions of authorship and authenticity.

6. Susanna has provided various artists with inspiration for portraying gendered relationships. Between the sixteenth and eighteenth centuries, the story offered painters a nude subject and – through the elders' gazes – a hint of pornography.

Typically, these paintings portrayed Susanna as sexually available. In 1610, Artemisia Gentileschi, a woman painter, reclaimed Susanna as an innocent woman who fell victim to male domination. Art historians have theorized that Artemisia was portraying the story of her own rape, trial, and subsequent damaged reputation (Mary Garrard, "Artemisia and Susanna," 146–171).

7. Chihuly's work connects to the plot's Seattle location and some of the play's Native American themes. Chihuly, who was born in Washington state and is based in Seattle, built the glass shop for the Institute for American Indian Arts in 1974. Two of his famous collections, Navajo Blanket Cylinders and (Northwest Coast) Baskets, were inspired by Native American artworks. In 1998, Chihuly began mentoring the glasswork of Taos Pueblo students through the Hilltop Artists in Residency program (Chihuly, "Chronology").

8. Justice notes that Talbert's language invokes the mythological figures of Cherokee lore (such as the Mississippi/Long Man and the spirit deer, Awi Usdi). He surmises that Riggs may have once "sought turtle shells in muddy red shallows, dropping them on anthills until they were cleaned out and ready to be worked into stomp dance leggings or hand rattles," for Riggs' separation and feelings of exile can't be necessarily conflated with an ignorance of the old ways" (Justice, *Fire*, 105).

9. Scolnicov states that the classical Greek use of theatrical space associated the doorway into the home with a woman's mouth and vagina. Consequently, a woman could keep her chastity through a series of closures: keeping her legs crossed, remaining silent, and staying behind closed doors (*Woman's*, 7).

10. For further discussion, see: Wiles, *Tragedy*; Scolnicov, *Woman's*; and Zeitlin, "Playing," 63–94.

11. For more see: Wiles, *Tragedy*, 175–186. Wiles argues that the thymele was used specifically for libations.

12. Due to the more recent invasion of the Hawaiian Islands, federal policies regarding lands and Native inhabitants were applied to Native Hawaiians somewhat differently from the traditional practice of creating reservation lands. It was not until August 12, 1898 that Hawaii was annexed by the United States, against the official protest of Hawaii's Queen Lili'uokalani, who claimed, amongst many injustices, that "said treaty ignores not only the civic rights of my people but, further, the hereditary property of the chiefs. Of the 4,000,000 acres composing the territory said treaty offers to annex, 1,000,000 or 915,000 acres has in no way been heretofore recognized as other than the private property of the constitutional monarch, subject to a control in no way differing from other items of a private estate" (Lili'uokalani, "Official").

In 1993, the US Congress offered an official apology to Native Hawaiians. The apology admits the illegal annexation of "1,800,000 acres of crown, government and public lands of the Kingdom of Hawaii, without the consent of or compensation to the Native Hawaiian people of Hawaii" ("United States Public Law 103–150"). The document recognizes the link between Native Hawaiians and the land, and offers the apology, in part, on the grounds that "*Whereas*, the health and well-being of the Native Hawaiian people is intrinsically tied to their deep feelings and attachment to the land; *Whereas*, the long-range economic and social changes in Hawaii over the nineteenth and early twentieth centuries have been devastating to the population and to the health and well-being of the Hawaiian people" (ibid.).

While the US apology directly speaks of "Native Hawaiians," there is no federally recognized Native Hawaiian Nation. Native Hawaiians are, however, recognized as "Indian Nations" in several listings of Native nations by Native American peoples (see Jaimes, "Index," 459). Native Hawaiians also have been active in advocating Native Hawaiian sovereignty. In this respect, Native Hawaiians are similar to the many other mainland indigenous nations not officially recognized by the US federal government.

In literature, Native Hawaiian authors often are studied alongside Native American writers. An example of this is Kneubuhl's inclusion in NAWPA. However, as Pacific Island literature grows, and with it academic studies in the region's literature, many Native Hawaiian authors will eventually be studied within that field of literature.

13. Other translations are: minko – chief, ishki – mother, inki – father.
14. Originating in the fourth century BCE, the stories in the Book of Daniel were not written down until 167–164 BCE ("Introduction to Daniel," 617).

5 NATIVE STORYTELLING

1. The formerly warring six nations (Oneida, Cayuga, Mohawk, Onondaga, Seneca, and Tuscarora) from what is now the north-eastern region of the United States and south-eastern region of Canada created peace amongst themselves when they formed the Iroquois Confederacy between AD 1000 and 1400. Through pledging their allegiance to the values of "freedom, respect, tolerance, consensus, and brotherhood" the Six Nations Iroquois Confederacy did not only thrive: it has lasted. Howe explains that the Iroquois perform their discourse, this story of how peace was achieved, through a Condolence Ceremony, an "oral drama which observed the unification of the Iroquois" ("Tribalography," 121). It was through seeing the performance of unification that immigrants were inspired, in part, to create the United States' constitution. Howe states, "The power and persistence of native storytelling and performance convinced the separate peoples of the Old World to merge for their mutual benefit. Ironically, unification would enable the colonizers to seize almost all of the homelands of the Indians" (ibid., 120). Thus, immigrants to the United States connected to the story of the Iroquois Confederacy and, from this point of contact, wove another section of US history.
2. In traditional clowning, laughter allows people's minds and hearts to open so that they can better hear and accept the serious messages that come later. Please see: Barbara Tedlock, "The Clown's Way," 105–118.
3. Spiderwoman premiered *Rever-ber-berations* at the Theater for the New City, in New York, March 8–25, 1990. The play was published in 1992 in *Women in Performance* (Spiderwoman Theater, *Rever-ber-berations*). The title, *Rever-ber-berations*, is spelled

differently in the publication of the play from how it is in Spiderwoman Theater's own publicity and other printed materials about the play. For consistency, I use the same spelling that Spiderwoman's publicity uses. However, the play is published under the spelling *Reverb-ber-ber-rations*.

4. For more information about the commission and the development of the production, please see Highway, "*Ernestine* Study Guide," containing Director's Notes from David Ross and information about the production's documentary video.

5. For more information on the Laurier Memorial see "Introduction to the Memorial to Sir Wilfrid Laurier."

6 STORYING AND TRIBALOGRAPHY IN NATIVE AMERICAN DRAMA

1. *Rever-ber-berations*' portrayal of the sisters' spirituality contrasts markedly with the type of spirituality lampooned in another of Spiderwoman's plays called *Winnetou's Snake Oil Show from Wig-Wam City*. *Winnetou* satirizes those whom Spiderwoman calls "plastic shamans," new-age spiritual leaders who, for a profit, guide followers through mystical ceremonies that perpetuate stereotypical representations of Native American religions. In a post-performance discussion of *Rever-ber-berations*, Muriel Miguel explained that when the company was creating *Winnetou*, she wanted to include in the play a serious moment that emphasized her own spirituality. However, this one serious scene did not work well within the satirical atmosphere of *Winnetou*. Spiderwoman decided that Muriel's scene belonged in a new play; consequently, the intensely personal *Rever-ber-berations* was born out of the overtly political *Winnetou* (Spiderwoman Theater, Post-performance).

2. Although the use of place and time was particularly powerful in the premiere production, the subject of land rights plays such a large role in Native American histories that *Ernestine Shuswap* retains a resonance for almost any audience in the Americas.

3. In ceremonial performances, drumming often symbolizes the heartbeat, in the same way as flute-playing represents the breath.

4. In the play, Muriel wears a V-necked tunic that has a Kuna mola outlining the neckline and wrists. A mola is a geometric pattern created by overlaying fabrics. A Kuna mola rests at the center of Spiderwoman Theater's backdrop quilt, and the performers' costumes often incorporate Kuna molas.

5. Casting Native American actors in Native American roles is an important issue in Native American theatre, especially when one takes into account the long history of non-Natives playing "Indian." The complexities of this political issue of representation are often debated within the field of Native American theatre, and even Native playwrights are at odds with regard to whether or not non-Native actors should ever be allowed to play Native roles. For history on the matter, see: Philip J. Deloria, *Playing Indian*.

7 REPRESENTING UNCONTAINABLE IDENTITIES

1. Edward Curtis was an early-nineteenth-century photographer, celebrated in his day for photographically "documenting" the lives of Native peoples. However, Curtis often reinforced stereotypes of Native people by having his subjects wear "authentic" clothing that he provided and by "touching up" the photographs to remove evidence of modern life. Chief Wahoo is the mascot for the Cleveland Indians baseball team. The trademarked caricature is often referred to as "Little Red Sambo."

2. Most often, magical realism is closely associated with Latin American authors. Of course, the designators "Latin American" and "Native American" become extremely complicated when one accounts for the indigenous heritage that many Latin American authors possess. Magical realism, as it traverses the southern boundary of the United States and draws upon the indigenous mythologies of both North and South America, presents a fascinating theoretical method for mentally eradicating national borders.

3. Transformations offer an effective subject matter though which researchers may locate points of contact between the wider-ranging cultural perspectives of "magical realism" and the Native-specific theories of Vizenor's we are about to discuss. Such a study, although far beyond the reach of this book, might provide new, liberating perspectives for viewing the contemporary literature of North and South America as founded upon ancient, indigenous intellectual traditions.

4. Prior to the colonial invasion, Native American nations exercised independent self-governance, or sovereignty. It was not until 1832 that the US Supreme Court recognized the sovereignty of Native nations. However, the kind of Native national self-rule that the federal government acknowledged was one that fitted neatly into the guardian–ward relationship that had been established by the United States in 1831. The kind of sovereignty that Native American nations possess today is pseudo-independence. Native nations have the powers of a sovereign state, possessing an internal law and organized self-government. However, externally, Native nations – like states – are subject to the laws of the federal government. For more information, please see Pommersheim, *Braid of Feathers*, 37–56.

5. A full discussion of the various forms of these metaphorical limits would be its own study. Such a study would likely address issues concerning the relationship between poverty and choice, the former ban on Native American religious practices, forced-sterilization programs, and adoption programs that removed children from Native homes. For more information see Pommersheim, *Braid of Feathers*, and Jaimes, *The State of Native America*.

6. For a fun account of this see Daniel David Moses, "The Trickster's Laugh," 107–111.

7. AITE eventually changed its name to the Native American Theater Ensemble (NATE). These titles are used interchangeably in Native theatre history. Here, I use AITE because that was the group's name when it premiered *Foghorn*.

8. For more information about the historical event known as Wounded Knee II, please see Wall, "A Warrior Caged," 291–310.

9. For more information about the relationship between AITE and La Mama see Heath, "Development."

10. Other significant productions included: March 1974, Tyrone Guthrie Theater for National Native American Unity Day; June 1974, the annual Festival of American Indian Arts in LaGranda, Oregon; and November 1980, the Indian Rights Association 98th Annual Convention in Philadelphia.

11. For a history of Native Voices that includes information on Clements' work, see Reinholz and Scott, "Native Voices," 265–282.

12. For this analysis, I will use the 1996 version of the script that coincides with these two performances. A different published version of the script may be found in Darby and Fitzgerald (eds.), *Keepers of the Morning Star*, published in 2003.

13. Throughout this and the following chapters, I will use Vizenor's *indian* in the manner that he uses it, to refer to stereotypical representations of Native American peoples.

14. As an example, Vizenor discusses the American school system with regard to Native issues. He explains that America, which has only recently seen itself as multicultural, has been multicultural since before the European invasion. "First, this is a diverse native continent," he argues, and an understanding of Native peoples, as well as their presence in American history, must begin with this knowledge (Vizenor and Lee, *Postindian*, 178).

15. Certainly, there are trickster figures in many other cultures, but the discussion of non-Native trickster figures is beyond the scope of this study. The use of trickster figures and tales for perspectives into cultural drama and performance is the subject of several studies. For examples please see: Dale E. Seeds' "Trickster by Trade" for an investigation of how Thomas Riccio uses trickster and other stories as inspirations for directing indigenous theatre groups from Alaska to Zambia; Rabillard's "Absorption, Elimination, and the Hybrid" for a discussion of gender deconstruction through trickster figures in the plays of Tomson Highway; Olorou's "Modern Scheming Giants" for an analysis of how Soyinka twists African trickster figures into contemporary versions of materialist pragmatists; and Wright's *The Trickster-Function* for a combination of trickster behaviors with philosophies from psychoanalysis, anthropology, and literary theory as a critical point of inquiry for Lorca's scripts. For an interesting theatrical portrayal of the relationship between Native and African tricksters, see JudyLee Oliva's play *99 Cent Dreams*.

16. For an example of trickster stories paired with critical perspective, see Radin, *The Trickster*.

17. Kalloch's *U Da Naa* and the Native American Theater Ensemble's *Coon Cons Coyote* are two plays that provide theatricalized portrayals of Trickster's voracious appetites and reincarnations.

8 ACTS OF SURVIVANCE IN NATIVE AMERICAN DRAMA

1. Charleen Teeters, a Spokane artist, professor, and leader in the political movement against American Indian mascots, speaks about the "noble"-looking

Indian profiles adorning schools and civic buildings. She traces the tradition to the Indian Wars, in which non-Native settlers could earn money for hunting Native American people. To mark where non-Natives could go to claim their rewards, the buildings hung signs or had stone engravings of "Indian" heads. Eventually, she states, the engravings became an architectural trend, appearing on city buildings and public schools (Teeters, "Racism and Contemporary Genocide").

2. "Captain Columbus! Look! Look! Look! There! Look! My God! Those chocolate men! The Indians! The Indians! They are the Indians!"

3. Please see chapter 3, "Native American Platial History," for a more detailed discussion of "ownership by right of discovery."

4. Here, Owens is borrowing phrases from Mikhail Bakhtin's discussion of comical proximity. See Bakhtin, *The Dialogic Imagination*, 23, 24, 60.

5. Rosemarie uses N. Scott Momaday's "blood memory," a term that Native literature, art, and scholarship has adopted to refer to the way that ancestors' stories remain within an individual who may have never experienced the story's events but who intimately feels them. Please see Momaday, *Rainy Mountain*, 7.

9 INTERCONNECTED THEORIES AND THE FUTURE OF NATIVE AMERICAN DRAMA

1. Stanlake, "Mapping the Web."

Bibliography

PLAYS, PERFORMANCES, AND FILMS

Borst, Murielle. *More Than Feathers and Beads*. Performance. Dir. Muriel Miguel. Miami University, Oxford, Ohio. Feb. 26, 1997.

Bruchac, Margaret. *molly has her say*. In Darby and Fitzgerald (eds.), *Keepers of the Morning Star*, 317–373.

Clements, Marie. *Burning Vision*. Vancouver: Talonbooks, 2003.

    Now Look What You Made Me Do. Adaptation for Illinois State University ts. 1995.

    Urban Tattoo. In Darby and Fitzgerald (eds.), *Keepers of the Morning Star*, 205–228.

    Urban Tattoo. Performance. Dir. Randy Reinholz. Native Voices in New York. American Indian Community House, New York. Aug. 9, 1996.

    Urban Tattoo. Performance. Dir. Randy Reinholz. NAWPA. Hall Auditorium, Oxford, Ohio. Nov. 7, 1999.

    Urban Tattoo. ts. 1996. NAWPA, Oxford, Ohio.

Dandurand, Joseph A. *Please Do Not Touch the Indians*. Performance. Dir. Randy Reinholz. 2001 Native Voices at the Autry Play Festival. Wells Fargo Theatre, Los Angeles. Mar. 11, 2001.

D'Aponte, Mimi Gisolfi, ed. *Seventh Generation: An Anthology of Native American Plays*. New York: Theatre Communications Group, 1999.

Darby, Jaye T. and Stephanie Fitzgerald, eds. *Keepers of the Morning Star: An Anthology of Native Women's Theater*. Los Angeles: UCLA American Indian Studies Center, 2003.

Daystar/Rosalie Jones. *No Home but the Heart*. In Darby and Fitzgerald (eds.), *Keepers of the Morning Star*, 77–106.

Dennis, Darrell. *The Trickster of Third Avenue East*. In *Darrell Dennis: Two Plays*. Toronto: Playwrights Canada Press, 2005.

Flather, Patti and Leonard Linklater. *Sixty Below*. In Grace, D'Aeth, and Chalykoff (eds.), *Staging the North*, 435–501.

Geiogamah, Hanay. *Body Indian*. In D'Aponte (ed.), *Seventh Generation* 1–37.

    Foghorn. In Geiogamah and Darby (eds.), *Stories of Our Way*, 103–126.

    49. In Geiogamah and Darby (eds.), *Stories of Our Way*, 195–226.

New Native American Drama: Three Plays. Norman: University of Oklahoma Press, 1990.

and Jaye T. Darby, eds. *Stories of Our Way: An Anthology of American Indian Plays.* Los Angeles: UCLA American Indian Studies Center, 1999.

Glancy, Diane. *The Woman Who Was a Red Deer Dressed for the Deer Dance.* In D'Aponte (ed.), *Seventh Generation,* 270–289.

Grace, Sherrill, Eve D'Aeath, and Lisa Chalykoff, eds. *Staging the North: Twelve Canadian Plays.* Toronto: Playwrights Canada Press, 1999.

Highway, Tomson. *Dry Lips Oughta Move to Kapuskasing.* In *The Harcourt Brace Anthology of Drama.* 2nd edn. Ed. W. B. Worthen. New York: Harcourt Brace, 1996. 1243–1270.

Ernestine Shuswap Gets Her Trout: A "String Quartet" for Four Female Actors. Vancouver: Talonbooks, 2005.

The Rez Sisters. Saskatoon: Fifth House, 1988.

Howe, LeAnne and Roxy Gordon. *Big PowWow: A Time to Change.* ts. NAWPA, Oxford, Ohio.

Indian Radio Days: An Evolving Bingo Experience. In D'Aponte (ed.), *Seventh Generation,* 101–147.

Huston-Findley, Shirley A. and Rebecca Howard, eds. *Footpaths and Bridges: Voices from the Native American Women Playwrights Archive.* Ann Arbor: University of Michigan Press, 2008.

Kalloch, Gina. *U Da Naa (A Long Time Ago).* Performance. Dir. Rose-Yvonne Urias. Native Voices at the Autry Play Festival. Wells Fargo Theatre, Los Angeles. Aug. 19, 2001.

U Da Naa (A Long Time Ago). ts. 2001.

King, Bruce. *Dustoff.* In King, *Evening at the Warbonnet and Other Plays,* 57–113.

Evening at the Warbonnet and Other Plays. Los Angeles: UCLA American Indian Studies Center, 2006.

Threads: Ethel Nickle's Little Acre. In King, *Evening at the Warbonnet and Other Plays,* 115–164.

Threads: Ethel Nickle's Little Acre. Performance Dir. Pat Melody. Thunderbird Theatre, Lied Center, Lawrence, Kans. Oct. 4, 2001.

Kneubuhl, Victoria Nalani. *The Story of Susanna.* In D'Aponte (ed.), *Seventh Generation,* 291–371.

Manuel, Vera. *The Strength of Indian Women.* In *Two Plays About Residential School.* Vancouver: Living Traditions, 1998. 75–119.

The Strength of Indian Women. Reading. A Celebration of Native Women Playwrights. NAWPA, Oxford, Ohio. Mar. 20, 1999.

Mojica, Monique and Ric Knowles, eds. *Staging Coyote's Dream: An Anthology of First Nations Drama in English.* Toronto: Playwrights Canada Press, 2003.

Momaday, N. Scott. *The Indolent Boys.* In *Three Plays: The Indolent Boys, Children of the Sun, and The Moon in Two Windows.* Oklahoma Stories and Storytellers Series 3. Ed. Teresa Miller. Norman: University of Oklahoma Press, 2007. 1–71.

Moses, Daniel David. *Almighty Voice and His Wife.* In Mojica and Knowles (eds.), *Staging Coyote's Dream,* 176–236.

Native American Theatre Ensemble with Hanay Geiogamah. *Coon Cons Coyote*. In Geiogamah and Darby (eds.), *Stories of Our Way*, 127–154.

Nolan, Yvette. *Annie Mae's Movement*. ts. 1997.

Blade, Job's Wife, and Video: Three Plays. Toronto: New Canadian Drama Series, 1995.

North American Indian Drama. 2006. Ed. Oliver Brearey. Alexander Street Press and University of Chicago. June 1, 2008. www.alexanderstreet2.com/indrlive/

Oliva, JudyLee. *The Fire and the Rose*. ts. 1998, 2003. NAWPA, Oxford, Ohio.

99 Cent Dreams: A Full-Length Play in Two Acts. ts. 2000. NAWPA, Oxford, Ohio.

Spirit Line. ts. 2001. NAWPA, Oxford, Ohio.

Te Ata. In Huston-Findley and Howard (eds.), *Footpaths and Bridges*, 200–268.

Te Ata. Reading. Native Voices in New York. American Indian Community House, New York. Aug. 10, 1996.

Te Ata World Premiere. Performance. Dir. Sherry Landurm. USAO. Te Ata Memorial Auditorium, Chickasha, Okla. Aug. 5–13, 2006.

Perkins, Kathy and Roberta Uno, eds. *Contemporary Plays by Women of Color: An Anthology*. New York: Routledge, 1996.

Ramirez, Vickie. *Smoke*. Performance. Dir. Elizabeth Theobald. Chuka Lokoli, Native Theater Ensemble. Native Voices in New York. American Indian Community House, New York. Aug. 9 1996.

Rendon, Marcie R. *SongCatcher: A Native Interpretation of the Story of Frances Densmore*. In Darby and Fitzgerald (eds.), *Keepers of the Morning Star*, 1–75.

The Cherokee Night and Other Plays. Norman: University of Oklahoma Press, 2003.

Riggs, R. Lynn. *The Cherokee Night: A Play in Seven Scenes*. 1932. In Riggs, *Cherokee*, 109–211.

Green Grow the Lilacs. 1931. In Riggs, *Cherokee*, 3–105.

Shorty, Sharon. *Trickster Visits the Old Folks Home*. In Grace, D'Aeth, and Chalykoff (eds.), *Staging the North*, 331–353.

Spiderwoman Theater. *Rever-ber-berations*. In *Women and Performance* 5.2 (1992): 184–212.

Rever-ber-berations. Performance. Dir. Muriel Miguel. Roy Bowen Theatre, Columbus, Ohio. Oct. 20–21, 2000.

Sun, Moon, and Feather. In Perkins and Uno (eds.), *Contemporary Plays by Women of Color*, 297–309.

Winnetou's Snake Oil Show from Wigwam City. In *Canadian Theatre Review* 68 (Fall1991): 54–63.

Taylor, Drew Hayden. *Girl Who Loved Her Horses*. 1995. In Mojica and Knowles (eds.), *Staging Coyote's Dream*, 316–359.

Teeters, Charlene. *In Whose Honor? American Indian Mascots in Sports*. Documentary. Dir. Jay Rosenstein. Ho-ho-kus, N. J.: New Day Films, 1997.

Tunooniq Theatre. *Changes*. In Grace, D'Aeth, and Chalykoff (eds.), *Staging the North*, 101–113.

In Search of a Friend. In Grace, D'Aeth, and Chalykoff (eds.), *Staging the North*, 279–292.

Yellow Robe Jr., William S. *Grandchildren of the Buffalo Soldiers*. Performance. Dir. Lou Bellamy. Penumbra Theatre, St. Paul, Minn. Sept. 23–Oct. 15 2005.

CRITICAL RESOURCES

Allen, Paula Gunn. "The Ceremonial Motion of Indian Time: Long Ago, So Far." In Geiogamah and Darby (eds.), *American Indian Theater in Performance*, 69–75.

Off the Reservation: Reflections of Boundary-Busting, Border-Crossing, Loose Canons. Boston: Beacon, 1998.

The Sacred Hoop: Recovering the Feminine in American Indian Traditions. Boston: Beacon, 1992.

Appleford, Rob, ed. *Aboriginal Drama and Theatre.* Critical Perspectives on Canadian Theatre in English 1. Toronto: Playwrights Canada Press, 2005.

Armstrong, Jeannette C. "Land Speaking." In Ortiz (ed.), *Speaking for the Generations*, 174–195.

Baird, David W. "Are there 'Real' Indians in Oklahoma? Historical Perceptions of the Five Civilized Tribes." *Chronicles of Oklahoma* 61.1 (1990): 4–23.

Bakhtin, Mikhail. *The Dialogic Imagination: Four Essays by M. M. Bakhtin.* Ed. Michael Holquist. Trans. Caryl Emerson and Michael Holquist. Austin: University of Texas Press, 1981.

Baudrillard, Jean. "Symbolic Exchange and Death." *Literary Theory: An Anthology.* Eds. Julie Rivkin and Michael Ryan. Malden, Mass. 1998. 488–508.

Bird, Gloria. "Breaking the Silence: Writing as 'Witness.'" In Ortiz (ed.), *Speaking for the Generations*, 26–49.

Blackstone, Tsianina. *Where Trails Have Led Me.* Santa Fe: Vergara Printing, 1970.

Blaeser, Kimberly M. "Like 'Reeds through the Ribs of a Basket': Native Women Weaving Stories." *American Indian Quarterly* 21.4 (1997): 555–566.

Brask, Per and William Morgan, eds. *Aboriginal Voices: Amerindian, Inuit, and Sami Theatre.* Baltimore: John Hopkins University Press, 1992.

Braunlich, Phyllis Cole. "Chronology." In Riggs, *Cherokee*, xvii–xx.

Haunted by Home: The Life and Letters of Lynn Riggs. Norman: University of Oklahoma Press, 1988.

Brecht, Bertolt. "Alienation Effects in Chinese Acting." In Brecht, *Brecht on Theatre*, 91–99.

Brecht on Theatre: The Development of an Aesthetic. Ed. and trans. John Willett. New York: Hill and Wang, 1992.

Carpentier, Alejo. *The Kingdom of This World.* 1949. Trans. Harriet de Onis. New York: Farrar, Straus, and Giroux, 2006.

Casey, Edward. *Getting Back into Place: Toward a Renewed Understanding of the Place-World.* Indianapolis: Indiana University Press, 1993.

Centre for Indigenous Theatre website. 2008. June 30, 2008. www.indigenous-theatre.com/

Chaudhuri, Una. *Staging Place: The Geopathology of Modern Drama.* Ann Arbor: University of Michigan Press, 1995.

Cherokee Nation official website. 2008. June 16, 2008. www.cherokee.org

"Cherokee Clans." Webpage. In Cherokee Nation official website.

"Cherokee Stomp Dance." Webpage. In Cherokee Nation official website.

"Traditional Cherokee Belief System." Webpage. In Cherokee Nation official website.

Chihuly, Dale. "Chronology." Webpage. See the Dale Chihuly official website. Updated regularly. Designer, Mark McDonnell. Artspot. www.chihuly.com/

D'Aeth, Eve. "Introduction to *Changes*" (by Tunooniq Theatre). In Grace, D'Aeth, and Chalykoff (eds.), *Staging the North*, 101–104.

"Introduction to *Sixty Below*." (by Patti Flather and Leonard Linklater). In Grace, D'Aeth, and Chalykoff (eds.), *Staging the North*, 431–433.

Darby, Jaye T. "Broadway (UnBound): Lynn Riggs' *The Cherokee Night*." In Stanlake (ed.), *Nations Speaking*, 7–23.

"Introduction: A Talking Circle on Native Theater." In Geiogamah and Darby (eds.), *American Indian Theater in Performance*, iii–xv.

Deloria, Jr., Vine. *God is Red: A Native View of Religion, A Classic Work Updated.* Golden, Colo.: Fulcrum, 1994.

"Trouble in High Places: Erosion of American Indian Rights to Religious Freedom in the United States." In Jaimes (ed.), *The State of Native America*, 267–290.

Deloria, Philip J. *Playing Indian.* New Haven: Yale University Press, 1998.

Diamond, Elin. *Unmaking Mimesis: Essays on Feminism and Theatre.* New York: Routledge, 1997.

Eliot, T. S. *Four Quartets.* New York: Harcourt and Brace, 1943.

"Burnt Norton." In Eliot, *Four Quartets* (1–8).

"The Dry Salvages." In Eliot, *Four Quartets* (19–28).

"East Coker." In Eliot, *Four Quartets* (9–17).

"Little Gidding." In Eliot, *Four Quartets* (29–39).

Favel Starr, Floyd. "The Artificial Tree: Native Performance Culture Research 1991–1996." 1997. In Appleford (ed.), *Aboriginal Drama and Theatre*, 69–73.

"The Theatre of Orphans/Native Languages on the Stage." 1993. In Appleford, *Aboriginal Drama and Theatre*, 32–36.

Filewod, Alan. "Receiving Aboriginality: Tomson Highway and the Crisis of Cultural Authenticity." 1994. In Appleford (ed.), *Aboriginal Drama and Theatre*, 37–48.

Garrard, Mary D. "Artemisia and Susanna." In *Feminism and Art History: Questioning the Litany.* Eds. Norma Broude and Mary D. Garrard. New York: Harper & Row, 1982. 146–171.

Geiogamah, Hanay. "Author's Note for *Foghorn*". In Geiogamah and Darby (eds.), *Stories of Our Way*, 106.

"Indian Theatre in the United States 1991: An Assessment." *Canadian Theatre Review* 68 (Fall 1991): 12–14.

"Introduction to *Evening at the Warbonnet and Other Plays*" (by Bruce King). Los Angeles: UCLA American Indian Studies Center, 2006. ix–xv.

"The New American Indian Theater: An Introduction." In Geiogamah and Darby (eds.), *American Indian Theater in Performance*, 159–164.

and Jaye T. Darby, eds. *American Indian Theatre in Performance: A Reader.* Los Angeles: UCLA American Indian Studies Center, 2000.

Gilbert, Helen and Joanne Tompkins. *Post-colonial Drama: Theory, Practice, Politics*. New York: Routledge, 1996.

Glancy, Diane. "Author's Statement for *The Woman Who Was a Red Deer Dressed for the Deer Dance*." In D'Aponte (ed.), *Seventh Generation*, 270–275.

"Further (Farther): Creating a Dialogue to Talk about Native American Plays." *Journal of Dramatic Theory and Criticism* 14. 1 (1999): 127–130.

"Native American Theater and the Theater That Will Come." In Geiogamah and Darby (eds.), *American Indian Theater in Performance*, 359–361.

"Native American Theater, Spiderwoman Theater, and Theater That Will Come." Conference paper. Women's Voices in Native American Theatre. Miami University. Oxford, Ohio, Feb. 26, 1997.

Hagan, William T. *American Indians*. 3rd edn. Chicago: University of Chicago Press, 1993.

Haugo, Ann M. "'Circles Upon Circles Upon Circles': Native Women in Theater and Performance." In Geiogamah and Darby (eds.), *American Indian Theater in Performance*, 228–255.

"Native Playwrights' Newsletter Interview: Lisa Mayo." In Geiogamah and Darby (eds.), *American Indian Theater in Performance*, 320–341.

Heath, Sally Ann. "The Development of Native American Theatre Companies in the Continental United States." Diss. University of Colorado at Boulder, 1996.

Hernandez, Martin. Review of *Urban Tattoo* by Marie Clements. *LA Weekly* Mar. 5–11, 1999: 82–83.

Highway, Tomson. *"Ernestine Shuswap Gets Her Trout, Study Guide." Western Canada Theatre, 2004–2008*. Western Canada Theatre, Kamloops, BC. June 20, 2008. www.westerncanadatheatre.bc.ca/esstudyguide.htm

Interview by William Morgan. "The Trickster and Native Theater." In Brask and Morgan (eds.), *Aboriginal Voices*, 130–138.

"Introduction to *The Rez Sisters*." Saskatoon: Fifth House, 1988. vi–ix.

"On Native Mythology." 1987. In Appleford (ed.), *Aboriginal Drama and Theatre*, 1–3.

Hill, Roberta J. "Immersed in Words." In Ortiz (ed.), *Speaking for the Generations*, 72–91.

Hobson, Geary, ed. *The Remembered Earth: An Anthology of Contemporary Native American Literature*. Albuquerque: Red Earth Press, 1979.

Howard, Rebecca. "Introduction." In Huston-Findlay and Howard (eds.), *Footpaths and Bridges*, 1–9.

Howe, LeAnne. "Tribalography: The Power of Native Stories." *Journal of Dramatic Theory and Criticism* 14.1 (1999): 117–130.

Howes, Craig. "Introduction." In Victoria Nalani Kneuhuhl, *Hawai'i Nei: Island Plays*. Honolulu: University of Hawai'i Press, 2002. ix–xxviii.

Huntsman, Jeffrey F. "Native American Theatre." In Geiogamah and Darby (eds.), *American Indian Theater in Performance*, 81–113.

Huston-Findley, Shirley and Rebecca Howard, eds. *Footpaths and Bridges: Voices from the Native American Women Playwrights Archive*. Ann Arbor: University of Michigan Press, 2008.

"Introduction to the Book of Daniel." *The New American Bible*. Grand Rapids: Catholic World Press, 1987. 617.

"Introduction to the Memorial to Sir Wilfrid Laurier." *Secwepemc Cultural Education Society*. 2007. Secwepemc Cultural Education Society, Kamloops, BC. June 20, 2008. www.secwepemc.org/about/laurier

Jaimes, M. Annette. "Index of Indian Nations." In Jaimes (ed.), *The State of Native America*, 459–460.

   ed. *The State of Native America: Genocide, Colonization, and Resistance*. Boston: South End Press, 1992.

Jemison, Peter. "Repatriation Law – Review of NAGPRA Committee Activities." Native American Regional Conference. Ohio Arts Council. Radisson Hotel, Cleveland. Mar. 23, 2001.

Justice, Daniel Heath. *Our Fire Survives the Storm: A Cherokee Literary History*. Minneapolis: University of Minnesota Press, 2006.

King, Bruce. "About the Authors." In Geiogamah and Darby (eds.), *Stories of Our Way*, 499.

   "Emergence and Discovery: Native American Theater Comes of Age." In Geiogamah and Darby (eds.), *American Indian Theater in Performance*, 165–168.

King, Thomas. "Godzilla vs. Post-Colonial." *World Literature Written in English* 30.2 (1990): 10–16.

Kneubuhl, Victoria Nalani. "Author's Statement for *The Story of Susanna*." In D'Aponte (ed.), *Seventh Generation*, 292–293.

Lee, A. Robert. "Introduction." In Vizenor and Lee, *Postindian*, 1–18.

Leupp, Francis. *The Indian and His Problem*. New York: Scribner, 1910.

Lili'uokalani. "Official Protest to the Treaty of Annexation: Presented by Lili'uokalani in Washington D.C. June 17, 1897." Online posting. Hawaiian Sovereignty Elections Council. Dec. 31, 1996. Ha Hawai'i. Feb. 8, 2002. www.planet-hawaii.com/hsec/treaty protest.html

Lynn Riggs Memorial. 2007. Gary Cundiff. June 20, 2008. www.members.cox.net/lynn.riggs/lrmem.htm

Macpherson, Crawford Brough. *The Political Theory of Possessive Individualism: Hobbes to Locke*. New York: Oxford University Press, 1962.

Malinowski, Sharon, ed. *Notable Native Americans*. New York: Gale Research, 1995.

Manuel, Vera. "Author's Note." *The Strength of Indian Women*. In *Two Plays About Residential School*. Vancouver: Living Traditions Press, 1998. 76.

   Post-performance Discussion. *The Strength of Indian Women*. A Celebration of Native Women Playwrights. NAWPA, Oxford, Ohio. Mar. 20, 1999.

Markowitz, Harvey, ed. *American Indian Biographies*. Pasadena: Salem, 1999.

Maufort, Marc and Franca Bellarsi, eds. *Siting the Other: Re-visions of Marginality in Australian and English–Canadian Drama*. Brussels: Peter Lang, 2001.

McNamara, Brooks. *Step Right UP*. Jackson, University Press of Mississippi. 1995.

Mojica, Monique. "ETHNOSTRESS." Conference paper. *Women's Voices in Native American Theatre.* Miami University. Oxford, Ohio, Feb. 26, 1997.

"Introduction to *Almighty Voice and His Wife*" (by Daniel David Moses). In Mojica and Knowles (eds.), *Staging Coyote's Dream,* 172–174.

"Introduction to *Girl Who Loved Her Horses*" (By Drew Hayden Taylor). In Mojica and Knoules (eds.), *Staging Coyote's Dream,* 311–14.

"Introduction to *Staging Coyote's Dream.*" In Mojica and Knowles (eds.), *Staging Coyote's Dream,* iii–ix.

and Ric Knowles, eds. *Staging Coyote's Dream: An Anthology of First Nations Drama in English.* Toronto: Playwrights Canada Press, 2003.

Momaday, N. Scott. "Preface." *Three Plays: The Indolent Boys, Children of the Sun, and The Moon in Two Windows.* Oklahoma Stories & Storytellers 3. Norman: University of Oklahoma Press, 2007. vii–viii.

The Way to Rainy Mountain. Illus. Al Momaday. Albuquerque: University of New Mexico Press, 1969.

Moses, Daniel David. "A Handful of Plays by Native Earthlings." 2001. In Appleford, *Aboriginal Drama and Theatre,* 134–149.

"The Trickster's Laugh: My Meeting with Tomson and Lenore." *American Indian Quarterly* 1–2 (2004): 107–111.

Native American Women Playwrights Archive. NAWPA website. Updated regularly. University Libraries and Department of Theatre. Miami University: Oxford, Ohio. www.staff.lib.muohio.edu /nawpa/

Native Earth Performing Arts website. 2008. June 30, 2008. www.nativeearth. ca/en/

New, Lloyd Kiva. "Credo for American Indian Theatre." 1969. In Geiogamah and Darby (eds.), *American Indian Theater in Performance,* 3–4.

Nolan, Yvette. "Selling Myself: The Value of an Artist." 1999. In Appleford (ed.), *Aboriginal Drama and Theatre,* 95–105.

Noriega, Jorge. "American Indian Education in the United States: Indoctrination for Subordination to Colonialism." In Jaimes (ed.), *The State of Native America,* 371–402.

Oliva, JudyLee. "Te Ata – Chickasaw Indian Performer: From Broadway to Back Home." *Theatre History Studies* June 15, 1995: 3–26.

Olorou, Samuel B. "Modern Scheming Giants: Satire and the Trickster in Wole Soyinka's Drama." *Callaloo* 11.2 (1998): 297–308.

Ortiz, Simon ed. *Speaking for the Generations: Native Writers on Writing.* Tucson: University of Arizona Press, 1998.

"Towards a National Indian Literature: Cultural Authenticity in Nationalism." 1981. In Weaver, Womack, and Warrior (eds.), *American Indian Literary Nationalism* 253–260.

Otis, D. S. *The Dawes Act and the Allotment of Indian Lands.* Norman: University of Oklahoma Press, 1973.

Owens, Louis. *Other Destinies: Understanding the American Indian Novel.* Norman: University of Oklahoma Press, 1994.

Pavis, Patrice, ed. *The Intercultural Performance Reader.* New York: Routledge, 1996.

Pommersheim, Frank. *Braid of Feathers: American Indian Law and Contemporary Tribal Life*. Berkeley: University of California Press, 1995.

Rabillard, Sheila. "Absorption, Elimination, and the Hybrid: Some Impure Questions of Gender and Culture in the Trickster Drama of Tomson Highway." *Essays in Theatre* 12.1 (1993): 3–27.

Radin, Paul. *The Trickster: A Study in American Indian Mythology*. New York: Schocken Books, 1972.

Reinholz, Randy. Post-Performance Discussion over Marie Clements' *Urban Tattoo*. NAWPA, Oxford, Ohio. Nov. 7, 1999.

and Jean Bruce Scott. "Native Voices: New Directions in New Play Development." In Geiogamah and Darby (eds.), *American Indian Theater in Performance*, 265–282.

Riggs, R. Lynn. "Preface." *Green Grow the Lilacs*. In Riggs, *Cherokee*, 4–5.

Ruffo, Armand Garnet. "*A Windigo Tale*: Contemporizing and Mythologizing the Residential School Experience." In Appleford, *Aboriginal Drama and Theatre*, 166–180.

Scolnicov, Hanna. *Woman's Theatrical Space*. New York: Cambridge University Press, 1994.

Scott, Vincent P. "National Museum of the American Indian Native Theater Program." In Stanlake, *Nations Speaking*, 135–141.

Seeds, Dale E. "Trickster by Trade: Thomas Riccio on Indigenous Theatre." *TDR* 40.4 (1996): 118–133.

Sequoya, Jana. "How (!) Is an Indian?" In *New Voices in Native American Literary Criticism*. Ed. Arnold Krupat. Washington: Smithsonian Institution, 1993. 453–473.

Silko, Leslie Marmon. "Interior and Exterior Landscapes: Pueblo Migration Stories." In Ortiz (ed.), *Speaking for the Generations*, 2–25.

Spiderwoman Theater. "About the Authors." In Geiogamah and Darby (eds.), *Stories of Our Way*, 501–503.

Post-performance Discussions. *Rever-ber-berations*. Ohio State University. Roy Bowen Theatre, Columbus. Oct. 20, 21, 2000.

Storyweaving Workshop. Ohio State University. Oct. 18, 2000.

Stanlake, Christy, ed. "Interview with JudyLee Oliva." In Stanlate (ed.), *Nations Speaking*, 109–120.

"JudyLee Oliva's *The Fire and the Rose* and the Modeling of Platial Theories in Native American Dramaturgy." *Modern Drama* 48 (2005): 819–841.

"Mapping the Web of Native American Dramaturgy." Diss. Ohio State University, 2002.

Nations Speaking: Indigenous Performances Across the Americas. Spec. issue of *Baylor Journal of Theatre and Performance* 4.1 (2007).

"Profile: DeLanna Studi." In Stanlake (ed.), *Nations Speaking*, 143–146.

Stiffarm, Lenore A. and Phil Lane, Jr. "The Demography of Native North America: A Question of American Indian Survival." In Jaimes (ed.), *The State of Native America*, 23–53.

Swisher, Karen Gayton and AnCita Benally. *Native North American Firsts*. New York: Gale, 1998.

Taylor, Drew Hayden. "Alive and Well: Native Theatre in Canada." 1996. In Appleford (ed.), *Aboriginal Drama and Theatre*, 61–68.

Te Ata World Premiere website. 2005. University of Science and Arts of Oklahoma. June 16, 2008. www.usao.edu/teata/

Tedlock, Barbara. "The Clown's Way." In Tedlock and Tedlock (eds.), *Teachings from the American Earth*, 105–118.

Tedlock, Dennis. *Rabinal Achi: A Mayan Drama of War and Sacrifice*. Oxford: Oxford University Press, 2003.

 and Barbara Tedlock, eds. *Teachings from the American Earth: Indian Religion and Philosophy*. New York: Liveright, 1975.

Teeters, Charlene. "Racism and Contemporary Genocide." *Third Annual Conference on Hate and Violence: Racist Images in Popular Culture*. Cleveland State University, Committee of 500 Years, and Racial Injustice Ministry Team/UCC. Cleveland, Mar. 31, 2001.

"Trinity Rep and Penumbra Theatre Company Announce Cast and Dates for Touring Production, Grandchildren of the Buffalo Soldiers." Sarah McGreer. 2005. Mid-America Arts Alliance. June 16, 2008. www.maaa.org/news/press/05/pr102605bs.html

Tuan, Yi-Fu. *Space and Place: The Perspective of Experience. 1977*. Minneapolis: University of Minnesota Press, 2003.

"United States Public Law 103–150: 103rd Congress Joint Resolution 19; November 3, 1993." Online posting. *Hawaiian Sovereignty Elections Council*. Dec. 31, 1996. Ha Hawai'i. Feb. 8, 2002. www.planet-hawaii.com/hsec/aplogy.html

Velie, Alan. "Magical Realism and Ethnicity: The Fantastic in the Fiction of Louise Erdrich." In *Native American Women in Literature and Culture*. Eds. Susan Castillo and Victor M. P. Da Rosa. Porto, Portugal: Fernando Pessoa University Press, 1997. 57–67.

 "Vizenor: Post-Modern Fiction." *Critical Perspectives on Native American Fiction*. Ed. Richard F. Fleck. Washington, D. C.: Three Continents Press, 1993. 155–170.

Vizenor, Gerald. *Fugitive Poses: Native American Indian Scenes of Absence and Presence*. Lincoln: University of Nebraska Press, 1998.

 "Trickster Discourse: Comic Holotropes and Language Games." In *Narrative Chance: Postmodern Discourse on Native American Indian Literatures*. Ed. Gerald Vizenor. Norman: University of Oklahoma Press, 1993. 187–212.

 and A. Robert Lee. *Postindian Conversations*. Lincoln: University of Nebraska Press, 1999.

Wall, Jim Vander. "A Warrior Caged: The Continuing Struggle of Leonard Peltier." In Jaimes (ed.), *The State of Native America*, 291–310.

Warrior, Robert Allen. "Native Critics in the World: Edward Said and Nationalism." In Weaver, Womack, and Warrior (eds.), *American Indian Literary Nationalism*, 179–223.

Tribal Secrets: Recovering American Indian Intellectual Traditions. Minneapolis: University of Minnesota Press, 1995.

Weatherford, Jack. *Indian Givers: How the Indians of the Americas Transformed the World*. New York: Crown, 1988.

Weaver, Jace. "Foreword." In Riggs, *Cherokee*, ix–xv.

"Introduction." In Riggs, *Cherokee*, 107–108.

"Splitting the Earth: First Utterances and Pluralist Separatism." In Weaver, Womack, and Warrior (eds.), *American Indian Literary Nationalism*, 1–89.

That the People Might Live: Native American Literatures and Native American Community. New York: Oxford University Press, 1997.

Craig Womack, and Robert Warrior, (eds.) *American Indian Literary Nationalism*. Albuquerque: University of New Mexico Press, 2005.

Wiles, David. *Tragedy in Athens: Performance Space and Theatrical Meaning*. New York: Cambridge University Press, 1997.

Williams, Robert A., Jr. *The American Indian in Western Legal Thought: The Discourse of Conquest*. New York: Oxford University Press, 1990.

Womack, Craig S. "The Integrity of American Indian Claims: Or, How I Learned to Stop Worrying and Love My Hybridity." In Weaver, Womack, and Warrior (eds.), *American Indian Literary Nationalism*, 91–177.

Red on Red: Native American Literary Separatism. Minneapolis: University of Minnesota Press, 1999.

Woody, Elizabeth. "Voice of the Land: Giving the Good Word." In Ortiz (ed.), *Speaking for the Generations*, 149–173.

Wright, Sarah. *The Trickster-Function in the Theatre of García Lorca*. London: Tamesis, 2000.

Zeitlin, Froma I. "Playing the Other: Theatre, Theatricality, and the Feminine in Greek Drama." *Representations* 0.11 (1985): 63–94.

Index

CPSIA information can be obtained at www.ICGtesting.com
Printed in the USA
LVOW13s0856220813

349031LV00002B/176/P